CARLETON RENAISSANCE PLAYS IN TRANSLATION

In print:

In preparation:

Carleton Renaissance Plays in Translation Series No. 9

COMPARATIVE CRITICAL APPROACHES TO RENAISSANCE COMEDY

Edited by Donald Beecher and Massimo Ciavolella

Dovehouse Editions Canada

1986

ACKNOWLEDGEMENTS

This book has been published with the help of funds provided by the Social Sciences and Humanities Research Council of Canada.

We are also indebted to Carleton University Dean of Arts Naomi E.S. Griffiths for financial assistance in the preparation of the manuscript.

CANADIAN CATOLOGUING IN PUBLICATION DATA

Main entry under title:
Comparative critical approaches to Renaissance comedy

ISBN 0-919473-55-5

(Carleton Renaissance plays in translation; 9)
L. European drama—Renaissance, 1450-1600—
History and criticism. 2. European drama (Comedy)—History and criticism. I. Beecher, Donald   II. Ciavolella, Massimo   1942-

PN2173.C64 1986 809.2'523 C86-090170-X

For information and orders write to:

Dovehouse Editions Canada
32 Glen Ave.
Ottawa, Canada
K1S 2Z7

INTRODUCTION

Comic theatre in the Renaissance was a pan-European development, though it has been studied preponderantly in segments created by language in turn leading to the national-schools-of-drama approach to criticism. For many years, crossing those lines meant going in search of sources and influences in relatively mechanical and linear historical ways. In the essays that follow there is a perpetual undercurrent of interest in "influence," but in ways that render that term misleading as it is conventionally understood. Influence becomes a less conscious matter, more a form of communication that takes place at the level of the ideogram, the basic unit of discourse, the pattern of fable, the character type, the theatrical sign, all of them the more implicit components of comic theatrical structures. The plays that together represent the genre, viewed across national lines, reveal not only the now familiar meeting of foreign with native elements, but a universal and universalizing process of transformation, mutation and resuscitation of a wide variety of these fundamental building blocks, to use an outworn metaphor, blocks which in one essay are viewed as elements drawn from a metaphorical wardrobe or prop room, in another as distinct micro-units of thought and structure that lend themselves to recombination, in yet another as mythic elements that compound to form generic character, and in a fourth as verities of aesthetic patterning. The value in these essays lies in their concerted effort to examine the underlying units of thought, form and sign that compose and recompose themselves in the creative process and in ways characteristic to the genre, transmutations that must prefigure historical analysis.

Until recently this kind of analysis was the unique preserve of the literary theoretician who was also an agile expert in the languages of Western Europe. The obstacle posed by language is being removed slowly by the appearance of a representative number of these comedies in English translation, permitting for the first time a far wider accessibility, enabling many more than before to examine at first hand the materials on which any such critical reassessments must be made, and which will in their turn contribute to that reappraisal—one that holds for its implicit premise that our understanding of comic theatre in the Renaissance has everything to gain by seeing individual works in the broadest European context.

Massimo Ciavolella and Donald Beecher

Comparative Critical Approaches to Renaissance Comedy

Towards a "Philosophy" of Renaissance Theatre

Riccardo Scrivano
University of Rome

During the period of Shakespeare's poetic career that is often referred to as the second phase, his comedies continue to exploit a considerable number of the conventional elements already widely tested and proven in Renaissance comic theatre together with others that are totally or partially new. *Twelfth Night*, to the best of our knowledge written around 1599 or 1600, and thus at the peak of this second period, is just such a play. Here the motif of the shipwreck is given new prominence and importance. From this single event all successive action evolves, and all that comes about looks back to that event as a permanent point of reference in a play that is largely concerned thematically with characters who have assumed new identities and have taken on the roles of others.

Of course, a person assuming the role of another through disguise is one of the most ancient of theatrical traditions.[1] For the Renaissance it can be traced to Plautus who gave the device two distinct directions, that of the *Amphitruo* in which two gods, Jupiter and Mercury, take on the identities of two mortals, Amphitruo and Sosias, and that of the *Menaechmi*, in which two twins, separated in their infancy, do not manage to rediscover one another until they are adults. In neither of these traditions of the mistaken identity plot did the shipwreck motif appear. In *The Comedy of Errors* (c. 1593) the shipwreck served as background and as a plotting device. In *The Tempest* (1611) it is of salient importance throughout the play, not only explicitly as the background to all the events, but implicitly as a governing principle in the entire dramatic action. It was incorporated even into the aereal presence of the immaterial beings populating the fantastic island.

Of the differences in the use of the shipwreck motif between *The Comedy of Errors* and *Twelfth Night*, one in particular stands out, namely the time span between the shipwreck and the opening action of the play for which it serves as the antecedent fact. In *The Comedy of Errors*, the event is lost to the memory of the protagonists, but remains obsessively present in the minds of the two characters called upon to solve all of the play's enigmas. These are Aegeon, whose own casual and abstract drama frames the main comic action, and the abbess, who, in the final scene, supplies the missing elements in the story of a family life which had been interrupted and suspended for the course of many years. In *Twelfth Night*, the shipwreck is quite recent, an antecedent fact very close to the events that make the play. It is therefore a flexible element, diversified in its functions according to the theatrical mechanisms it is employed to create.

Another salient motif is that of twinship,[2] which has the fundamental characteristic of being a fact of nature, while shipwreck belongs solely to the universe of possible events. On this level, the motif of the twins establishes its common ground, though there is room for wide variation: the loss of one of the twins in the crowd of a feast; a forced separation brought about by plundering Turks. These are the circumstances that generate, respectively, the *Menaechmi* of Plautus and the *Calandria* of Bibbiena.

Twinship in *The Comedy of Errors* is an original motif, an antecedent to the play and yet a natural condition with its particular characteristics. It is presented according to the scheme of the *Menaechmi*, but with the doubling of the twins through the addition of the twin servants, Shakespeare produces the doubling of the theme of the exchanged character role according to the scheme of the *Amphitruo*. The two young masters, both males of course, are separated in their infancy. Their paths nearly cross on several occasions before they actually meet, and after various complications, they manage to recognize each other. Paralleling Antipholus of Syracuse and Antipholus of Ephesus, derived from the *Menaechmi*, are the two corresponding servants, Dromio of Syracuse and Dromio of Ephesus, derived from Sosia-Mercury of the *Amphitruo*. Though this duplication has been considered a baroque-like affectation, yet, considered in terms of the conflation of schemes from these two plays, it takes on complex and significant dimensions. In this sense Shakespeare has drawn upon a well-established and highly stratified repertoire of theatre elements which he has deliberately altered and recombined in order to make them function in a different network of communication, a network providing an original whole, even if its component parts are familiar.

In Shakespeare's procedures an important dimension of Plautus's conception is lost, namely the differences in personality, character and virtue which distinguish the physically identical protagonists. In a word, that moral diversity is parallel and inverse to the physical identity.[3] It has been stated, though perhaps too hastily, that this loss accounts for the mechanical nature of *The Comedy of Errors*, suggesting that it is a meagre and dry reworking of materials drawn from the erudite tradition, that it is merely a document of the apprenticeship of a young Shakespeare. Not yet accounted for, however, are the theatrical effects of that doubling, which are at least of two kinds. The first establishes a relationship between the audience and the play itself. It is a way of familiarizing the viewer with the text being performed, creating certain expectations regarding a text which, although well known, can still generate comparisons between performances. The second effect is gained from fixing the differences of tone between the comedy of the masters and that of the servants. Perhaps even further factors should be considered, since the levels of discourse in *The Comedy of Errors* are not so elementary as to allow us to relegate the play to the periphery of Shakespearean criticism. I do not mean the levels in the writing, of which I would make a rather poor judge, but the other factors that enter into the theatrical structure, such as the handling of the plot, the sequences and the continuations of the scenes—factors which, when considered, weaken the charge of erudite pedantry.

What should be remarked about *The Comedy of Errors* is that the modalities of invention achieved through variations in the use of materials— that is to say, in concrete terms, of the time-honoured and critically sanctioned plot situations, themes and motifs, dead and then revivified with greater audacity and eccentricity (modalities today referred to as manneristic)—are controlled and well-devéloped. The diminishing of characterological and moral differences in the twins reveals the generic nature of their dilemma and of their adventures, highlighting more clearly the predetermined nature of the situations, the contrast between the destiny of individuals in motion and the fixity of nature. In literary terms, it signifies a symbolic structure yet to be discovered, to be identified in the intersection of events. We should perhaps work towards a different conception of the comic.

In *Twelfth Night*, the twinship scheme of Plautus' *Menaechmi* undergoes further transformation: the twins are of different sexes. This is not the first time, however, that the motif has been varied in this way. By creating twins of different sex in the *Calandria*, who are separated as infants and whose destinies lead them together again as adults, Bibbiena discovers a formula for enriching the structures of his comedy. The nature of the twinship accounts for the nature of the amorous events in the play and the network of desires that arise, and in turn leads to the particular satisfactions and delusions of those desires. That twinship is the very condition which gives rise to the disguising and exchange of roles bears in itself specific thematic significance: it suggests that nature herself is no guardian of essential distinctions, that she is, in fact, a matrix of confusion and misunderstanding, a turmoil that must be set at rights in the end through the regulating intervention of the mind that, alone, is capable of mastering these experiences. More specifically, this variant on the twinship theme means that even when nature introduces her diversifying elements, the chain of confusion and misunderstanding is not reduced; on the contrary, it becomes more entangled. In direct proportion to this entanglement is the increasing eagerness to disentangle the chain and hence to clarify events. In this procedure there is further indication of the maturation of a different conceptualization of the comic, one that increases its intellectual responsibility.

At this point it is important, at least for me, to table a methodological consideration. The two motifs, shipwreck and twinship, treated so far, could be delineated in far greater detail simply by referring to other Shakespearean plays. Since the first was Shakespeare's own invention it does not require further amplification. The second one, however, can be traced from variant to variant throughout the Renaissance back to antiquity, just like the theme of the exchanging of roles. The methodological observation I would like to make concerns this chainlike transformation of thematic motifs which positivistic criticism recognized and set out to anatomize by collecting the single concrete examples that are, in turn, to be arranged in a sequence of modulations from one example to another. There is considerable value in their work since in many cases they were able to identify specific sources and to reveal the channels through which these motifs passed from one work to another. But I must candidly affirm that such is not my purpose nor my critical horizon. Without wanting to compromise myself with a declaration in favour of innate ideas, it is my view that these chainlike transformations of motifs are to be accounted for in the natural repetitiousness of the mental operations which can be performed. As a parallel, one need only consider the artisans' shops where certain secrets and certain techniques were handed down from one person to another. In much the same way, actors handed down one to another, not only such stock-in-trade items as the comic types (the miser, the old amoroso, the *miles gloriosus* and the others), but also comic themes and situations, including role exchange motifs. To this can be added certain models of dramatic execution—those which are relegated to the background of the story, and those which must be shown on stage.

Among these modules, there is a whole series of actual mechanisms which have always been common ingredients of the theatre. In order to understand their various levels of functionality, it is useful to examine them according to the levels of analysis which, in parallel with narrative structures, have been clearly defined by Cesare Segre:[4] the discourse (*discorso*), as the linguistic aspect of the text's surface; the plot (*intreccio*), as the unities of content resulting from the segmentation of the discourse; the fabula (*fabula*), as the selection and rearrangement in succession and consecution of the unities of content; the narrative model (*modello narrativo*), as a series of functions traceable in kindred narrations of which they constitute the fundamental structure. I do not think there is need to make a special case for this association between theatre and narrative, because theatre and narrative share, by definition, a common spatio-temporal nature, and because this association is, in any case, useful and meaningful only in the analytical phase of the investigation.

When we ask ourselves what position is occupied in this scheme by the motifs and themes we have singled out in our observations concerning Shakespeare, we meet with uncertainty. The scheme of the levels of analysis proposed by Segre is fundamentally an articulation of the progression from superficial structure (discourse) to deep structure (narrative model). I wonder if the scheme does not also imply an idea of generation by means of an appropriation of elements from the second structure for use in the first. This appears probable, though there is no need to decide upon the question now. There is always a certain amount of distortion in any attempt to apply to the analysis of a particular language (in our case that of the theatre) the analysis of language *tout-court*. The uncertainty we experience with regard to Shakespeare must therefore come from another source and be of another kind. The problem is, in fact, related to the legitimacy of assuming that the exchanging of roles is the narrative model for *The Comedy of Errors* and for *Twelfth Night*. Strictly speaking, the assumption proves to be obvious for the first play, less so for the second, where the substitution of one character for another is not an end in itself, but is translated into a web of desires. The comedy concerned with errors, in a word, becomes the comedy concerned with love intrigues in a way which manifests a compounding of the model with its now two-fold meaning. More certain is the assigning of the motifs of twinship and of shipwreck to the level of the fabula, encouraged in this by Segre's view that "at the level of fabula we cannot find elements which may allude to or anticipate the theatrical performance."[5]

What is assigned to the level of discourse is totally obvious. We accept the fact that in the dialogue between characters, that which goes on between them—and which constitutes the true superficial structure—must be separated from its implications for the progression of the action, or for what happens or has happened off the stage. Such material does not belong to the dialogue between the characters, but rather to the dialogue between the characters and the audience. These elements must, in fact, be assigned to the level of the plot, which comprehends all the specifically theatrical elements which allude to or prelude the discourse. Among these are gestures, scenography, music, noises, but particularly those mechanisms we have already referred to.

I must add here a further point of clarification. I have just mentioned as being at this same level those mechanisms which I am trying to define, mechanisms which, for the sake of convenience, I can as of now identify in such things as the effect of the doubling, the agnition, the disguising, and in elements such as gesture, scenography, music, and others. All of these have been earmarked as the single systems of signs that the theatre sets in action, joining them into a "bundle" which, at any given time, can comprise them all, or only a part.[6] Both classifications of signs must be assigned to the level of plot, but in two separate categories. Gestures, scenography, music, and related signs belong to this level because they are elements from among which preliminary operative choices are made. These choices manifest themselves at the level of discourse, and therefore they go alongside the dialogue as non-linguistic factors which, nevertheless, constitute particular codes of communicative or performative language. On the other hand, doubling, agnition and disguising directly reify the units of content resulting from the segmentation of discourse. Naturally, one is tempted, for the sake of simplifying, to categorize the former (gestures, scenography, etc.) as signs at the level of discourse, and to keep only the latter as signs at the level of plot. Yet such a desire for simplification could cause us to misconstrue the connection they have with the definition of the units of content. Moreover, with regard to the linguistic aspect, one should take into account the phase which precedes its appearance on the surface, just as we have done in differentiating the dialogue between the characters from the dialogue between the characters and the audience.

The usefulness of this probe into the structures of theatre can be clarified, if not actually justified, by a consideration of certain elements which are closely aligned with gestures and scenography and which, just like these, constitute particular systems of signs flowing together in the bundle of codes that gives life to the theatrical event. I am thinking of elements such as costumes and make-up, which can easily be isolated from the others in as far as, although some of these can be omitted, they are always, of necessity, part of the performance. As one can see, they concern more directly the actor in his process of identification with the character who in turn sets himself up as the centre of the stage fiction. To such elements one can associate even the movements on stage, even if only to arrive at that point on stage specified for recitation.

Costumes, make-up and movement on the stage are essential determining elements in the definition of the unit of content, which can identify itself with several scenes, one scene only, or even with part of a scene. These elements are even more determinant when they are altered in a way that goes beyond the primary fictions they represent in former instances. In

Renaissance comedy, this function of altering is often accomplished through the use of disguise. With that device, a fiction is created within the fiction. In *The Comedy of Errors* there are no disguises. There are only the mistaken identities which serve in the place of disguise to set the action in motion. This is a more expansive but simpler mechanism. Through it Antipholus of Syracuse receives from Angelo, the goldsmith, the bracelet which was to be bestowed upon Adriana, wife to Antipholus of Ephesus. The latter is turned away from his own house as a nuisance because his own twin, unknowing and unknown, is already comfortably ensconced at his table. Meanwhile, the two Dromios generate other paradoxical misunderstandings predicated on the theory that reality is beyond comprehension, on the confusion and astonishment of not being able to recognize even things once certain and of not being recognized, and on a forced reading of the world as a place defying all sense. In *Twelfth Night* disguise is the theatrical mechanism which prevails from the outset; Viola, as soon as she is safe on the shores of Illyria and has the prospects of refuge in the court of Orsino, transforms herself into Cesario. As a consequence, she takes on the same appearance as her own brother Sebastian, from which fact flows a series of misunderstandings that are at times comical, at times pathetic, and at times erotic.

The disguise as a fundamental plot mechanism has been looked upon critically as a simple, even facile, expedient, a sign of a poverty of invention drawn from the repository of more traditional theatre props. This is far from the case. As in the *Calandria*, the disguises in *Twelfth Night* translate into a theatrical dimension the motif of twinship at its most intricate level— the changing of sexes—granting a means to desire and to the rise of a complex series of amorous intrigues: by its very appearance it creates the first instance of collusion between the audience and the protagonist. The audience knows more than all the other characters in the play, and, in consequence, is superior to them, since it has the knowledge necessary to master the events on the stage. To be sure, this superior knowledge is also a superior power, or an illusion of power, which is entirely congruous with the fiction of the theatre with its elusive and temporary quality. But such factors do not detract from the significance of that power in the minds of the spectators. We should not forget that over the course of Shakespeare's development as a writer, there is an incremental use of disguise. It occurs singly in *The Two Gentlemen of Verona*, *The Merchant of Venice* and *Much Ado About Nothing*, but twice in *The Taming of the Shrew* and six times in *Love's Labour's Lost*.

A mechanism similar to disguise is the "mask," which makes use of other signs such as costume, make-up, movement, and of course the mask itself. While disguise entails taking on another identity, the mask can be employed simply as a means of hiding or of cancelling one's own identity. The mask is used in this elemental way in *The Merry Wives of Windsor*, where it remains a marginal and supplementary, even mechanical, device, especially if we reject the romantic notion that character is the essence of the play. In *A Midsummer Night's Dream*, the parade of masks in the Pyramus and Thisbe episode creates an exceptional atmosphere. Here there is a special fascination shown for the joyous release that accompanies the entrance into theatrical performance, with all its attendant cross-references to festival and the theatre of carnival. Already widely recognized is the fact that carnival and the feast provided the context and space out of which modern theatre was born, the space for which the performance was written and in which it was given.[7] The play-within-the-play is a further manifestation of that continuous layering of scene upon scene which Shakespeare never refrained from using. The show-within-the-show is an open avowal of that desire to duplicate performance according to a manneristic procedure that seems to find its own justification in the repetitive nature of the theatre itself.[8]

The merit of this idea of the theatre squared lies in the fact that it insists upon the non-mimetic nature of theatre. This is no minor consideration, even if it may seem paradoxical to apply it to a culture which had discovered and meditated at length on Aristotle's *Poetics*, where theatre is defined as "mimesis in action." Nevertheless, there can be little doubt that great theatre appears at the very moment when it amplifies itself on the stage, when it reflects upon itself, as in the case of Pirandello's texts dealing with the theatre-within-the-theatre: *Sei personnaggi in cerca d'autore, Questa sera si recita a soggetto, Ciascuno a suo modo.* I will not dwell here on the problem of the interpretation of Aristotle during the Renaissance, a problem which must be looked at separately, and following a re-examination of the Aristotelian texts. Yet I would be remiss if I did not review, briefly, the notion of imitation, which the aesthetics of realism has deprived of all symbolic connections, and limited to the realm of pure reproduction, the mirror image, while forgetting that the mirror does indeed reflect things, but that it also reverses them. Every imitation is a recreation in the mind, subject to relationships, to the use of materials, and to effects which differ totally from their sources. Imitation, in a word, is the result of the institution of a code or a bundle of codes.

The usufructuary of this revelation is, naturally, the public, which, by means of this institution of codes, is invited to enter into the spectacle, to make use of it from within, since failing this, the revelation itself is lost. In short, the audience is an integral part of the theatrical event. This concept leads, inversely, to the realization that even when one is in the world of reality, and believes he is squarely in that world, he is, at the same time, in a theatre. This concept is an integral part of the idea of the "great theatre of the world," which was so obsessively promulgated in various forms throughout Europe in the late sixteenth and early seventeenth centuries.[9] Shakespeare, himself, gave voice to the idea in his own particular way in a famous passage in *As You Like It* (II, vii):

> All the world's a stage,
> And all the men and women merely players:
> They have their exits and their entrances,
> And one man in his time plays many parts,
> His acts being seven ages. At first, the infant,
> Mewling and puking in the nurse's arms.
> Then the whining school-boy, with his satchel
> And shining morning face, creeping like snail
> Unwillingly to school. And then the lover,

Sighing like furnace, with a woeful ballad
Made to his mistress' eyebrow. Then a soldier,
Full of strange oaths, and bearded like the pard,
Jealous in honour, sudden, and quick in quarrel,
Seeking the bubble reputation
Even in the cannon's mouth. And then the justice,
In fair round belly with good capon lin'd,
With eyes severe and beard of formal cut,
Full of wise saws and modern instances;
And so he plays his part. The sixth age shifts
Into the lean and slipper'd pantaloon,
With spectacles on nose and pouch on side,
His youthful hose, well sav'd, a world too wide
For his shrunk shank; and his big manly voice,
Turning again toward childish treble, pipes
And whistles in his sound. Last scene of all,
That ends this strange eventful history,
Is second childishness and mere oblivion,
Sans teeth, sans eyes, sans taste, sans everything.

With this statement we have reached a kind of limit, or, put another way, we have gone very far towards making an inventory of a repertoire of ideas and notions which have been accumulating, like the props themselves, in the storeroom of materials of Renaissance theatre. In this storeroom there is a little of everything: masks found in the old chests where, unknown to the world for centuries, the texts of ancient comedies have been preserved; costumes of every kind, somber or ridiculous, stately or ragged—an immense array that can be more easily imagined than recorded. All is of equal importance; every object, even the most unworthy, can be a generative resource, can be invested with a new significance beyond all previous dimensions. In this storeroom there is a place belonging to the themes and motifs relating to twinship and to the duplication of identities. Moreover, one finds there the mechanisms which set the system of signs in motion. There they are near the surface and in full display: the doubling, the duplication, the disguising, the masking, the agnition.

This repository was formed slowly, but not too slowly. In less than a century it became full to overflowing. Attempts were made to record its entire inventory, or a least parts of it. Even the universal classification of the materials of the theatre did not yet seem impossible. Alessandro Piccolomini, the learned Sienese scientist and theorist of behaviour, dialogist and writer of comedies, let it be known that he had undertaken a project designed to catalogue all the comic figures in the form of a canonic system of witticisms and dialogues to be used as repertoire. It was a bizarre idea which has stirred up considerable speculation—bizarre in that one could even think of achieving faster results in the preparation of texts as well as a greater freedom by using pre-fabricated materials. The conclusion, probably a wise one, was that it was a prelude to the *commedia dell'arte*. Considering Piccolomini's eclecticism, we are safe in assuming that he believed that everything deriving from antiquity or that was simply old had to be continually revisited, reread, reintroduced, for fear of losing its original version or its practical import. With regard to the usefulness of translations, Piccolomini argued that there is no science except that found in the great inheritance left to us by the classics, that the study of dead languages— Latin, Greek, Hebrew—in which the ancients wrote requires much time and can end up by absorbing all our intellectual activity, that we will finish by knowing the ancient languages but not the knowledge the ancients have handed down to us, and that therefore it is necessary to have good, specialized translators and to use translations. This is an exemplary paradigm of what happened, in the course of the rebirth of humanistic culture, and which was a process particularly evident in the field of theatre, which had been resuscitated with great enthusiasm and, out of intrinsic necessity, opened up to new experimentation.

But just as Piccolomini's project was probably never realized or, in any case has not come down to us,[10] in much the same way the sense of the enormous theatrical operation promoted by the Renaissance has grown dim and impoverished. This is what happened with the Italian Renaissance theatre, essentially a comic theatre, which, as is well known, had an enormous flowering in the early decades of the Cinquecento. With such rare exceptions as Machiavelli's *Mandragola*, this theatre has, for a long time, succumbed to a negative critical judgement that labelled it as an erudite, fossilized and pedantic art form. Given the rediscovery of Plautus, and, to a less extent, the retrieval of a reconstituted medieval and moralized Terence, and given, besides, a humanistic culture totally concerned with the renewal of the ancients, every new work offering events based upon ancient models was, by definition, transformed into an archaeologism. Thus Italian comedy of the Renaissance came to be considered erudite and dead. When later on, much later, it became apparent that this comic theatre occupied too much space in the whole of that cultural phenomenon to be considered only as a marginal and secondary experience of little or no significance, an attempt was made to save it by finding in it the capacity to reflect realistic motifs, events from contemporary life, and figures known to the audience to whom the play is addressed. Thus Nicia became the faithful prototype of the Florentine bourgeois, whom Machiavelli takes upon himself to dress with the mask of stupidity, while Ariosto's Lena becomes one of the bawds of sixteenth-century Ferrara.

I have no doubt that between those two critical moments some progress has been made, albeit in a rather curious manner, as if critics assumed that chronicles work better than history, and that the path of true theatrical success passes through the transformation of the stock character types not into an actual character, but into an object person materialized in the referent, and therefore verifiable. This type of methodological behaviour, from every point of view, belongs to idealism, even if those who employed it believed in good faith that what they were using was pure historical materialism. But, as if to say no human effort is entirely lost, they did acknowledge that there could be a breath of life in an art form which was tenaciously pursued by such writers as Ariosto and Machiavelli, and which enjoyed success in the presence of such audiences as Guicciardini, governor of the Romagne, the court of Ferrara, which also opened certain performances to the citizens of the town, and the Venetian public, which was the first paying audience in the history of western theatre.

I will be forgiven if I have outlined a history of the misfortunes of Italian theatre in the Renaissance from a perspective that is bound exclusively to the events of cultural history, which are in their turn, isolated and examined from an Italian point of view. To be sure, there are very instructive episodes in this kind of enquiry but from which no general statements can be drawn. I am thinking, for example, of the rediscovery of Ruzante in France toward the middle of the nineteenth century, within a framework barely related to specific facts of theatre culture, but rather to folklore. The intellectual by-products of that discovery appeared in Italy in the form of a debate over the interest fifteenth-century Italian intellectuals had shown both for atypical characterizations and for the use made of the language of the Po valley as opposed to a more standard Italian—debate which was to become heavily distorted by ideological interpretations. But with the exception of these few episodes, the renewed interest in the theatre of the Italian Renaissance is entirely connected with the retrieval of the Renaissance as a civilization, not only concerned with images and texts, but also with performance.

The reconstruction of the conditions and objects garnered in the great storeroom of theatre props arose from this retrieval. Placed first into the storeroom were the mechanisms which allowed paradigmatic episodes and fabulae to function concretely at the level of theatre, elements which prior to that time had been adaptable only to narrative. Indeed, one of the most important transformations to take place, namely from narrative to theatre, involved the use of short stories, especially those of Boccaccio, within the context of the theatre. The sixteenth-century comic dramatists developed a program of adaptation that allowed them to appropriate the narrative models of Boccaccio for the theatre. The significance of that transformation goes well beyond the scope of the surveys which deal with the critical fortune of Boccaccio as the first modern short story writer, or, if you prefer, as the intermediary between medieval narrative based upon the *exemplum* and a new narrative style which had for its basis the multiplication and compounding of events, and the free play of human actions *vis à vis* fortune and destiny.[11] One need only consider that in this process of transforming narrative into theatre, certain processes of perception and of materialization were set into action. New dimensions of visualization, hearing and physical presence were activated that the art of reading could not offer; in the different categories of reception, set in motion through a process of theatrical extension and amplification, a new availability of the mind was manifested, a more diversified mental rapport with reality was instituted; this transformation also transformed the models of knowledge.

The first of the great theatre experiments of the Italian Cinquecento is the one attempted by Ariosto. This is followed by the innovations of Machiavelli, Ruzante and the anonymous writers of *La Venexiana* and *Gli Ingannati*, all of whom made substantial use of Ariosto's plays because of their wide circulation up and down the Po valley and beyond. I am mentioning only the most outstanding plays from a period crowded with theatrical activity. Ariosto, as an author of comedies, progressed, of necessity, through all of the critical phases outlined above. He was at first seen as the erudite playwright who, with varying degrees of ability, worked with schemes taken from rediscovered classicism. Later, he was admired as an acute observer of the civic life of Ferrara, including its characteristic figures conducting their affairs in such true-to-life places as streets and taverns. Still later came the self-conscious revaluation of his specific professionalism as a theatre intendant, manager, stage director and impresario, as it were. Only then could the author of comedies, the supplier of texts, be seen as the founder of a great theatrical age, with its diversity of paths, multiple developments, its interruptions and recoveries, differing from phase to phase of its development. We see the transformation of theatrical practices and elements from their primary to alternative territories, such as tragedy, which afterwards leads to the most singular of Renaissance inventions, tragicomedy or pastoral drama. Within this great adventure, Ariosto's initiative has the function of stimulus, and especially of defining the nature of an operative space for the new theatre.

During this process of development which Ariosto patiently pursued, he made use of materials which were simultaneously flowing into the great storeroom of theatrical props, resetting and refocussing them as he went. With *Cassandra* (1508), the idea of the comic plot woven around a material object comes into currency, in this case the coffer of valuable gold yarn that touches off the actions of the characters who are, in turn, derived from a cautious readaptation of classical types: the severe old merchant, the profligate and enamoured son, the thief, the scoundrel, the parasite, and the gallery of servants, modified and enriched for his purposes. We also find the mechanism of the substitution of roles which will become, soon after, the fertile source of the expediences of the *Suppositi* (1509): a comedy constructed entirely upon the misunderstandings caused by mistaken identity— in a word, belief in a character who is, in fact, different from the one he is believed to be.

If, as an expert of theatre, Ariosto occupies an important place in a flourishing centre of theatre entertainment, one which will continue to evolve throughout the century, he has an even more important place in making that theatre—from within its function as a moment of evasion and escape, and as the climax of a festive occasion—an instrument of knowledge, an arrangement of the things to be learned, a structural machine. In the first direction, Ariosto's presence is found in the defining of the structure of the theatre space, as well as in the use of detailed suggestions in the text that effect the delineation of the scene (indications of certain movements that the actors must execute on stage, elements that must be distinguished from the simple physical presence of the actor on the stage). In the second direction, Ariosto establishes the terms of the relationship between performance and communication, that is to say between the performance in itself and the performance that must be received by the public. This is an aspect I have dealt with at greater length elsewhere,[12] and which I can only summarize briefly here.

In Ariosto's first three comedies, the correct decoding of the nature of the space by all those present at the performance, both actors and public, is a critical factor. There are two orders of space distribution. One is the scene, the direct object of the perception of the actor-characters who perform within it, and of the spectators who contemplate and decipher it. This space is absolutely real, assuming the shape of a city street with houses and shops, their doors and windows opening onto the street. This perceivable reality is, however, fictitious, provisional, false, illusory. All this is well known to the spectator who has accepted, by the very act of going to the theatre, the conventions which are at the foundation of theatrical communication. Beyond this finite space, real yet false, there is circulating throughout the comedy, down to its smallest elements, a continuous reference to another space, a purely mental one, a space of the imagination, which is nevertheless true, just as the world is true. It is not just the space represented by the city in which the action takes place, which the character-actors enter, leave and move through; it is this, but also a much larger space intrusted to the imaginative abilities of the spectator. This space is not susceptible to nor in need of fictitious recomposition, which is the perennial cause of falsified perceptions. All the identifiable mechanisms set in motion by the theatre event are interconnected, or better, comprised in this general container. From this event these mechanisms receive their sense; within it they carry out their connections; through it they are purified of their fictitious nature.

Quite rightly, we should ask ourselves if this articulation does nothing but repeat the previously described process of the levels of analysis leading from the superficial to the deeper structures. Perhaps this is indeed the case, though we should not let that stand without pointing out one important consequence. If the mental horizon which circumscribes the physical dimension of the stage is to be identified with the deepest structure, that is to say, the narrative model, then it must be posited that the narrative model already contains some theatrical proclamations of its own, and that it is not indifferent to the future concrete manifestations of the event. I do not think, however, that it is useful to long for a primordial magma from which all forms must be derived that the times demand. This means then that the various levels of the structure condition each other at every moment, that between them there is not a real before or after, but there is a moment when materials of distant, different and contrasting origins begin to interact and proceed—if they proceed—to define the structure of the theatre that we enjoy, or that in any case we know.

Illustrating these methodological proposals by gathering meticulously analyzed data could be, in fact must be, a lengthy undertaking, clearly something that cannot be done here. Sufficient for now is an invitation to recognize how much the theatre of the Renaissance offers to the means of human knowledge. It is much more than an occasion for escapism. With the audacity of its fictions, its hypotheses, its capacity to cancel the usual modes of conduct, it reveals to us different ways of organizing knowledge, and thus different ways of knowing.

NOTES

1 A vast register of the modalities in which the theme manifests itself in the comic theatre of the Italian Renaissance can be found in G. Ferroni, "Tecniche del raddoppiamento nella commedia del Cinquecento," in *Il testo e la scena. Saggi sul teatro del Cinquecento* (Roma: Bulzoni, 1980), 43-64.
2 *Q.v.* G. Ferroni, " Il sistema comico della gemellarità," in *Op. cit*, 65-84.
3 Cfr. E. Paratore, "Notizia," in Plauto, *I Menecmi*, transl. into Italian by E.P. (Mazara: Società Editrice Siciliana, 1957), 10.
4 C. Segre, "Narratologia e teatro," in *Teatro e romanzo. Due tipi di comunicazione teatrale* (Torino: Einaudi, 1984), 15-26.
5 Ibid., 17.
6 Cfr. T. Kowzan, *Littérature et spectacle* (La Haye-Paris: Mouton, 1975), 182-205 and table of p. 206.
7 See F. Cruciani, *Il teatro del Campidoglio e le feste romane del 1513* (Milano: Il Polifilo, 1968), e F. Taviani, "La festa recisa, o il teatro," in *Biblioteca teatrale*, 15-16 (1976), 16-49, an issue dedicated to "L'invenzione del teatro. Studi sullo spettacolo del Cinquecento," ed. by F. Cruciani.
8 See L. Mango, "teatro del teatro," in A. Mango and L. Mango, *Teatro della follia. Teatro del teatro, Saggi su Shakespeare* (Napoli: Società Editrice Napoletana, 1984), 73-93, and C. Segre, "Shakespeare e la scena 'en abyme'," in *Op. cit.*, 51-60.
9 See in general M. Costanzo, *Il "Gran teatro del mondo." Schede per lo studio dell'iconografia letteraria nell'età del Manierismo* (Milano: Scheiwiller, 1964).
10 Piccolomini himself mentions it in his dedication to the treatise *Della sfera del mondo* (Venetia: Bevilacqua, 1561). On this see my *Cultura e letteratura nel Cinquecento* (Roma: Edizioni dell'Ateneo, 1966), 43-44 and 49-50, and the specific contribution by D. Seragnoli, "La struttura del personaggio nel teatro del Cinquecento: il progetto di A. Piccolomini," in *Biblioteca teatrale*, 6/7 (1973), 54-64.
11 See V. Branca, *Boccaccio medievale* (Firenze: Sansoni, 1956), 18 and 108-09.
12 In the volume *Finzioni teatrali da Ariosto a Pirandello* (Firenze: D'Anna, 1982), especially 54-76.

Theatregrams

Louise George Clubb
University of California, Berkeley

As a question for historians, the relation between Italian and English Renaissance drama is a hardy perennial, never prevented by radical scepticism from sending up new interrogative shoots. One line of scholarship stretching back before W.W. Greg brings forward into our time the negative conclusion that analogues, common sources and numerous instances of borrowing will not add up to evidence of significant "influence" of Renaissance Italian theatre on the Elizabethan. The conclusion follows logically from methods of source study standard in Greg's time, and from the premise that in critical comparisons, differences are more revealing than similarities. But, in a paradoxical inversion of intent this conclusion also mirrors the dissatisfaction of addicted readers of Italian and English plays who meet in the contrary conviction that there existed what is better conceived of as a common system than as an influence; for them too, the constantly rising number of discrete but apparently unconnected connections between Italian and English drama discovered by the tradition of *Quellenstudien* is not enough to account for the broader kinship insistently suggested by the collective testimony of theatrical texts.

Nowhere is the suggestion stronger than in relation to Shakespeare's comedies, and nowhere does the conspicuous position of the classical sources that he shared with Italian drama more obstruct a comprehensive view of the cultivation of comic genres in the Renaissance. Source studies which acknowledge the pretextuality of Plautus and Terence to Shakespeare necessarily, if sometimes unintentionally, raise again the question of the relation of the nonpareil of the English Renaissance to the powerfully fashionable Continental genres that were also rooted in Attic-Roman New Comedy. Ruth Nevo's demonstration that the "stratagems of the New Comedy supplied Europe with its comic fictions for two millenia" and "Shakespeare with his plots from *The Comedy of Errors* to *The Tempest*"[1] is sound genealogy. Certainly, from Menander to Dustin Hoffman is a long span in Western Culture, and doubtless there are things to be learned about culture in general from the fact, for example, that the complications of Menander's *Sikyonios* and those of the television play-within-the-play in Hoffman's *Tootsie* are dismissed by identifying one of the major characters as the long-lost brother of another. Something more particular can be learned, however, from the fact that *Tootsie* is punctuated by allusions to Shakespeare, the principle one being the articulation of the title-character as a transvestite male whose motives and actions reconstitute those of Viola in *Twelfth Night*, but with the sexes reversed; and that although this familiar theatrical phenomenon can be traced to numbers of Cinquecento Italian comedies, its genealogy does not go back as far as Plautus, the latter's much imitated boy-bride (in *Casina*) notwithstanding, for the Renaissance stratagems of Viola and the modern ones of Tootsie are altogether different in both components and consequences from classical identity shifts.

Twelfth Night, which Nevo treats as the summit of the peculiarly Shakespearean genre, romantic comedy, is emblematic of the current state of our question. A play permeated by unequivocally Cinquecento theatrical structures, signally by those adapted from medieval romance and contingent upon the exploitation of the combinatory possibilities of the transvestite heroine in an Italianized New Comedy framework, *Twelfth Night* testifies to an English-Italian relationship the more pervasive for being unspecific, although Shakespeare's contemporaries could see that *Twelfth Night* was closer to *"Inganni"* than to its distant Plautine source.[2] It has proved impossible to fix the relationship by old-fashioned source studies, resistant as they are to historicizing synthesis. On the other hand, the undeniable existence of a relationship has been conducive to metahistorical contrasts, as well as to diachronic demonstrations of Shakespeare's drama as the apex, even the final cause, of an evolution in genre.

Incorporating some of the best of such teleological theory into his admirable comparative analysis, Leo Salingar has made it impossible ever again to doubt that Shakespeare's use of Italian elements was "not mere imitation of New Comedy or Italian plots, but application of Italian methods to new purposes." And by adding a voice to Coghill's and Doran's perceptions of Shakespeare's participation in the classicism of his time, "Jonson associated classical comedy with . . . satire, following a sixteenth century tradition, while Shakespeare, also, however, following tradition, associated it with romance,"[3] Salingar helps to return Shakespeare to the central community of Renaissance theatre from which often he is still barred by the disposition to order cultural history toward a previewed end by means of polar oppositions.

Whether the antipodal concepts are labelled classical/romantic or have been further de-historicized as learned/spontaneous or artificial/natural, or have evolved politically into conservative/progressive or élite/popular, most polarizations divide European theatre into regular, "Aristotelian," theoretical Italian and French, on one hand, and irregular, pragmatic Spanish and English, on the other. In local contexts, they line up Jonson against Shakespeare and pit *commedia erudita* against *commedia dell'arte*, as well as "pure" genres against mixed ones. The oppositions are not historically unfounded, of course. Jonson himself provided a view of two camps, himself in one and the colleague he loved "on this side Idolatry"[4] in the other. Lope de Vega paraded his acquaintance with the road not taken.[5] Italian *trattatisti* warred over the permissibility of mixing tragedy and comedy. But positions destined to become the right and left banks of a Great Divide of cultural history may in the late Cinquecento and early Seicento have appeared rather as hypotheses about issues internal to the new institution of the theatre. Ordering of the past according to such contrasting pairs of timeless concepts as classical and romantic has obscured the common premises of Renaissance drama and has skewed modern perceptions of Italian theatre.

Italian scholarship long tended to apologize for Cinquecento theatre, even in the act of discovering its remarkable achievement. Romantic and post-Romantic criticism generally shied away from the imitative principle at the humanistic core of a literarily transmitted theatre, and instead praised whatever in it could be called "unclassical," as if only by deracinating self-assertion could the identity of Italian drama be maintained against its Latin and Greek antecedents.

The Shakespeare revered in Italy, moreover, is still a Schlegelian one, a version of Coleridge's bard of truth to Nature and knowledge of the human heart, his comedy admired for being so much farther from Plautus and Terence than the Italian genre, which is reproached by the comparison. The political implications of such metahistorical polarization appear in Gramsci's rebuke to Sanesi for observing that the anonymous author of the extraordinary but structurally old-fashioned *La venexiana* had not followed the avant-garde model of humanistic comedy produced by Ariosto, Bibbiena, and Machiavelli. For Gramsci theatre was ideally a *vox populi* and neoclassicism at all times of Italian history an exhalation of authority, a conservative enemy to innovation, costumed in his imagination as a "codino," or pigtailed aristocrat, target of the French Revolution.[6] The late Ludovico Zorzi, too good a historian to let stand this anachronism, acknowledged the accuracy of Sanesi's view of the *commedia erudita* as innovative and the linear medieval play model as old-fashioned, but he residually shared Gramsci's conventional anti-classicism. Zorzi felt it necessary, therefore, to isolate Ruzante from the standard idea of Italian Renaissance comedy, and, in so doing, subscribed for Marx and for himself to a cliché opposition of *commedia erudita* to the comedy of Shakespeare. In *La moscheta* and the dialogues, wrote Zorzi, Ruzante

. . . per dirla con Marx, scopre veramente sé stesso e shakespeareggia: se shakespeareggia significa, secondo il concorde giudizio, rappresentare la genuina natura umana contro gli schemi convenzionali e la costruzione di personaggi secondo idee preconcette e modelli moralistici.[7]
(. . . as Marx says, discovers himself and Shakespearizes, if by Shakespearize is meant, as is generally agreed, to represent true human nature, as opposed to conventional patterns and character construction according to preconceived ideas and moralistic models.)

Here the character of *commedia erudita* is obliterated in the romantic/classical polarization reinvoked long past its usefulness, and Shakespeare's greatness is used to shut out the light that would show him standing in the theatre of his time, instead of merely towering over it. Here another sort of "idea preconcetta" obscures what a mass of fragmentary, disorderly but substantial evidence points to: that the same theatrical movement which promulgated imitation of classical models produced romantic comedy and mixed genres, in Italy as well as in England, and did so through a common process based on the principle of contamination of sources, of genres, and of accumulated stage-structures, or theatregrams.

If we look synchronically at Shakespearean and Italian theatre, we find the latter in a state of broad development and diversification. The century that had begun with Ariosto's "Nova comedia" fostered a self-consciously modern system of imitating reality by contract between spectators and playmakers for forming an alternative physical space, a place for controlled play within the uncontrollable play of life around them, in which kinds, means, and goals of representation and things represented could both reflect and exclude aspects of the encompassing outer world. The idea that distinct genres were necessary to such representation and were available in ancient models was a strong determinant established well before theoretical debate was sparked by commentaries on Aristotle. The premise was one underlying the Renaissance practice of *imitatio* in general, and rested on a choice as deliberately calculated as were the choices of forms and materials from antiquity that Quattrocento humanists had made to achieve some independent definition of their present, in resistance to the undifferentiating and massive pressure of their immediate past.[8]

The prospect of wielding power over perceptions of reality by using as an instrument of selection the luminous clue of ancient comedy promised ideological, political and economic gain; it also provided technological motivation that led inevitably to comic excursions into tragedy and to more far-reaching experiments in crossbreeding of genres. By the late Cinquecento innumerable conjunctions had been tried, and there had proliferated various kinds of plays, of audiences, of auspices, and, most consequentially, of actors, private and professional, male and female. The difference within the range of drama could be as great as that between a five-act academic, Sophoclean pastoral tragicomedy in verse prepared for a royal wedding, such as Guarini's *Pastor fido*, and a three-act prose *zannata* improvised in a piazza by a hat-passing travelling troupe; nevertheless, viewed from the measured distance that permits historical periodization, such representations were but separate branches of a common enterprise.

Constant as a principle from the time of Ariosto on, was construction by contamination, the meditated and usually explicit combination of pretexts. But in addition to the mere fusion of borrowed plots, it demanded the interchange and transformation of units, figures, relationships, actions, topoi and framing patterns, gradually building a combinatory of theatregrams which were at once streamlined structures for svelte playmaking and elements of high specific density, weighty with significance from previous incarnations. The "elementi drammaturgici" which Ferruccio Marotti identifies as common building blocks of the *commedia dell'arte* that often frustrate attempts to make precise historical connections and attributions,[9] constitute a class of these resources. When the work Zorzi bequeathed to his Florentine circle is finished and all the scenarios in extant collections have been cross-referenced, we shall see more of theatregrams at work in the professional theatre. But the process of transformational theatre from the common repertory of theatregrams is immensely larger than the *commedia dell'arte* branch of Renaissance drama can suggest. It is the activation of the essential principles of Cinquecento comedy, contamination and complication, illustrating how (whatever the primary sources of any comedy, literary or improvised, may have been) theatre came from theatre, self-nourishing, self-reproducing and evolving.

The practice of several generations of playwrights in a century of testing their principles and expanding their process stretched combinatory structures to new lengths, made new reverberations, sometimes generating philosophical overtones in unexpected settings, and brought to Italian theatre an inwardness which only critical commonplaces about "conventional patterns," "preconceived ideas," and forced contrasts with Shakespeare can prevent us from recognizing as effects characteristic of much of his work too. Construction by contamination of plots and theatregrams was soon extended to produce contamination of genres. From the cultivation of comedy and tragedy arose a movement toward a third genre, a predictable next step in the long humanistic competition with antiquity. It coincided with a response to the challenge thrown down by the dissemination of the *Poetics*, with an answering attempt to make perfect plots in Aristotle's sense by adapting to comic structure the Sophoclean peripety he acclaimed, but displacing the dynamics of fate and predestination with a theatrical expression of the essential Counter-Reformation tenets of divine providence and free will. The results were mutations of the comic repertorial structures to allow imitation of kinds of reality previously unattempted in Renaissance drama but without abandoning the controllable, alternative, represented space achieved by Cinquecento playmaking and without returning to the linear "illustrated narration" technique of medieval drama.

"Nova comedia," which had been called "commedia grave" to denote the high theoretical claim of its neoclassical form, became grave in content too as playwrights increasingly charged the genre with loans from tragedy. There appeared more kinds and levels of action, higher ranking or more exotic characters, integrating designs in aid of polysemous representation; a comedy that was more romantic, more serious; and a pastoral drama that was tragicomic. These take shape by fission and fusion of theatregrams under pressure from new materials and directions. I propose to illustrate this phase of expansion and diversification by following the fortunes of one particular theatregram, one of the humbler ones, through the century: or by pursuing, more precisely, a complex of specific theatregrams, for to speak of one alone is to reduce it to the abstraction of "stock" character or situation. Of the latter a superrational analyst once claimed there were only thirty-six. My aim is the opposite, to show the unlimited fertility and transformational capability implicit in each theatregram. Any of them is the demonstration of the core process: permutation and declension by recombination with compatible theatregrams, whether of person, association, action or design.

* * *

The choice of a sexual centre differentiating Renaissance New Comedy from its Roman model (in which a bed-bound action was optional only, and nubile or otherwise marriageable female characters could easily be dispensed with as stage presences) directed the mainstream of the Cinquecento genre toward the figure of the woman desired and desiring, a requisite datum of plot and, with usage, to become the staple *giovane innamorata*. This theatregram of person called for and partly defined itself by another, with which to form a theatregram of association, which in turn motivated certain stageworthy actions. The young woman in love requires specifically a confidant, encourager, agent, messenger, or perhaps all of these, so that from the association there may arise expository scenes and plot-forwarding motions toward the lovers' unions and toward connections with other characters whose own associations and actions may further or oppose such ends.

In the cornerstone comedy of the genre, Ariosto's prose *Cassaria*, which he introduces as *"Nova comedia . . . piena / di vari giochi, che né mai latine / né greche lingue recitarno in scena" (Prologo)*,[10] the women in love are mere merchandise, their assignment to wait for their respectively Greek and Turkish lovers to buy them and set them up as mistresses. When Ariosto revised the comedy in verse he made important changes, transferring the action closer to the spectators' world, from the Greek Metellino to Sibari in the Italian Magna Grecia, turning the lovers into an Italian and a Spaniard and the girls into sisters, but still slaves. As before, they function as confidants to each other and receive assurances and Petrarchan compliments directly from their lovers without intermediaries. Ariosto adds the character of an old *fantesca*, by status eligible to act, as the theatregram of the maidservant would later do, in a variety of associations, including that of confidant/go-between to the *innamorata*, but he does not put her into communication with the sisters nor engage her in the intrigue, reserving her for the purely ethical function of showing the procurer's bad character and contrasting the advantages of pretty girls with the condition of used-up old servants whom love will not liberate (III. 4).

With his second comedy, *I suppositi*, Ariosto confirmed the inclination of the Italian genre toward a looking-glass perspective that distanced it increasingly from Plautine and Terentian Hellenizing by bringing the plot home to Ferrara; the woman in love is now marriageable, and her lover is a Sicilian student who has reached her bed by exchanging identities with his servant and obtaining work in her father's house. Polimnesta's associate is her nurse (anonymously "Nutrice" in the prose version, "Balia" in the verse revision); the expository scene establishes that after an attack of love at first sight, Polimnesta has been encouraged to sleep with Erostrato by the nurse, who first praised and then brought him to the bedroom (I. 1). It is also established that the Nutrice, later called "puttana vecchia" (III. 3) and "ruffiana" (III. 4), has accepted money for this aid; but she claims hypocritically to have acted simply out of pity and now advises Polimnesta to forget the "famiglio" and turn her mind to a more "onorevole amore." The nurse's status and significant stances have taken on shades of the Roman Comedy *anus*, as in *Hecyra* and *Mostellaria*, as well as of *La Celestina* and her antecedents, and the resulting cluster of traits and deeds fits her to represent the first of the false "suppositions" forming the comedy's warp. Polimnesta, moreover, defines her own character by contrast with the nurse, revealing that she and Erostrato aim at marriage, that she does not share the nurse's comfortable acceptance of a plurality of lovers and that she has been keeping her own counsel as to the true identity of her future husband.

From a cultural accretion of clues to the variability of two contrasting feminine *personae*, separately and in associations triggering an even more variable series of actions and attitudes, a theatrical combination has been worked to answer the demands of plot plausibly and dramatically, that is, representably onstage, within the urban domestic space that *commedia* claimed as its site. While Polimnesta and her nurse declare and supersede their own history, they authorize the recombinations to come, of theatregrams of person (*innamorata, balia, fantesca*) with theatregrams of association (specific pairings in the *serva-padrona* range) that would generate theatregrams of motion (actions and reactions with apposite speeches, kinds of encounters, use of props and parts of the set for hiding, meeting, attack, defense, seduction, deceit and so forth), all of which produce variations of plot and character united in theatregrams of design, patterns of meaning expressed by a disposition of material reciprocally organizing the whole comedy and the spectators' perception of its form. Ariosto's great reputation with later connoisseurs and playwrights for bringing coherent structure to the genre[11] may owe something to his success in patterning this second comedy by permutations of substitutions and suppositions or, as Gascoigne would translate, of "supposes" of one thing for another,[12] clinched with porno-puns on suppository acts at the beginning of the prologue and the end of the last act, intensified and doubled in the verse revision.

Though relegated to a single scene, Polimnesta and her nurse demonstrate at the outset of Cinquecento comedy a relationship and attendant points of behaviour perpetually useful and variable. In countless plots these theatregrams of action recombinable for new structures reappear, often reassigned to alternative *personae*. In Bibbiena's *Calandria* the *innamorata* is a *malmaritata*, an unhappy wife old enough to have a grown son, but the variation impedes none of the standard operations: messages are carried, disguises are put on, clandestine meetings arranged, and the character of the *innamorata* is thrown into relief by that of the *serva*. In Francesco D'Ambra's *Furto* many, but not all, of these functions are performed, with a different final effect, by a professional free-lance *mezzana*, or procuress. In *La mandragola*, a comedy launched by the mainstream but not quite in it, the young wife Lucrezia is not an *innamorata*, or not at first: that she becomes one at all is a triumph of the lover's machinations, requiring several persuaders and confidants. Within a decade of Ariosto's first comedy, Machiavelli's corrosive satire of corrupt institutions, of the Church in the person of Fra' Timoteo and of the family in those of Messers Nicia and Sostrata, is already testing the limits of what is generically possible in the "Nova commedia" by recombinations of person, association and action, dividing the pimping action of a *mezzana* between a priest and a mother who urges her daughter to adultery for economic and social security, but also for fun, having herself been a "buona compagna" (I. 1), or playgirl in her youth. By this shuffling of associations, Machiavelli confirms Lucrezia as the only reluctant party to the hilariously vicious fraud by which her husband cuckolds himself. The equally famous and still more influential *Gl'ingannati* contains two *innamorate*: one has a *balia* and the other a *fante*, between whom portions of the theatregrams of association and of action subsisting among such *personae* are divided or shared.

In *Twelfth Night*, the play supposed to prove that Shakespeare imitated *Ingannati*, there is no *balia* for Viola; and though the lady Olivia has in Maria a variety of the *fantesca*, their relationship does not run to confidential chat or to plans in aid of Olivia's love for Cesario/Sebastian. Shakespeare uses the *balia* for such actions in *Romeo and Juliet* (only some of which are to be found in Arthur Brooke's *Romeus and Juliet*, whose source was, *nota bene*, a play) as he uses the maid in *Two Gentlemen of Verona*, or, with still other

variations, in *The Merchant of Venice*. His not using either *persona* in the associations and actions in which they were to be found in *Ingannati* is another
demonstration of his working on the principles of "Nova comedia," not
by borrowing plots from sources, but by *contaminatio* of structures, recom-
bining in novel ways theatregrams that had become part of a large common repertory, discarding those that were not to the purpose of the highly
individual structure of each of his plays.

In Shakespeare's time, of course, many other actions were being used
in cross-combinations with those attributed to Ariosto's Nutrice. The *balia*,
old *fante*, or *mezzana* may natter earthily about maidenheads and marriage
and invite reprimand, like Bernardino Pino's Frosina[13] or Juliet's nurse;
perhaps her nattering is joined to a manipulative opportunism, like Pas-
quella's in *Ingannati* or Mistress Quickly's in *The Merry Wives of Windsor*;
she can be a flirt, old or young, encouraged or rejected; or, rather than
flirt, she may indulge in slanging matches with insulting boys; there is name-
calling between the old *ancilla* and the *ragazzino* in *Suppositi*, a theatregram
which by the time of *Ingannati* had ripened into the sexual-flavoured mockery
with which the transvestite *innamorata* accosts her *balia* before revealing
herself; and the flavour is still riper in Shakespeare's recombination, in
the dialogue of Mercutio and the Nurse.

*   *   *

Pursuit of signifying form in the Italian theatre eventually attached the power
of abstract representation to the design of comedy. The radical *contaminatio*
of genres that enriched the second half of the Cinquecento with comic structures and possibilities of unprecedented expressive scope touched even the
homely little theatregram of the *innamorata*'s abettor. In *La balia*, as in *La
Cecca*,[14] Girolamo Razzi gives the title role and a great manipulative power
to the earthy succourer of lovers. With their dexterity in sneaking suitors
into their young mistresses' bedrooms, both the Balia and Cecca (identified as "serva") continue the tradition of this particular servant-mistress
relationship, but whereas Cecca counsels *carpe diem* and propounds for the
more husbands being the merrier, *La balia* attests Razzi's shift toward serious
comedy, a move that earned him condemnation from Sanesi and Herrick
in our century,[15] but put him in the van of a kind of tragicomedy that is
a major clue to the constitution of the Renaissance theatre and to its claims
in that period of cultural history. The melodramatic and almost tragic matter
itself is less interesting than the form that the choice of such matter entailed. The Balia engineers a quadruple mistaken-identity bedtrick, a dark room
substitution which causes the *innamorata* to think she has committed incest
with her half-brother (Herrick emphasizes the resemblance to Tasso's
Sophoclean tragedy *Torrismondo*). Of course she has not done so; such violent
transgression of genre limits would lose the name of *commedia*. But the
manipulation of familiar theatregrams of association and action to weave
such a potentially tragic nexus, subsequently untied by a dénouement of
revealed changes of identity and substitution of children, show Razzi participating in the theatrical movement toward a third genre, thus undertaking what the ancients had not achieved, and doing so in the only way it was

imagined they would have approved: by adhering to Aristotle and imitating in comedy the form of tragedy that he had ranked highest, that of Sophocles' *Oedipus Rex*. Through the temporary investment of the *balia* with an unaccustomed semiotic weight as the designer, unwittingly providential, of this intrigue plot with pretensions to tragic formal gravity, Razzi's otherwise undistinguished play joins the many *commedie, tragicommedie,* and *favole pastorali* that variously attempted the ultimate imitation of classical models which would be at once transmission and exploratory transgression.[16]

The pastoral play was swept into fashion by a confluence of the movement toward the third genre with attempts to adapt the "perfect" Sophoclean plot to comedy, and with an ideological hope of replacing the representation of fate (in which pagan concept Catholic Counter-Reformers descried a perilous correspondence to Lutheran predestination) by the image of providence, guaranteeing free will. A providential pattern emerged in some *commedie gravi* as a theatregram of design by which an intrigue plot could become a metaphor for the labyrinth of life and could invoke the timely analogy of the *theatrum mundi*: the world as a stage where God is both spectator and dramatist, with the reverse corollary expressed in ritual quotation from Aelius Donatus, that the play is a mirror of the world, in which a human audience may see not only the *imitatio vitae* of physical reality but also its meaning, the *imago veritatis* of a transcendent order.

As a setting, Arcadia was better suited than the city of comedy or the court of tragedy to represent immaterial reality and universal psychological or spiritual experience, by virtue of being a mental space, natural, private and oneiric, the inner side of the civilized public and waking scene of city and court. And yet, when the pastoral world took to the stage and playmakers reached for theatrical instrumentation for the ancient abundance of pastoral situations, characters, topoi, attitudes and stories, the repertory of tried and proven structures of the established genres were at hand, and theatregrams, of comedy especially, were put to work in Arcadia.

The experience of love, self-knowledge and the vision of harmony which could be felt straining against the limits of *commedia grave* committed to urban economic realities, could be approached directly and expressionistically in pastoral drama. Change of heart and self-discovery could be acted out more freely than in a genre still oriented to love primarily as the winning force in a conflict of interests. Even in the most romantic *commedie* the loves of the young couples to be mated by the victory are relatively static: when love changes it is usually because an impediment, such as consanguinity, demands, or because a prior claim is filed, a first engagement renewed when rationally presented as the alliance best suited to the social resolution of the intrigue. In the pastoral, on the contrary, there are always psychological mutations and developments, and the irrationality together with the experience of gradually falling in love is a centre-piece of the action, an action which, taken as a whole, is simply love's motions dramatized. But whether the theatrical image of love in its varieties made possible by the Arcadian Elsewhere is mounted as a comedy of mistakes, errors produced when love is blocked by circumstances, or as elevated Sophoclean actions of dramatic irony modulated into a happy major key, with courtly or even regal characters threatened by the blindness of their passions, by tragic *antefatti* and portentous oracles, revealing through the motions of their loves the benignity of providence, repeatedly the theatregrams of comedy declare themselves as the process for giving stage presence and form to the pastoral matter.

The action of persuasion to love becomes more essential in pastoral drama than in comedy, the gradual education of the virgin heart being a principal motif of the developing genre, a design of conversion, in this instance of the devotee of Diana to the service of Venus. The action of the practical go-between, with its subsidiary actions assignable to the range of *balia-serva-mezzana* characters in associations with *innamorate* and *innamorati*, shows up in the pastoral all the more prominently because it is almost indispensable to plots in which psychological movement toward true love is paramount; but it relies for stage presence on redirections of familiar relationships and actions. The persuader is commonly a *ninfa attempata*, a middle-aged nymph, whose experience in love, *carpe diem* advice, propensity to flirt and practical impatience with idealistic scruples or ascetic notions define her relationships and her function within the pattern made by the total range of positions on love in a given play. Even if she is on an equal footing with the *innamorata* in a classless or one-class Arcadian society, the old nymph inevitably suggests to an audience wise in the ways of *commedia* both the function and aims of the *balia-serva* type, while at the same time her presence measures how far from that theatregram of person a variation moves when tuned to the inner world of the heart that is the venue of the third genre.

Even in Tasso's atypical but persistently imitated *Aminta*, with its severely economical offstage action and its distance from the ethos of *commedia*, there transpires the useful comic model. Dafne, the aging persuader who dominates much of the play, moves on the invisible wheels of comic theatregrams as she reminisces about the joys of love in her youth, chides Silvia in the famous "Cangia, cangia consiglio / pazzarella che sei: / che'l pentirsi da sezzo nulla giova." (I. 1. 121-31),[17] flirts cautiously with Tirsi and is as delicately mocked by him, laughs knowingly at signs of Silvia's awakening to love and hints with a vestige of the typical *balia-serva* coarseness that a little force from Aminta might be more effective than respectful adoration (II. 2. 933-39).

Taking *Diana pietosa, comedia pastorale* of Raffaello Borghini,[18] already an established author of *commedie gravi*, as an example of the post-*Aminta* play more openly incorporating the pastoral matter into theatre by fusion and redistribution of comedy's associations, persons and actions, we find the function of Tasso's Dafne performed by Cariclea, a *vecchia* with a distant origin in Greek romance and an immediate presence keyed to *balia-serva* models. Her behaviour and attachments contribute to a *commedia* design of deception and error, but here are redirected toward pastoral revelation of love's blindness and its cure and of hope crowned with joy by a sympathetic providential goddess, to which end the power of Fortune, traditionally supreme in comedy, is geared and subordinated.

In such calculated *contaminatio*, functioning as in comedy but without its socio-economic context, old Cariclea is essentially a woodland *balia*, an accomplice to Silveria's disguise and to the tricking of Ismenio into marriage, the "dolce inganno" (V. 8) approved by the oracle of Diana. Like the *balia-serva* who carries messages and beseeches the reluctant *giovane* of comedy, Cariclea solicits Ismenio for Silveria, but she does it with a pastoral topos, a reversed echo of the words Tasso's Dafne uses to Silvia: "Cangia, cangia voglia / Semplicetto che sei" (III. 1).

Cristoforo Castelletti's *Amarilli, pastorale*[19] illustrates the Ovidian magical pastoral comprising country clowns in *servo-padrone* associations with refined *pastori* and *ninfe*, and the theatregram of metamorphosis, of which Shakespeare's Bottom with his ass's head would be the supreme version. Castelletti's bumptious *capraio* is turned into a tree by a naiad whose waters he has profaned. His master obtains his release and scolds, like a jollier Prospero to a grosser Ariel: "havresti meritato, ch'io t'havessi / Lasciato star nel tronco eternamente" (IV. 4). To the design formed by this combination of rustic farce and fantasy with poetic revelation of love's providence, an experienced older *ninfa* brings an analogous psychological and conceptual amalgam of *mezzana*, *serva*, and classically learned initiate in love's mysteries. She carries messages and urges several shepherds and nymphs to love, employing a curiously mixed battery of familiar arguments: *carpe diem*, the material advantage of marriage to prosperous sheepowners, regret for beauty's loss and missed opportunities, and divine examples, such as Jupiter's transformations for love, with which Terence's "Eunuch" had egged himself on to rape (III. 584-91) and which Falstaff remembers when he awaits his assignation with one of the merry wives in Windsor forest, disguised as Herne the Hunter wearing a buck's head (V.5. 1-15).

Another recombination of *Aminta* with the magical pastoral and its repertorial actions and associations produces Pietro Cresci's *Tirena, favola pastorale*,[20] in which the title-figure is an old nymph like a nagging nanny, who preaches *carpe diem* to the Arcadian *jeunesse dorée* but angrily rejects the clown's gross advances, and who manipulates the plot toward a providential pattern linked to the idea of Time in its flight and its fullness.

Guarini brought the pastoral play, the movement toward the third genre and the adaptation of theatrical form to ideological representation into definitive integration, with *Il pastor fido, tragicomedia pastorale*.[21] Only deconstruction or refraction can identify vestiges of the theatrical microstructures that Guarini reassembled for his ambitious transformation. The human manipulator of a plot that is Sophoclean tragedy in design and intrigue comedy in the disposition of its theatregrams (Guarini termed it "l'ordine comico")[22] is Corisca, a character who seems so distant from the nurse-servant figure that to allege the antecedent makes a point only in an analysis of theatrical recombination and contamination. Corisca is not quite a *ninfa attempata*, although she is somewhat older and vastly more experienced than the other nymphs. Her function by association with this family of characters and actions would expectedly be that of a subordinate well-wisher of the young lovers, like Cresci's manipulative Tirena or Tasso's Dafne, but on the contrary, Corisca is not benign. She wants to contrive the death of the *innamorata* Amarilli in order to have the faithful shepherd Mirtillo for herself. To deceive the lovers, she adopts the role of conventional well-wishing confidant and go-between: she exhorts Amarilli to love, urges Mirtillo to boldness and arranges a rendezvous for them. All this Guarini fuses with another staple of comic action, the compromising discovery of lovers in a dark room. As the scene is Arcadia, the function of the comic *camera terrena* is assigned to a grotto, appropiately dark. Corsica's strategy of deception and her pragmatic dismissal of moral ideals bear the stamp of long use by comic servants, and the scene of a violent encounter with the *satiro* whom she has loved and cast aside and who grabs her by the hair, but is left with only a wig in his hands and taunts in his ears, evokes the city streetcorner of comedy. In the cursed and tragic Arcadia of *Il pastor fido* city noises, the physical clashes, and the verbal wrangling of *servi* and *cortigiane* strike the mind's ear as a faint but distinct tone in the measured discord that Guarini composes.

His redistribution and reversal of elements of action and association make of Corsica as wicked a variation on the clever manipulator of comedy as that constituted by Iago in the ultimate distortion of *commedia* achieved by Shakespeare in *Othello*. Moving, as in *Othello* or *Oedipus Rex*, but toward a happy rather than tragic ending, the comprehensive theatregram of design in *Il pastor fido* draws new significance from the old patterns: the tragic inescapability of fate, by a providential reversal, becomes a comic image of blind human pursuit of error, which takes good for evil and *vice versa*, misinterprets divine oracles, and in unwitting self-enmity works against the ineffable plan for men's happiness that heaven implements by the least expected means. In *Othello* the design of the tricker-tricked, of mischief hoist by its own petard, which in comedy works to the benefit of the good, is horribly turned inside out, and innocence as well as guilt works its own downfall. The function of "improvising manipulator" assigned to the complex character of Iago is both adapted to this design and contributes to its formation, interacting with the credulity of Othello and the naiveté of Desdemona, who helps to do herself in by her inability even to imagine what she is suspected of. Corsica's machinations throughout *Il pastor fido* surprisingly become the means whereby truth is at last discovered and the oracle fulfilled. The fusion and reversal in her of attitudes and actions shared with the *serve*, *balie* and *ninfe attempate* in comedies and other pastorals are appropriate and necessary to an ironic final peripety that includes her in the universal and divinely foreseen happiness against which the Arcadians have blindly struggled. In short, there is a structural kinship between the designs of *Othello* and the *Pastor fido*: both are reversals of the tricker-tricked, and, as such, add to the technical and conceptual range of the mixed genres under exploration by a theatrical movement that had become international. *Othello* is made by its new *contaminatio* of genres into unrelieved tragedy and *Il pastor fido* by an even-handed blending into tragicomedy, both ventures in genre conducted by the recombination of persons, associations, and actions from the repertory of *commedia*.

*   *   *

Il pastor fido was to become the single most influential example of pastoral drama and of the calculated mixture of comedy and tragedy, but contamination of theatregrams in all declensions, effecting contamination of the two genres, continued to propose other versions of the third genre.

When professionals of the *arte* began using the combinatory process for improvisation from scenarios, they tailored their mixtures of comedy, pastoral and tragedy to the semi-fixed roles assumed as specialties by given actors and to the compact size of an acting company. The result has repeatedly been cast as the antithesis of regular theatre, but when it is reattached to the cultural system it belonged to originally, the *commedia dell'arte* appears rather as an alternative style of participation in the accretive repertory begun in *commedia erudita*, polished by the practice of *contaminatio* into an arsenal of classical playmaking and then directed afield to the dialectical modern triumph of a third genre. By the late sixteenth century the great theatrical enterprise belonged not only to a primarily private and festival drama but to Italian commercial show business and, more or less, to all the players and playwrights of Europe.

Although the acting troupes who developed the *commedia dell'arte* participated in more than one kind of pastoral play, the variety of the third genre that they preferred for their characteristic improvisational mode was, to judge by extant scenarios, the mixture of magic and romance in which exiled nobles, raucous peasants and servants mingled in Arcadia with shepherds, sorcerers, satyrs, tutelary deities and other supernatural beings. With limitations on the size of the cast and with emphasis on the potential for spectacle and physical action of the fantasy that was permitted to this Ovidian kind of pastoral, the role of *innamorata*'s confidant was more dispensable than in psychologizing literary versions, and such functions of persuading to love, remembering lost love, juxtaposing experience to naiveté and so forth, that the plot left room for, were redistributed among the necessary stock types.

The scenarios of Arcadia unearthed by Ferdinando Neri and Flaminio Scala's *Arbore incantato*, together with related pastoral elements in other *giornate* of his *Favole rappresentative*[23] document a preference among Italian professional players for the same ingredients of the magical pastoral that Shakespeare chose for *A Midsummer Night's Dream* and *The Tempest*. As usual, Shakespeare pitched his variations at new frequencies and even went so far as to leave out the shepherds; but the familiar features identify the genre. The magician with rod and book, the spirits, the urban refugees, wandering lost and hallucinated, the transformations into animal, vegetable or mineral forms, the boisterousness of self-infatuated clowns with their minds on drink and license jarring with the arcane or spiritually rarefied ethos of the wood or island to which they wander: these are repertorial features of literary *favole pastorali* like Cresci's, Castelletti's, Pasqualigo's or Guazzoni's[24] that the *comici dell'arte* and Shakespeare took up for some of their excursions from the city and the court.

It is illustrative of the way the common fund of theatrical coin was drawn upon that a theatregram suppressed or subdivided past recognition by the exigencies of one generic formation, such as the magical pastoral, might in another remain indefinitely in use in all its varieties. Of Scala's fifty model scenarios the first forty are labelled "commedia" and display the credentials of the genre in their contemporary urban settings and actions of a stock cluster of variable characters, whose individual functions could be increased in inverse proportion to the size of the troupe; the frequent double duty of Capitano Spavento as both braggart comic butt and worthy *innamorato* is an example.

In the comedy scenarios the figure of Franceschina is the oldest and most essential of the various female servants. Ricciolina, Olivetta and others come and go, but Franceschina is always on hand and comes into play as confidant, *balia*, *mezzana*, innkeeper, sexy *serva*, as the permutations and redistributions of theatregrams continually form new plays. Her range includes actions of the *balia* as repository of the *innamorata*'s secrets (*Finta pazza*, Giornata 8) and associations which had been acclimatized to the stage a century earlier when Ariosto wrote the scene between Polimnesta and her Nutrice. Franceschina is a buxom bawdy foil to her lovesick *padrona* in *Li tragici successi* (Giornata 18), which was Scala's reduction for improvisational purposes of Borghini's *Donna costante*. But in *Il marito* (Giornata 9) Franceschina becomes the *nutrice* and is not only an inciter to virtue, confidant of the *innamorata* and manipulator of the plot, but is also singularly enterprising: assuming the transvestite disguise which is more commonly the prerogative of the *innamorata* herself, Franceschina poses as the jealous husband of her young *padrona*, whom she thus saves from an unwanted marriage.[25] When Scala expanded his scenario into a complete five-act text, *Il finto marito*[26], with the characters renamed, his additions and changes were all further recombinations from the repertory of theatregrams.

*   *   *

Neither the *commedia dell'arte* nor Shakespeare as we know them would have been conceivable except at this moment of a movement which had acquired great formal variety and geographical extension,[27] but not so great as to have shifted its centre of intelligibility, resting on basic developmental principles, codes, vocabularies and the memory of a common beginning in the specifically Renaissance Will to Genre that Shakespeare recapitulates in the advance publicity of the players in *Hamlet*, where he underlines the choice of Latin models, the transgressive creation of new genres from the fusion of old and the function equally of the "writ" and the "liberty," that is, of the literary dramatic text and the actor's improvisation.[28] Polonius' famous description of the players sums up a large and mature dramaturgical system in which both the *commedia dell'arte* and Shakespeare worked.

When Shakespeare dramatized the tale of Romeo and Juliet he did not do what Borghini in literary comedy or Scala in scenarios did with the same story nor what dozens of Italian *commediografi* did with similar combinations of theatregrams, but instead kept the dark outcome of da Porto's, Bandello's and Brooke's versions, to make a "lamentable tragedy." The code of its construction, however, places Shakespeare's play squarely in the experimental theatre of mixed genres as a comi-tragedy. At any moment *Romeo and Juliet* could be turned by an accident of good fortune or simply by the failure of one of the accidents of bad fortune into a romantic comedy. Even Tybalt's death could be assimilated by the *commedia grave*, as that of the *innamorata*'s cousin is in the analogous *Donna costante*.

The perception of Shakespeare's use of the world of romantic comedy as the matrix of tragedy which Susan Snyder comes to by comprehensive genre theory with psychological underpinnings and global premises about comedy as a "rejection of singleness" and tragedy as an isolation in a unique fate, is arrived at without reference to the Italian forays into genre combinations.[29] Salingar brings the specificity of cultural history to his study of comic traditions and recognizes Shakespeare's mastery of Italian techniques. But Salingar sees this primarily as a mechanical feat, learned from Italian comedies of the early sixteenth century and most clearly illustrated by *The Merry Wives of Windsor*, one of Shakespeare's least romantic comedies; he points to the doubling of plots, the use of a repertoire of casts and situations from joint narrative and stage traditions, and the construction of comic actions as networks of tricks and vicissitudes of Fortune. It is to an ulterior addition of elements from Ovid and medieval romance, rather, that Salingar attributes the motif of transformation, the changes within characters, the poetic and moving spectacles of illusion opening the way to self-knowledge and of restoration and reconciliation that are the essence of Shakespeare's romantic comedy and have caused the late plays especially to be called commonly "romances," or individually by Robert G. Hunter "comedies of forgiveness" and by Thomas McFarland "pastoral."[30]

Absent from these views of Renaissance drama (an omission that diminishes both Italian theatre and Shakespeare) is the middle term between distant sources and individual achievement, that is, the resources of the theatrical movement that in Italy produced not only neat intrigue comedies in the early Cinquecento but also subsequently, romantic comedy, experiments with tragedy and a pastoral drama cultivated with intent to stage the kinds of visions at which Shakespeare would excel.

Evidence that Shakespeare used Arthur Brooke's verse narrative as a source for *Romeo and Juliet* suggests how complex the relationship was between source, dramatization and contemporary dramaturgy, but it need conflict neither with Snyder's conclusion that Shakespeare made tragedy out of romantic comedy nor with Salingar's that he deployed Italian techniques. Brooke said that he "saw the same argument lately set foorth on stage,"[31] and even without his statement it could be deduced from the figure of the "noorse" alone, whose character and behaviour he establishes by a cluster of associational attitudes and actions from the lexicon of the stage. The "noorse's" tantalizing an impatient *innamorata* by dragging out her lover's message, her earthy reminiscence of the pleasure of losing a maidenhead, encouraging and contrasting with Juliet's high passion, her practical, unprincipled and uncomprehending advice to Juliet to commit adultery, that is, bigamy with Paris, her taking Romeus' money and glossing it with silence: such moves, long familiar in various combinations of the *balia* or *serva* in Italian comedy, are, as we have seen, not essential to the tragic narrative. They confirm Brooke's statement that he saw the story in a play, and they tell us that the play's theatregrams were comic ones. Shakespeare accepts this generic placement and intensifies it. Adding more bawdy nattering for the Nurse, a rebuke from her *padrona* Lady Capulet, and taunts and sexual slurs from Mercutio on the street, the latter here assuming the action most commonly assigned to the impudent *ragazzo* in association with an old *serva* (or often with a *pedante*), Shakespeare supplements the current coin of the genre *commedia* with more of the same.

Simultaneously he employs the principle of dramatizing specific narrative sources by contaminations of theatregrams pointed toward contamination of genres. But instead of bringing comedy to the verge of tragedy, then reversing it into a happy ending, as his Italian contemporaries were doing, he pushes it all the way. In the process he disposes the units in an integrating comic theatregram of design redirected; the Nurse's function as messenger, for example, takes its place in the pattern of missed messages, disastrous gaps in understanding, and crossed stars, that finally illuminates the tragic nature of the play. The same elements had long been intrinsic to the "ordine comico" which Guarini adduced in his construction, as even the titles of many comedies announce. Just the label *"Comedy of Errors"* names a pattern of mistakings and *"Much Ado About Nothing"* an intricate figure of over-reactions to misinterpreted "noting" or ocular impressions, so *"Gl'ingannati"* and *"I suppositi"* had described early designs of deceits and impersonations, while later *"La cangiaria"* (the play of identity changes), *"Gl'intrichi d'amore,"* *"Gl'ingiusti sdegni,"* *"La furiosa"* and such pastoral titles as *"I sospetti,"* *"Gl'intricati,"* *"La danza de Venere"* point to the theatregrams of design constantly being formed like snowflakes from recombinations of smaller parts.

Juliet's Nurse, although she is Shakespeare's only *balia* proper, shares functions with other characters whose individual distinctions illustrate Shakespeare's inventiveness as much as their partial similarities do his mastery of theatregrams—Margaret of *Much Ado*, Lucetta of *Two Gentlemen of Verona* and Nerissa of *The Merchant of Venice* are all identified in the First Folio as waiting-women, but of different social rank, and they all have assignments appropriate to the *serva* in association with the *innamorata*, but not the same ones: Margaret is not a confidant, but she is a mildly bawdy foil to Hero and is closely involved in the shaping design of seen things misconstrued about which there is so much ado; Lucetta is not bawdy, only teasing and more blasé than her lovesick mistress; Nerissa is the most intimate with the *innamorata*, Portia, and also shadows her in other associations and actions, falling in love, putting on male disguise and participating in the merciful deceit that saves the merchant's pound of flesh. Mistress Quickly of *Merry Wives of Windsor* is listed as "Caius' servant" but functions primarily as a freelance *mezzana*.

In *Othello*, Emilia is identified only as Iago's wife but, as Barbara Heliodora De Mendonça is not alone in observing, she plays the *"servetta"* to the *"innamorata"* Desdemona.[32] Earthy, practical and outspoken, a *serva-ninfa attempata-balia* spinoff more than the ensign's wife she is labelled, Emilia represents the kind of acute distortion of models which was one of Shakespeare's characteristic skills. She and Juliet's Nurse are related through comic theatregrams and both belong to tragedies, but they and the tragedies are each a unique recombination of parts and kinds. Shakespeare contaminates the same two genres, but in *Othello* he does not make a *commedia grave* with an unfortunate end as he does in *Romeo and Juliet*; rather he begins with comic commonplaces and allows their farthest imaginable psychological weight and consequence to overpower the scenario and subvert all the theatregrams. The design of the adultery trickery plot, with jealous cuckold, *malmaritata*, young *innamorato* and the rest, is transferred to Othello's mind, evoked by Iago. To deny the obscene farce he imagines himself in, he turns it to tragedy, with his own hands killing Desdemona and himself (tragic theatregrams of action, incidentally, with visual and semiotic substance radically differentiating them from the ways in which "Disdemona" and the Moor meet their deaths in the Giraldi narrative which was Shakespeare's source). Othello thinks in theatregrams; Shakespeare reveals the distance between them and reality. But to do so he uses them as signs which can be joined with other signs, carrying over old meanings against which the result defines itself as new.

Positivistic *Quellenstudien*, concentrating on precise sequence of linear transmission, contribute little to our perception of movement by continual recombination and variation, but many of the other roads of historical criticism do lead to Rome, that is, to Italian theatre. Modern editors' accounts of Shakespeare's handling of materials, and individual analyses such as the one Salingar makes of Italian techniques in what Jeanne Addison Roberts defines as Shakespeare's "English" comedy,[33] *The Merry Wives of Windsor*, in synthesis testify to a layer of dramaturgy called into action somewhere between the choice of specific sources and the finished play, to a central process comprising *contaminatio*, patterned complication and variation of theatregrams.[34] Unlike most Italian playwrights and all the scenario-smiths, Shakespeare never repeats himself; each play, distinct even from those of his other plays nearest to it, is like a solution to a problem in theatrical genre. The system that generated such problems and concomitantly offered terms and a process for their solutions was one made in Italy, but enlarged and used wherever in Europe Renaissance drama flourished.

NOTES

1 "Shakespeare's Comic Remedies," *Shakespearean Comedy*, ed. Maurice Charney (New York, 1980), 4. For comparison of Shakespeare's comedy with the Terentian model, see her *Comic Transformations in Shakespeare* (London and New York, 1980).

2 John Manningham's diary note on a 1602 performance, "At our feast wee had a play called 'Twelve Night, or What You Will,' much like the *Commedy of Errores*, or *Menechmi* in Plautus, but most like and neere to that in Italian called *Inganni*," surely refers not to Secchi's or Gonzaga's *Inganni* but to the much imitated, adapted and translated *Ingannati*, the collective work of the Sienese Accademia degli Intronati performed in 1531 and printed in 1537. I quote from Geoffrey Bullough, *Narrative and Dramatic Sources of Shakespeare*, V. 2 (London and New York, 1958), 269.

3 *Shakespeare and the Traditions of Comedy* (Cambridge, 1974), 225 and 77.

4 *Timber: or, Discoveries*, in C.H. Herford and P.E. Simpson, *Ben Jonson*, V. 8 (Oxford, 1947), 584.

5 *El arte nuevo de hacer comedias*, 1609.

6 Antonio Gramsci, *Letteratura e vita nazionale* (Torino, 1955), V. 4, 70-71.

7 Ruzante, *Teatro, prima edizione completa. Testo, traduzione a fronte e note*, a cura di L. Zorzi (Milano, 1967, rpt. 1969), lxvi, n. 64. Zorzi refers to Marx's letter to Lassalle, 19 April 1859, on the subject of revolutionary tragedy.

8 Particularly valuable among numerous works on the subject, though not concerned with the theatre, are Nancy S. Struever, *The Language of History in the Renaissance: Rhetoric and Historical Consciousness in Florentine Humanism* (Princeton, 1970), and Thomas M. Greene, *The Light in Troy: Imitation and Discovery in Renaissance Poetry* (New Haven, 1982).

9 "La figura de Flaminio Scala," in *Alle origini del teatro moderno: La commedia dell'arte*, ed. Luciano Mariti (Rome, 1980), 23-24.

10 *La cassaria* (prose version, 1508), in Ludovico Ariosto, *Opere minori*, a cura de Cesare Segre (Milano, Napoli, 1954), 242.

11 Gianmaria Cecchi, for one, on Horatian critical grounds praised Ariosto especially for setting up standards for the logic of successive action, "Cede a te nella comica palestra/ Ogni Greco e Latin, perche tu solo / Hai veramente dimonstrato come /Esser deve il principio, il mezzo e'l fine/ Delle comedie . . . ." Intermedio VI, *Le pellegrine*, quoted in L. Ariosto, *Commedie e satire*, annotate da Giovanni Tortoli (Firenze, 1856), lxii, but Ariosto's other devices for structural coherence also moved Cecchi to imitation in more than one of his own comedies.

12 "El nome è li *Suppositi*, perché di supposizioni è tutta piena," Ariosto announces in the prologue, *I suppositi* (prose version, 1509) in *Opere minori*, ed. Segre, 298: "our Suppose is nothing else but a mystaking, or imagination of one thing for an other . . . . I suppose that euen already you suppose me very fonde that have so simply disclosed unto you the subtilties of these our Supposes; where, otherwise, in-deede, I suppose you shoulde haue heard almoste the laste of our Supposes before you could haue supposed anye of them aright." *Supposes . . .* Englished by George Gascoygne . . . 1566, Prologue, in *Chief Pre-Shakespearean Dramas*, ed. Joseph Quincy Adams (Cambridge, Mass., 1924), 537.

13 *Gli ingiusti sdegni comedia* (Roma, 1553), II. 1.

14 *La balia*, comedia (Fiorenza, 1560); *La Cecca*, comedia (Fiorenza, 1563).

15 Marvin T. Herrick, *Italian Comedy in the Renaissance* (Urbana, 1960), 178; Ireneo Sanesi, *La commedia*, 2ª ed. riv. e acc. (Milano, 1954), 344.

16 The semitragic thrust of the late *commedie gravi* naturally led also to assigning moralizing to nurses and maids but though it is not uncommon to hear virtuous resolutions from *balie*, as in Sforza Oddi's *Prigione d'amore* (Fiorenze, 1590) and Raffaello Borghini's *Donna costante* (Fiorenza, 1578), even in very grave romantic comedies it often suited the design to keep them to the usual coarse or commonsensical actions in their associations with the *innamorate*.

17 Torquato Tasso, *Aminta, favola boschereccia* (1573), I. 1. 129-31, in *Opere*, a cura di Bruno Maier (Milano, 1963), 95.

18 *Diana pietosa, comedia pastorale* (Firenze, 1585).

19 *Amarilli, pastorale* (Venetia, 1582).

20 *Tirena, favola pastorale* (Venetia, 1584).

21 Battista Guarini, *Il pastor fido, tragicommedia pastorale* (1589), in *Il pastor fido e Il compendio della poesia tragicomica*, a cura di Gioacchino Brognoligo (Bari, 1914).

22 *Compendio*, 231.

23 Neri, *Scenari delle maschere in Arcadia* (Città di Castello, 1913); Scala, *Il teatro delle favole rappresentative* (1611), a cura di Ferruccio Marotti, 2 vols. (Milano, 1976).

24 Luigi Pasqualigo, *Gl'intricati, pastorale* (Venetia, 1581); Diomisso Guazzoni, *Andromeda, tragicomedia boscareccia* (Venetia, 1587).

25 The fact that Franceschina, unlike other *commedia dell'arte serve*, was often played by a male actor, adds another digit to the multiplier by which the action theatregram of disguise-within-disguise could be readapted inexhaustibly. The possibilities were still being exploited in the 1970s in Jean Poiret's *Cage aux folles*, when Albin tries to conceal his being a drag queen by posing as conventional Uncle Al, and, that failing, as Maman.

26 *Il finto marito, commedia* (Venezia, 1619).
27 The resemblances that justly have persuaded comparatists from Allardyce Nicoll, O.J. Campbell, Winifred Smith, and Kathleen M. Lea to Ninian Mellamphy of the *commedia dell'arte*'s importance to Shakespeare and led Walter L. Barker to credit itinerant *comici* with the "eruption" of Elizabethan drama (*Three English Pantalones: A Study in Relations Between the Commedia dell'arte and Elizabethan Drama* [University of Connecticut dissertation, 1966], 204) in most cases point back to features which originated in earlier Cinquecento literary theatre and continued there, often modified by the reciprocal pressure of the art of the *comici*.
28 "The best actors in the world, either for tragedy, comedy, history, pastoral, pastoral-comical, historical-pastoral, tragical-historical, tragical-comical-historical-pastoral; scene individable, or poem unlimited. Seneca cannot be too heavy, nor Plautus too light. For the law of writ and the liberty, these are the only men." *Hamlet* II. 2. 387-83, ed. W. Farnham, in William Shakespeare, *The Complete Works*, general editor A. Harbage (New York, 1969).
29 *The Comic Matrix of Shakespeare's Tragedies* (Princeton, 1979), 4 ff.
30 Hunter, *Shakespeare and the Comedy of Forgiveness* (New York and London, 1965); McFarland, *Shakespeare's Pastoral Comedy* (Chapel Hill, 1972).
31 Preface "To the Reader," *The Tragicall Historye of Romeus and Juliet* (1562), in Shakespeare, *Romeo and Juliet*, ed. Brian Gibbons (London and New York, 1980), 240.
32 " 'Othello': a Tragedy Built on a Comic Structure," *Shakespeare Survey* 21 (1968), 35.
33 *Shakespeare's English Comedy: The Merry Wives of Windsor in Context* (Lincoln, Neb. and London, 1979).
34 See the Introduction to my edition and translation of Giambattista Della Porta, *Gli duoi fratelli rivali/The Two Rival Brothers* (Berkeley, Los Angeles and London, 1980) for further discussion of the process and for comparison of *Much Ado About Nothing* with a contemporary *commedia grave* on the same source plot.

The Stage in the Text: A Theatrical Stratification of Italian Renaissance Comedy

Domenico Pietropaolo
University of Toronto

The formal and systematic analysis of the theatre, as distinct from the literary study of drama, is a recently constituted area of theoretical and empirical research founded on the principle that the nature of theatrical discourse is radically different from that of other forms of linguistic expression. Its chief goal is the discovery and convalidation of evaluative paradigms and analytical categories proper to its object of investigation, on the premise that within its real boundaries the conceptual apparatus of adjacent fields—such as literary criticism and intellectual history—can shed only an inadequate sort of light, possibly capable of clarifying a few of its issues while inevitably disfiguring or altogether concealing others. The current status of the discipline as a whole is marked by the internal tension of rapid growth, but the theoretical frameworks which it has so far constructed have proven to be sufficiently free of indeterminacy to elucidate many hitherto imperfectly perceived problems. The empirical foundation of the best known contributions has been predictably restricted to a few plays, carefully selected either as a basis for inductive arguments or as test cases for deductive theories. Among these, Renaissance classical comedies constitute a prominent genre.

There are several reasons for this, and the first of them is the methodological challenge represented by the prospect of discovering the formal mechanisms of laughter-inducing communication. From the point of view of the structural relation of the whole to its parts, comedy—however conventionalised it may be—is considerably more complex than its rival genre, tragedy, since in the latter all sorts of details may often be cursorily treated without appreciable prejudice to the overall tragic effect, while in the former details play an absolutely vital role, given that comic effect does not principally depend on the general pattern of their succession, but on the specific character of each one of them. In comedy, as Paul Goodman observes, "the tiniest touch deflates the biggest balloon,"[1] and because individual works may be replete with "touches" and "balloons" of many different types, it is clear that the rigorous formalisation of comic theatrical discourse is a more intricate problem than that of its tragic counterpart. Furthermore, on the Renaissance stage the popularity of contemporary comedies by far outweighed that of all other dramatic genres,[2] and the realisation of this fact has recently brought great pressure to bear on the traditional approaches to the individual comedies, which made use of the various theoretical tools of literary criticism in order to uncover their significance in the history of literature and in the history of ideas, while largely neglecting the central issue of their inherent theatricality. The fallacy consists in assuming that the essential nature of a work written for the stage is not artificially assimilated to the nature of works directed at a reading public when it is forced to undergo a critical process designed for the latter. Centuries of subjection to such perspectives have radically altered the common sense perception of the textuality of Renaissance comedy, which has been treated by the dominant traditions as if it were a subspecies of narrative, indeed of post-Renaissance narrative, meant, that is, to come to fruition in a silent and private reading experience.

This process of disfiguration began in the Renaissance itself, when the very concept of text—independently of genre—started to undergo a profound transition, as the art of printing developed to industrial proportions and books became ordinary commodities, readily available and increasingly conceived for quiet and private reading rather than communal recitation. Later, as it lost all traces of its acoustic and kinesthetic dimensions, the text came to be regarded as lineal and sequential as its conventional representation in print and was finally taken to be essentially identical with it.[3] The text was now perceived as being able to communicate directly with the receiver of its message, having overcome by technological evolution its earlier need for rhapsodic mediation and the reader could now engage in the repeatable perusal of a permanently fixed text completely disregarding its previous synesthetic complexity. What had made St. Ambrose appear like a prodigy, when he let his eyes glide across the page without moving his lips, comes instinctively and effortlessly to the average reader in an age of mass typographic literacy.[4] In the Renaissance, oral reading was still the conventional practice and hence constituted a limiting factor in all forms of writing, necessarily affecting diction, syntax and style.[5] But we modern readers are such refined products of typographical conditioning that we must constantly remind ourselves not to bring our biases of lineal textuality and direct communication to texts that are historically prior to the advent of mass literacy and ontologically alien to the reading experience.

That theatrical discourse is not logically reducible to lineality must have been a very obvious fact to the Renaissance men concerned with its creation, from the dramatist who contributed its verbal text, to the director and cast who gave it its kinesthetic dimension, to the set designer who constructed the artificial spatial context in which words, actions and characters could acquire significance. For it was precisely at that time that the non-verbal theatrical arts, indispensable as they may have been regarded in the past, developed to the dignity of full professionalism, each with its foundation of systematic theory and each with an enabling as well as a limiting function to play in the collaborative production of sense.[6] And in each of these contributing arts there are clear signs of the interdependence that links them all together. To write for the stage does not mean only or principally to write in the virtual presence of an audience analogous to the implied reader of narrative texts, but to write something that can be effectively staged, making, that is, reasonable demands on the other theatrical arts and complying with their technical limitations. It is to write with a reliable knowledge of the stage as a multichanneled means of communication. In a real sense, a play is the transcription of a hypothetical performance, imagined by the author on the basis of current stage practices and posited by him as his immediate ideal of attainment. The recovery of the "production script" that is implicit in such a text should be the primary aim of a theatrical reading of a play.

The conceptual apparatus necessary to retrieve the inherent theatricality of a Renaissance comedy cannot therefore be derived from the principle of textual lineality, which in this case must be rejected as historically anachronistic and logically inadequate. But it can be induced from the manner in which the text allows us to see its dependence on the other theatrical arts. Since they were composed before the spectacular advent of Baroque stagecraft, which would immensely complicate the nature of theatrical discourse, Renaissance comedies bear the signs of only three relatively simple acts of communication, respectively taking place (i) among the playwright, the designer and the director, (ii) between the director and the cast, and finally (iii) between the cast and the audience. Three radically different types of communication are however involved: the first is bidirectional and has the character of an exchange meant to define the limits of reciprocal dependence, the second is unidirectional and is in the nature of a command awaiting assent and execution, and the third is indirect and involves overhearing and looking in—rather than hearing and mutual seeing —as the principle manner of communicative reception. This heterogeneity within the chain of communication will obviously require the use of different methodological concepts, since questions regarding the third act of communication would not be appropriate to the first.

At the level of gross description, therefore, Renaissance comedies may be regarded as consisting of three superimposed textual strata, each containing the matter of a different communicative transaction and subject to a different mode of analysis. This model pretends to be neither the playwright's compositional matrix nor a universally valid perspective on dramaturgy, but an analytical construct applicable to the comedies of the Serlian period, in which *ex machina* solutions to stage and plot problems are not frequent occurrences. As an heuristic device it has the powerful advantages of rendering immediately obvious the stage consciousness of the playwright and of forcing upon the reader an indispensable degree of theatrical depth of view in his study of a particular play.

On a higher order of reflection, we may recall that during the Serlian period there was no proscenium arch, the function of which is to enhance theatrical illusion by focusing the audience's attention on the action and by giving each spectator the impression that he is watching a real situation from an unseen window. In the absence of this framing device, the invention of which marks a profound change in the history of the theatre,[7] the vanishing point of the scenic architecture automatically becomes the point of convergence of all space, artificial as well as real, and hence the referential centre from which the significance of both the feigned and the real worlds could be logically determined. The question of the dialectics of illusion and reality, which was to play such an important role in Baroque poetics, could not have been a primary concern of Renaissance comedy. Once the reality of the fictional world is conventionally conceded as a necessary condition of meaningful perception, one cannot speak of an opposition but of a continuum from reality in its fullness to reality seen under a few of its aspects, separated from the rest, filtered through literary modules, and amplified for comic exposure.

Once the Serlian scene became the orthodox setting, the playwright had little to say on the matter.[8] The spatiality of his play was not something of his making, but rather an independently determined starting condition which imposed obvious restraints on his imagination. Of course, he could choose to locate the action in any city, but this would mean at the most that the Serlian flats would have to show one or three buildings typical of that city. The space to which the flats gave shape, the types of buildings that they represented, and their relative configuration remained unaltered: three houses shown in perspective on the right, three on the left, and a church at the back of the stage defined the performance space of virtually every comedy. Pictorial adaptation to a specific city was not a matter of great concern. In a letter to Lorenzo Strozzi, Donato Giannotti remarked that his *Il vecchio amoroso*, which was set in Pisa, could just as easily be imagined in Genoa.[9] And Machiavelli, in the prologue to *Mandragola*, says quite clearly: "Vedete l'apparato, / qual or vi si dimostra; / questa è Firenze vostra; / un'altra volta sarà Roma o Pisa / cosa da smascellarse dalle risa." ("Watch now the stage, as it is set up for you; / this is your Florence; / another time perhaps, Pisa or Rome / don't laugh too hard, or you'll break your jaw.")

There can be no doubt that the Serlian stage was a determining influence on the conventionalisation of Renaissance comedy, since the number of situations representable in a city square was quite limited. After some time, variation could occur only within the canonical forms rather than at the level of larger structural strategies. Even so, it can be easily argued that such restraints were not of necessity a negative factor. The overwhelming appeal of perspective staging made that kind of scenic architecture a desirable feature of every performance. Modern perspective science had taken the shallow space of Roman comedy, which was represented by two or three doors opening onto a street that ran laterally along the stage, and had given it depth and complexity, transforming it into a demographically centripetal area where representatives of all the classes and professions in the city could converge and cross each others' paths without great prejudice to their social status. From a more technical point of view this meant that the actors could move from back to frontstage as well as laterally, and could make use of at least thirteen entrances, represented by the doors of the buildings and the several streets that separated them. Indeed, an advantage of the Serlian set not shared by earlier and later perspective designs was that it allowed stage business to be carried out directly against the rear flat. Serlio had in fact wisely insisted that in order to counteract the negative effect of perspective architecture, which reduces the size of an object as it approaches the vanishing point, the buildings were to be arranged in order of real vertical dimension, thus avoiding the consequence that an actor standing upstage might have a roof or a cloud at shoulder height. Furthermore, the upward slope of the rear portion of the stage guaranteed visibility from all audience positions.

From the playwright's point of view this meant several things. First of all he was not compelled to connect adjacent scenes by including at least one character in both of them in order to avoid the awkwardness of an empty stage during scene transition, since the depth of the performance space made possible, with appropriate blocking, the simultaneous ending of one episode and the beginning of another with different characters. Although this new license was sparingly used by some authors, the majority of them took great advantage of it. It appears, for example, only twice in Grazzini's *Il frate* and four times in Giannotti's *Il vecchio amoroso*, but ten times in the Intronati's *Ingannati*, seventeen in Bargagli's *La pellegrina*—in which the entire second act is structured on such a staccato pattern—and eighteen in Piccolomini's *L'amor costante*.

Secondly, since in the set for comedy the highest building is a church, the newly created upstage area could be used to resolve an important dramaturgical problem in classical comedy, which consisted in finding a way of preserving the decorum of a lady or of a girl of good family engaged in a dialogue with a male character in a public place.[10] Stratagems such as disguises and concealed identities, usually ending with the revelation of the character's true social status when prolonged street appearances were no longer required of her by the plot, ceased to be indispensable, because encounters of this type could now conveniently and decorously take place near the church, as the ladies in question went to or returned from service, confession or prayer. This is especially significant in episodes involving a friar. Frate Timoteo's conversation with Lucrezia and Sostrata in *Mandragola* and the scene between the prior of San Nicola and Dianora in *Il vecchio amoroso* would lack propriety in a street set and would be very awkward against the painted backdrops of the pre-Serlian stage as well as in the upstage area enclosed by the heavily reduced structures of later three-dimensional perspective designs. On the other hand, when such a lady-friar meeting takes place relatively far from the church, it immediately appears suspect and compromising. "Qui bisogna, padre, che noi andiamo in casa," says Caterina to Frate Alberigo in *Il frate* (II, 5), "acciocché noi nos dessimo da pensare a qualcuno." ("At this point, father, we must go into the house so that no one will jump to conclusions.")

In addition to this, the church interior could house offstage meetings which required secrecy from others as well as physical proximity to the public square, in order to justify a character's re-entry into the performance space without thereby having to complicate the plot any further. Giorgetto and Giulio in Cecchi's *L'Assiuolo* use the church precisely in this fashion, without the least suggestion that what they do is extraordinary or even uncommon. Being the meeting place accessible to all social groups, the church—on whose door is significantly located the vanishing point of the parallel plane of the set—is another centripetal focus of demographic motion and may, for present purposes, be regarded as the enclosed counterpart of the public square that extends in front of it. In the theatrical experience, the dramatist, the stage designer and the director could collaborate in playing with the spectators' consciousness, taking it, as if on a Möbius strip, from the inside of the theatre to the outside space of the square and back to the inside of the church, where all space seemed to come to an end, without losing architectural continuity or requiring abrupt adjustments in critical and aesthetic perspective.

The plot, however, had to be tightly controlled, since situations could easily arise that would force the spectators to alter in a radical manner their mode of aesthetic perception. By calculating the correct slope for the stage floor and by selecting the proper axis and vanishing point, the Serlian architect could geometrically create in the spectators' consciousness the illusion of great depth, but the actor had in reality only seven metres from the middle point of the front edge of the stage to the church. And while this real space was considerably deeper than that of the classical street set, it still required only one or two seconds to cross at normal walking speed. This meant that the dramatist had studiously to avoid scenes in which at one end of the square two characters carry on a dialogue while a third walks toward them from the opposite end. Such scenes, which are structurally fine in narrative discourse, would be very problematic on stage, since the science of perspective affects only the audience's view of space and not also their perception of time. However skilled the director might be, blocking episodes of this kind with a modicum of verisimilitude would be too difficult a task. However, not everyone was willing to accept such an imposition on the dramatist, and Piccolomini took issue with it when, in an attempt to vindicate the playwright's freedom from the designer and director, he said that the spectators can easily adjust their mode of perception to temporary lapses in verisimilitude.[11] But it is difficult to rationalise the awkwardness in *Il vecchio amoroso* (II, 5-6) where, between the moment when Lionetto sees Dianora and the prior on the church steps and the moment when he gets there, they each go through several speeches.

Furthermore the ground plan of the Serlian theatre did not permit a close relationship between the audience and the actors. Unlike the outer stage of the Elizabethan playhouse, the booth stage of *Commedia dell'Arte* productions, and the apron stage of Restoration theatres, the performance space of Renaissance comedy not only did not extend into the large area occupied by the audience but was actually quite far from the first row.[12] This essentially means that the ideal style of recitation must have been declamatory, with voice projection at right angles to the outer edge of the stage, and slow, respectively in order to avoid loss of syntactical clarity at a distance, to prevent wing muffling and sound dispersion, and to maintain distinctness of word utterance, since the speed of easily comprehensible speech varies inversely with the size of the hall and the proximity of the spectators. This last point was especially emphasized by Leone de' Sommi. "Come vizio pestilente, poi, li proibisco lo affrettarsi, anzi le costringo, potendo, a recitar molto adagio," he says about his standard instructions to his actors. ("Then I forbid them to speak too fast, just as if it were a pestilential vice, and when possible I compel them to recite very slowly.") "Et dico molto, facendoli esprimere con tardità le parole fin all'ultime sillabe, senza lasciarsi mancar la voce, come molti fanno, onde spesso lo spettatore perde con gran dispiacere la conclusione della sentenza."[13] ("And I mean very slowly, compelling them to pronounce slowly their words down to the last syllable, without losing their voice as many do, so that often the spectators regretfully miss the end of the sentence.")

A major consequence of this consideration is that a comedy could not possibly contain many asides requiring quick stage whispering and an extensive use of cheating techniques, by which an actor turns his head away from his interlocutor in order to deliver a line in another direction, but not his body. Asides, in other words, could not be witty and derisive remarks productive of quick humour, since the degree of audience complicity and intimacy that such lines must arouse is too difficult to achieve without physical proximity. That is why the vast majority of asides in Renaissance comedy occur while another character is either temporarily offstage (e.g. Lamprida's aside in *L'Alessandro* I, 3), or else is present but unseen by the speaker (e.g. Moro's aside in *Il vecchio amoroso* I,3). In such cases the actor is not required to whisper or to cheat.

It is clear from the preceding considerations that the interdependence of the verbal and non-verbal theatrical arts is governed by a rigid set of rules, which may be regarded as the code of laws of the stage peculiar to a given historical period. These rules are presupposed by the dramatist as his operational premises in the composition process, and later should be called upon to sanction his play as a performance text of a determinable level of excellence. While such premises may be gleaned only from a theatrically orientated reading of many plays and technical works, they are behind every scene meant for performance. It is useful in this respect to think of each moment in a dramatic plot as the verbal realisation of a formal compositional matrix, which is defined by a fixed aspect, constituted by the code of the stage in its systematic entirety, and by a variable one, represented by the actual strategy of plot development chosen by the dramatist among the several permitted by the code.[14] A rigorous theatrical stratification of Renaissance comedy involves both aspects, since it aims to retrieve from within the text the stage code that delimits its universe of discourse and legitimates the plot-building strategies that it employs. The first textual layer thus identified concerns the code; the second and third layers concern the strategies, that is, the substance of what the author accomplishes within the framework of the code's enabling and forbidding axioms, possibly violating some of them and possibly exploiting others to their maximum.

A significant advantage of this model is its implicit guarantee that the theatrical appraisal of a text will not be determined by judicial principles from alien aesthetic categories, such as the one in which the text figures as a variety of poetry and is evaluated in relation to poetics. Excellence in one category does not imply excellence in the other. An episode which, from a literary perspective, may appear to be a highly original treatment of the subject matter may be the result of insufficient skill in practical dramaturgy and based on a gratuitous violation of the stage code. On the other hand, a deliberate violation, carried out with the intention of denouncing the shortcomings of the code itself and with the resolution to bring an improvement to it, should be regarded as an attempt to inject theatrical originality into forms that have become too rigid. Lorenzino de' Medici's *Aridosia*, for example, cannot possibly be blocked on a traditional *piazza* scene without erecting another structure in its centre.[15] To realise fully the significance of a dramatist's view of the stage code, the best thing to do is to read the text from the perspective of a director of the time.

Actually except for the actors, who use the script to memorise their parts, the director is ideally the only one who reads the written text, and while his response to its literary qualities may be comparable to that of any other reader, his manner of reading is definitely not. For him, a line of print is truly like a line of music, meant, that is, to be read vertically as well as horizontally.[16] A page of dialogue activates in his mind a stratificational mode of perception by which he simultaneously and distinctly sees the text in terms of verbal exchange, costumes, stage configurations, action blocking and bodily expression, all within the spatiality of a given set. In his reading, which he later imparts to his cast and technicians, the director keeps in mind the stage code, recognising that its prescriptions and prohibitions are meant to guarantee a minimum of representational character to the performance, which may have to be safeguarded from the playwright's tendency to exercise stage-independent license as well as from the director's propensity to favour text-independent spectacle. But in comparison to the dramatist, the director is less hampered by the code, and in fact can enjoy considerable latitude in the interpretation and application of its principles. Costumes, stage configurations, gestures and the like may vary greatly from the illusion-seeking representational extreme of exclusive adherence to the written text to the spectacular extreme of self-conscious theatricality. Within this wide range, the director makes precise choices, bearing in mind that in each case there will be the two ingredients of representation and spectacle, present in mutually inverse proportions. If the elements of this relation could be precisely quantified for each performance, the spectacle/representation ratio would be an exact measurement of the director's artistic autonomy from the text and a precise assessment of the importance that he attaches to his art vis-à-vis that of the playwright. But such rigour and precision are hardly necessary for a reliable estimate.

Certainly there is no need for exact quantification in the case of a director such as Leone de' Sommi, since he fully endorsed the premise that good theatrical discourse owes much less to the written text than it does to the efforts and skill that go into a production. For example, he states regarding the importance of good actors: "Et oso dire, anzi affermo per vero, che piú importi avere boni recitanti che bella commedia."[17] ("And I dare say, or rather I declare it as truth, that it is more important to have good actors than a good comedy.") In his direction, de' Sommi scrupulously adhered to the text, but he knew that the text went only so far. The dramatists provide the dialogue but most of them are usually silent on how a speech should be delivered and on what the actor should do in between speeches. The director has the task of defining these actions for each character, bearing in mind the need for textual representation as well as the audience's taste for text-independent stage business and spectacle. The most effective way of accomplishing this was the addition of textually non-significatory and non-contradictory elements, such as gags and lavish costumes, since in this manner it was possible to preserve textual integrity and to provide at the same time some guarantees of success to the overall performance-interpretation of the comedy. As seen by an audience, therefore, the play depended to a large extent on the director and on his perception of the dominant theatrical taste.[18]

Faced with such a range of possible stage interpretations of his play, the author might take certain measures, meant to contain the director's liberty and to ensure that the actual performance of his work would be acceptably close to the hypothetical one that he had imagined. Ordinary stage directions are in effect such interpretive co-ordinates, but, in an age when dramaturgical conventions did not include elaborate authorial interventions in the mechanics of production, they can hardly be the whole answer. Furthermore, stage directions are by their very nature ambiguous, since they may be perceived as being part of the text, and hence mandatory, or else as being authorial accretions which may be safely disregarded and even considered attempts to interfere with the reading process. The solution was to incorporate the stage directions as interpretive guidelines into the dialogue itself, so that to stage an episode differently from its internally prescribed manner would be tantamount to the creation of an irreducible and conspicuous contradiction between its verbal and its non-verbal expressions. The only alternative would be to disfigure the text by altering the prescriptive passages, and this was not acceptable for obvious reasons. Leone de' Sommi, for example, reports that he always instructed his actors to learn their parts and cues to perfection. Directorial creative reading for him involves only those things that the playwright "nella testura della favola non può esplicitamente insegnare."[19] ("in writing the story cannot explicitly teach.") Clearly it is against this background that we should study a text's self-protective and metatextual disposition, which is what a modern scholastic might call its *esse intentionale*, orientated toward the perceiving intellect of the director and eventually transferred by him to the cast and technicians.

Renaissance comedies exploit their metatextual potential to varying degrees. It is an easy matter to quote examples of dialogic indications governing facial expression ("E di che piangi tu, bacchillona?") ("And you, silly girl, what are you crying for?"), gestures ("E' mi pare molto pieno di pensieri. Questo dimenare le mani e tenere il capo basso, mi paiono segni di cattive nuove") ("He seems to me to be burdened with thoughts. His throwing his arms around, his keeping his head down, seem to me signs of bad news"), costumes ("Ella è vestita di turchino, con acconciatura alla moresca") ("She is dressed in deep blue, with her hair done in the Moorish style"), properties ("e questa è la barba che io accattai dal profumiere") ("and this is the beard which I bought from the perfumer"), sound effects ("i' sento venir giú per le scale") ("I hear someone coming down the stairs"), restrictions on use of cheating devices ("vo' mi guardate in viso?") ("Why are you looking at me in the face?"), stationary character configurations ("fermiamoci qua dal nostro uscio e aspettiamo il vecchio . . .") ("let's stop here by our door and wait for the old man . . ."), action without walking ("che mastichi tu?) ("what are you chewing?"), and crossing the stage ("ma io lo veggo col nostro priore, e viemmi incontro correndo")[20] ("But I see him with our prior, and he's running towards me"). But it is immediately obvious that such instances—in which the playwright assumes the role of the director and effectively forces upon the actors and production personnel the essential elements of any stage reading of his text—are as scarce and brief in some plays as they are abundant and detailed in others. It would no doubt be profitable to survey a very large number of comedies from this point of view and to order them according to ascending degrees of explicit stage-metatextuality. Such a distribution would enable us to compare at sight the comedies of different authors, periods and cities in relation to their reliance on local directorial conventions. This would imply, for example, that the theatrical *esse intentionale* of a play like *Mandragola*, which would appear near the low end of the stage-metatextuality scale, lies almost completely in the area of the local performance traditions, on which it heavily relies for all possible stage interpretations and which constitute therefore the necessary and sufficient paradigm for this phase of a modern theatrical stratification of the play. On the other hand, the theatrical *esse intentionale* of a play like *L'Assiuolo*, which would figure near the other end of the scale, is only in part rooted in current and local directorial conventions, the scope of which the text severely limits with respect to itself, while issuing, from within, the indispensable parameters of its own potential performances, including, for instance, a delightful costume change in full view of the public and with the help of a stage assistant (II, 8).

Whether it is extensive or not, the explicit stage-metatextuality of Renaissance comedies constitutes a necessary part of the communicative transaction that takes place between the director at the emitting end and the cast and production staff at the receiving end. A rigorous theatrical reading of the texts, as we have seen, entails the reconstruction, largely from within, of the essence of that act of communication, the purpose of which is to establish authorially the manner of presenting individual scenes to the audience. And here we come to the final part of the theatrical stratification of the text, which is to consider its disposition to audience perception. What does an audience perceive in a play and how does it perceive it? This question is as inevitable as it is difficult and ultimately determines the methodological difference that separates the study of theatrical works from the study of other genres. Texts meant to be read can count on the fact that the reading process may be conducted at a personally suitable speed and is repeatable as well as interruptable, thereby allowing the reader time for intermittent analytical or reminiscent reflection and the opportunity to acquire the linguistic and background information needed to resolve cognitive difficulties that may arise along the way. Performance texts can count on no such thing. Performance perception is uncontrollable, unrepeatable and uninterruptable. In the theatre there are no quick reference works to check, and prolonged analytical reflection is as negative as distraction, since, by anchoring the mind to a particular incident, it causes the imperfect reception of another episode in the continuously unfolding text. This is especially true of comedy, which more than tragedy and the opera libretto relies extensively on the correct perception of details. The literary, philosophical and structural issues that now require considerable scholarly effort for their retrieval and elucidation could not have been the immediate concern of an audience intent on watching a new play, and in any case would not have been within the cognitive capacity of the average spectator during a performance. We must admit that while the audience of Renaissance comedy was indeed "being invited to perform the dual mental action of observing the pleasing fiction and perceiving the truth of which it was a sign,"[21] it was the former rather than the latter that dominated actual performance reception.

The textual modes of this dominance are visuality and orality, since sight and hearing are the only two sensory channels through which the performance of a Renaissance play was apprehended. Visuality and orality, which are manifested principally as character ostension and speech comprehensibility, are therefore the only two paradigms that may be used to analyse the text's special susceptibility to performance fruition. These paradigms are related hierarchically, with visuality occupying the higher level, since, as the psychology of the art of memory abundantly proved to Renaissance men of culture, visual images produce more lasting and deeper impressions than words. The first consequence of this consideration is that what the spectators saw on stage determined their global perception of the play to a greater extent than what they heard. Specifically this means that such questions as the relative significance of a character in the plot, and therefore his contribution to the perceived thematic configuration of the play, must be described in terms of his active presence on stage. The most important character is the leading actor, and so on down to the least conspicuous member of the cast. Understood in this manner, "character importance" may or may not coincide with the significance attached to him in a literary analysis of the text. Furthermore, "importance" ceases to be a vague notion and becomes a precisely quantifiable parameter, being as it is nothing other than the proportion of the total performance dominated by the impersonating actor.

The textual strategy with respect to the visual perception of character interaction may be appraised using the formalisms—in a properly adapted form—developed by Solomon Marcus and currently being explored by the "Bucharest school" of theatrical analysis.[22] The first step is preparatory and consists in translating the text into a matrix whose rows correspond exactly to the *dramatis personae* and whose columns represent all the scenes—or discrete units of stage appearance—in sequential order, indicating in the intersection of the mth row with the nth column whether character m is on stage in scene n and the number of lines that he delivers if he is. Once Machiavelli's *Mandragola* is so charted, for example, we may determine by little more than simple inspection the total duration of a character's presence on stage, the frequency of his appearances, his temporal proximity to hostile or friendly characters, his probability of occurrence in a particular scene, and the character configurations in which he appears—which may be easily correlated respectively with perceived total importance, active involvement in plot development, the dramatic suspense that he produces, the effectiveness and memorability of his entrances, and the motifs that he is associated with, whether collaboratively or antagonistically. In the case of Lucrezia, for instance, most of these factors have a very low value: whatever significance she may have in an analysis of the text as a world built on Machiavellian *virtú*, in the audience's visual perception of the play she is hardly present, her "importance" being only slightly higher than that of the unnamed woman in III, iii—who is only a device to introduce Fra Timoteo—and lower than that of all other characters, including Sostrata. On the other hand, Siro, who appears in 11 of the 37 scenes, is considerably more "stage important": he is on stage for a long time, is dynamic in his many entrances and exits, and appears with all the characters except the three women. However, Siro can only be perceived as an instrument of others, almost as a stage assistant to more important characters, since in all he has only 43 lines in 54 speeches, which means that thematically what he says cannot amount to very much.

Similarly, from the scene-character matrix we may infer the relative instability of each episode involving more than two characters, including supernumeraries, since in all such groups there may be collaboration among all the members or else collaboration among some of them pitted against the others. Scene instability is an indication of the imbalance in character orientation resulting from collusion with respect to the action of the play. In the perception of a performance it corresponds to the phenomenon of comic suspense, which is the audience's premonition that the scene is susceptible of imminent radical change. In *Mandragola*, until the seduction of Lucrezia has occurred, Messer Nicia is the only character who does not appear in at least one perfectly stable configuration, since the other characters on stage with him always feign collaboration but in reality conspire against him. The implication of this is that the audience's mental involvement in the comic action of the play is necessarily more intense whenever Messer Nicia appears on stage with two or more other characters. The most unstable scenes are those in which the conspiring characters are most numerous: the episode when Callimaco discusses with Messer Nicia his solution to the problem of Lucrezia's impregnation, in feigned professional collaboration with him and in the collusive presence of Ligurio and Siro (II, 6), and the scene in which Callimaco, disguised as a lute player, pretends to be captured by Messer Nicia and his supposed helpers (IV, 9). Machiavelli skillfully takes advantage of these instances of maximum audience involvement and fills them to capacity with laughter-inducing devices, the most important of which are the chamber pot, the urinalysis, the medical demeanor of Callimaco in the first of the two episodes, and the individual disguises, the military configuration of the characters and the actual capture of Callimaco in the other. Furthermore Machiavelli, in the first of these episodes, describes the essential features of the second ("Dipoi ci travestiremo, voi, Ligurio, Siro ed io, e andrencene cercando in Mercato Nuovo, in Mercato Vecchio, per questi canti; e il primo garzonaccio che noi troviamo scioperato, lo imbavaglieremo, e a suon di mazzate lo condurremo in casa, e in camera vostra al buio") ("Then we'll disguise ourselves, you, Ligurio, Siro, and myself, and we'll go searching in the new market, in the old market, in places like those; and the first young rascal we find loafing around, we'll gag him and, with the help of a few good blows we'll bring him in the house, and into your room, in the dark") and thereby exploits the audience's powers of anticipation and memory to enhance the overall comic effect of the action.

The text's oral mode of perception dominance can be analysed (i) in terms of its linguistic availability to contemporary spectators during a performance and (ii) in terms of its intended communicational function in its transaction with them. With respect to the first of these, if we begin with the premise—easily derived from the celebrated empirical principle known as Zipf's law—that in a given text the frequency of occurrence of a word or a structure varies inversely with the effort entailed by its usage,[23] and if we further consider, as we must, that in comedies written for the stage the effort involved is ultimately that required of an audience for it to recognise a sign and to call to mind its range of significant associations, we may conduct our appraisal of a play's textual proclivity for performance apprehension by means of audience related parameters. It is immediately obvious, in fact, that the recognitory proficiency of the ideal audience "implied" by the text is a function of the Zipfian character of its diction, from which it follows that in a lexically and syntactically accessible play the linguistic discrepancy between the implied and the real audiences must be negligible. Unfortunately the measurement and characterisation of this difference at present can be no more than a desideratum, since the currently available data do not warrant precise observations. One can say, for example, that Caro's and Cecchi's predilections for archaic expressions[24] is a sign that in the implied audiences of their texts there are traces of artificiality without referential correlatives in the world of real contemporary audiences. But without the appropriate statistical breakdown of the language of *Cinquecento* comedy, it is not possible to quantify that hiatus and hence to estimate the linguistic accessibility of every part of their plays. However, it is conceivable that a systematic application of computer methods to the theatre of the Italian Renaissance could bring all of this within the reach of any graduate student in only a few years. What is principally needed is a rank and frequency distribution of the diction of each play and of the language of comedy *in globo* for every major theatrical centre in Italy. This would enable us to compare a particular comedy with the universe of discourse of its own stage tradition as well as with that of other areas, allowing us thereby to measure its accessibility to audiences of different dialectal backgrounds and hence to trace the geographical extension of its potential communicational appeal as signalled by its paradigmatic self-restraints.

The syntagmatic dimension of comic language calls for a somewhat different consideration. For a given range of vocabulary, the oral comprehensibility of a temporally unfolding text is correlated with its syntactic structure. In contrast to works meant to be read, in which sentence structure is largely idiosyncratic, texts meant to be heard necessarily favour syntactical linearity to intricate clausal subordination and to parenthetical developments embedded in a basic pattern. Accordingly the fundamental parameter to be used in the syntagmatic study of the linguistic openness of Renaissance comedies must be the structural complexity of their discourse, understood as an indirect gauge of the effort required in its oral reception. Ideally the individual speeches in a play could be mapped onto a gradient spectrum stretching from maximum parataxis to maximum hypotaxis. We would inevitably find that soliloquies and speeches with a narrative content are much more prone to hypotactical organisation than the rest of the play.

In Machiavelli's *Mandragola*, for instance, the majority of such speeches belong to Callimaco, whose role by virtue of this fact alone makes exceptional demands on an actor. Unlike sequentially ordered paratactic segments, the following sentence requires considerable skill in voice modulation and speed control:

Ma poi che io me le fu' dato a conoscere, e chi io l'ebbi dato ad intendere lo amore che io le portavo, e quanto facilmente, per la semplicità del marito, noi potavàno vivere felici, sanza infamia alcuna, promettendole che, qualunque volta Dio facessi altro di lui, di prenderla per donna; ed avendo ella, oltre alle vere ragioni, gustato che differenzia è dalla iacitura mia a quella di Nicia, e da' e' baci d'uno amante giovane a quello d'uno marito vecchio, dopo qualche sospiro disse . . . . (V,4)
("But then, when I was finally able to tell her who I was and how much I loved her and how easily, because of the simple-mindedness of her husband, we could find happiness together without the slightest scandal, promising her that whenever God should will to take him away I would make her my wife; and when, on top of these good reasons, she had tasted the difference between my embrace and that of Messer Nicia, and between the kisses of a young lover and those of an old husband–after sighing a little, she said . . . .")

The clause "Ma dopo qualche sospiro disse" governs the supporting intonation pattern of the entire sentence; what occurs between the first word and the last, which is the long awaited principal verb, is entrusted entirely to the actor's command of voice inflection in the presence of a living, and therefore continuously reacting, audience. Such intricately constructed sentences are more comprehensible and enjoyable to the reader than they are to the average spectator.

By a logical extension of the same analytical principle, we could map onto a structural complexity scale the individual plays of the whole genre during a given period for each of the theatrical centres of Italy. This would give us a useful comparison of the syntagmatic orality of different texts. For example, in comparison to *Mandragola*, Cecchi's *L'Assiuolo* is bound to be syntactically more awkward on stage, since the inflectional characteristics of Callimaco's role are here extended to several *dramatis personae*.[25]

As for the second mode of perception dominance, or the communicational function of each textual utterance, a play may be considered in relation to its capacity to govern the spectators' reaction to its unfolding on stage. To this effect, it is useful to approach Renaissance comedies from the standpoint of Bühler's well known *Sprachtheorie*, according to which a linguistic act may function to express a state of mind, to describe an external reality, or to arouse a specific response in the listener.[26] Predictably enough, all three functions of language can be found in Renaissance comedies, since expression or character revelation is the principal purpose of soliloquies, ostensive and deictic description the chief task of the dialogue, and arousal of laughter the purpose of the more or less skillfully devised and distributed humorous passages. While it is important to consider all three functions for each play, since their relative proportions can by themselves provide us with an insight into the conception of the genre that is presupposed by the text, it goes without saying that in the analysis of a comedy the function of arousal, which the text may carry out in concomitance with the other two, merits greater attention, since "comic catharsis" during a performance depends almost entirely on its efficacity.

In general it can be said that the Renaissance repertoire of devices actually used in comic arousal is quite limited. The principal ones were clearly sketched out by Machiavelli in the prologue to *Clizia*, where he says that "volendo dilettare, è necessario muovere li spettatori a riso, il che non si può fare mantenendo il parlare grave e severo; perché le parole che fanno ridere sono, o sciocche, o iniurose, o amorose." ("But in order to bring pleasure, a comedy must also make people laugh, which cannot be done if the dialogue is always grave and dignified, for the words which make people laugh are either witless, slanderous, or salacious.") It follows therefore that "quelle commedie che sono piene di queste tre qualità de parole, sono piene di risa; quelle che ne mancono, non trovano chi con il ridere le accompagni." ("Comedies full of words of these three types evoke laughter; those which lack them do not.") This statement is very significant because it is not derived from first principles, but is rather based on empirical evidence. As such it is a picture of contemporary taste which can be used to analyse the arousal function of the text. In *Mandragola*, for example, the first category of arousal, "parole sciocche" or witless remarks, is limited to the self-duping performance of Messer Nicia. Good illustrations of such textual facetiousness are his comparison of the Arno to the sea (I, 3), his reaction to Callimaco's Latin (II, 2), and his suggestion that he too should have inserted two nuts into his mouth in order to disguise his voice (IV, 9). In these instances Messer Nicia reveals his obtuseness and by so doing moves the audience to laughter. The second category, "parole iniurose" or the language of mockery and scatology, is again centred on Messer Nicia, being either emitted by or directed at him. Among the utterances produced by him we can recall his expletory imprecations, such as "cacasangue" ("blood and crap") and "potta di San Puccio" (II, 6) ("cunt of Saint Puccio"), and his coarse mode of being emphatic, as when he says "ho cacato le curatelle per imparare due *hac*" (II, 3) ("I've had to shit blood just to learn my *hics*, *haecs*, and *hocs*"); those directed at him include Ligurio's deformation of Verrucola in "carrucola" (I, 3) ("pulley"), his remark that Messer Nicia had urinated his way through a lot of snow (I, 3)—by which he meant that he had travelled widely—and his reference to his imminent status as a cuckold by describing his position between his two companions as being "intra le due corna" (IV, 9). The devices of the third category, "parole amorose" or phallic and erotic references, are also focused on Messer Nicia, who uses them in a scene dense with comic arousal (V, 2) when he recounts the episode of the "forced" impregnation of Lucrezia. On the other hand, Callimaco's account of the incident is clearly intended as description and expression rather than arousal. If to these considerations we add that comic arousal through action is also centred on Messer Nicia—in such scenes as that of his appearance in the piazza with a chamber pot or that of his shoddy disguise—we can conclude that the success of the play depends almost entirely on the actor who impersonates his role, since it is this character who governs most of the audience's response to the play's comic stimulus.

The foregoing analysis of a comedy's disposition to visual and oral apprehension describes the textually controlled aspects of its encounter with the spectators during any performance of it. Together with the prior examination of its necessary spatiality and of its metatextual capacity to circumscribe its possible stage interpretations, this analysis defines the formal

co-ordinates of a comedy's theatrical fruition, to the extent that they depend on the skill of the playwright, as he builds up an imaginary performance on the basis of its communicational presuppositions and then verbally hypostatizes it in his text-transcription. The level of generality to which
it seemed desirable to work out such an approach to Renaissance comedy
carries with it the consequence of detachment from the peculiarities of specific
texts as well as the advantage of a rigorous treatment of the common traits
of the genre. Ultimately its aim is to suggest the questions that should be
asked in the theatrical stratification of any comedy of the period. The fundamental claim it makes is that it is only by asking such questions that we
can deal with the text in terms of its indubitable distinctive features, which
are that it was written to be performed on a contemporary stage for the
entertainment of a contemporary audience.

NOTES

1 *The Structure of Literature* (Chicago, 1954), 81.
2 Cesare Molinari, "Strutture drammaturgiche e sceniche del teatro cin-
   quecentesco,"*Quaderni del teatro municipale 'R. Valli,'* I (1981), 27, estimates that
   comedies accounted for 90% of all performances.
3 On these points see Marshall McLuhan, *The Gutenberg Galaxy* (Toronto, 1969),
   105-16 and passim.
4 This famous episode is narrated by St. Augustine in *Confessions* V, 3.
5 Walter J. Ong, *Orality and Literacy* (London, 1982), 158.
6 Lee Simonson, *The Stage is Set* (New York, 1963), 261.
7 The first permanent proscenium arch was that of the Teatro Farnese in Par-
   ma (1618), but its origin in theatrical history is an unresolved issue. For an
   overview see O.G. Brockett, *The Theatre* (New York, 1964), 149-50. The following discussion of the Serlian stage is based on the selection from *The Second
   Book of Architecture*, tr. A. Nicoll, in *The Renaissance Stage: Documents of Serlio,
   Sabbatini and Furtenbach*, ed. B. Hewitt (Coral Gables, Florida, 1958), 21-36.
8 The Serlian period lasted approximately from 1514 to 1560—see L[otte] H.
   E[isner], s.v. "Scenografia," in *Enciclopedia dello spettacolo*, VIII, 1596.
9 See *Commedie del Cinquecento*, ed. N. Borsellino (Milano, 1962), I, 5. All tex-
   tual references to the plays themselves are to this edition and —for works not
   included by Borsellino—to the following: Pietro Aretino, *Le commedie*, ed. E.
   Camerini (Milano, 1962); Nicolò Machiavelli, *La Mandragola*, ed. G. Davico
   Bonino (Torino, 1975); Id., *Clizia*, ed. G. Davico Bonino (Torino, 1972);
   Alessandro Piccolomini, *L'Alessandro* (Venetia, 1560); Lorenzino de' Medici,
   Aridosia, ed. E. Faccioli (Torino, 1974).
10 On the question of female characters in Greek and Roman comedy, see F.B.
   Millet and G.E. Bentley, *The Art of Drama* (New York, 1963), 91-92, 231.
11 *Annotationi di M. Alessandro Piccolomini nel libro della poetica d'Aristotele* (Vinegia,
   1572), 23-24, on which see B. Weinberg, *A History of Literary Criticism in the
   Italian Renaissance* (Chicago, 1961), 547, for a translation and an analysis of
   the relevant passage.
12 Cf. Millet and Bentley, 44-50, and Richard Southern, *The Seven Ages of the Theatre*
   (New York, 1963), 159-62, 171-84, 235-43.
13 *Quattro dialoghi in materia di rappresentazioni sceniche*, ed. F. Marotti (Milano, 1968),
   40.
14 This concept is based on Arthur Koestler, *The Act of Creation* (London, 1975),
   38-42.

15 See Faccioli's "Introduzione" to his edition of the text, vi.
16 The analogy with music was first pointed out by M. Pagnini, "Per una semiologia del teatro classico," *Strumenti critici* II (1970), 121.
17 In *Quattro dialoghi*, cit., 39.
18 Cf. for example, the following passage in de' Sommi, 41-42: "Et se farà la parte di uno sciocco, oltre al risponder mal a proposito (il che gl'insegnerà il poeta con le parole) bisogna che, a certi tempi, sappia far anco di piú lo scimonito, pigliar delle mosche, cercar de' pulci, et altre cosí fatte sciocchezze."
19 Ibid., 42.
20 Respectively: *Il Vecchio amoroso* IV, 4; Ibid., I, 2; Ibid., IV, 3; *L'Assiuolo* III, 1; Ibid., IV, 9; Ibid., III, 1; Ibid., V, 2; *Il Vecchio amoroso* IV, 1; Ibid., V, 7.
21 Louise G. Clubb, "Italian Renaissance Comedy," in *Versions of Medieval Comedy*, ed. P.G. Rugiers (Norman, 1977), 204.
22 Brief accounts of Marcus' method are found in: B. Brainerd and V. Neufeldt, "Marcus' Analysis of the Strategy of a Play," *Poetics* X (1974), 31-74; M. De Marinis and G. Bettetini, *Teatro e comunicazione* (Firenze, 1977), 73-76. By Marcus, see *Poetica matematica* (Bucharest, 1970) and "Stratégie des personnages dramatiques," in *Sémiologie de la représentation* ed. A. Helbo (Bruxelles, 1975). The April 1984 issue of *Poetics* is edited by Marcus and contains the latest developments in the field.
23 On Zipf's law and its potential applications see J.R. Pierce, *An Introduction to Information Theory* (New York, 1980), 238-40. On p. 294 Pierce states Zipf's law as follows: "the number of occurrences of a word in a long stretch of text is the reciprocal of the order of frequency of occurrence."
24 Borsellino, *Commedie del Cinquecento*, cit., xxiii.
24 Cf. for example Giulio's and Rinuccio's long speeches in V, 2 and Oretta's in V, 6.
26 Karl Bühler's most important work is *Sprachtheorie—Die Darstellungsfunktion der Sprache* (Jena, 1934). For a clear and concise exposition of Bühler's ideas in the context of modern linguistics see Oswald Szemerényi, *Direcciones de la lingüística moderna*, tr. M. Martínez Hernández (Madrid, 1979), I, 122-29.

Intriguers and Trickster: the Manifestations of an Archetype in the Comedy of the Renaissance

Donald A. Beecher
Carleton University

The play of intensified trickery found favour with the early erudite dramatists in Italy because of the authority granted to such procedures by the plays of Plautus and Terence.[1] Moreover, the antics of the ruseful servant, which so often resembled the extended practical joke, accorded well with the spirit of carnival, for which occasion so many of the early comedies were written. Wit, laughter and the satisfaction of raw sexual desire, disguise and knavery in the streets—all served as the stuff and substance of intrigue. The strategems of the inventive lovers in the *novelle* were superimposed upon the logistics of carnival in a way that gave new latitude to comic experimentation. The "reality" of carnival gave credibility to the license of the intrigue plot and substance to its conventions. That is to say, the annual festival of aberrant impulses mediated a social realism to the comedy of the *machinatore*. Experimentation with actions predicated on extended *burle* produced a repertoire of characters and routines, a repertoire that possessed an identity of its own in the traits it contained of a generic character type whose "psyche" and cultural contents came to dominate the plays he manipulated and controlled. There were many elements both structural and social that contributed to an expression of the type in comedy, elements that allowed for a true "comedy of the trickster" to emerge in England early in the seventeenth century.

Risking bounding generalization, it would appear that the desires to be addressed in the erudite comedy led to an art form of intrigue that superimposed the conventions of the ancient comedy and the Renaissance *novelle* upon a contemporary setting, creating an ethos reconcilable in terms of carnival.[2] This formula led to the invention of a series of tool characters who structured the actions from within the plays through their intrigues, and in turn to an elaborate vocabulary of characterological codes from which subsequent playwrights could draw. This phase of expansion and experimentation was essential in every way to the future development of intrigue comedy. And while the northern playwrights who brought trickster to his apogee in the theatre may not have drawn upon the carnival ambience of the Italians, they, perforce, drew from their vocabulary of characterological and situational codes. Thus, that a proto-trickster configuration emerges *sui generis* from the intrigue structures in Italian comedy few would deny, but that the intriguer becomes a conscious "psychological" entity and a "hero" in the erudite theatre, such that the play becomes a medium for the thematic examination of his powers and inherent nature is doubtful.

Nevertheless, the "Italian phase" in the development of the intriguer

was essential to whatever prospects there were for the formation of a composite type, capable of assuming a generic psychology and identity that
were unique and true to him alone. Already in those plays are certain of
the traits belonging to the trickster of the anthropologists. And while the
emphasis remains on the trickster figure reborn as if "by accident" from
the conflation of structural and characterological elements necessary for
satisfying the conventions of the learned and erudite play, there is an inevitable sense of the archetypal which appears by dint of the essential an-
thropomorphization of the forces which animate carnival—forces that are
an inherent part of the trickster essence.

The trickster as an archetype was first articulated by Carl Jung in a
brief but influential essay.[3] Jung made certain assumptions about the way
in which this characterological force was embodied in literature. His point
of departure, however, was essentially folklore where the trickster renders
up his traits in the form of short, seemingly contradictory episodes which,
in sum, take the full measure of his paradoxical nature. Quite predictably
Jung makes associations between the symbolic structures of lore and stages
in the development of consciousness, placing trickster as a mediating figure
at the earliest phases of the dawning of moral consciousness out of a state
of preconscious amorality. He is a memory of outlaw freedom confronted
by a repressive collectivity to which he attaches, but never reconciles,
himself.[4] It is his nature to torment the social collective by satisfying his
instinctual love for knavery in pursuit of a reckless violation of taboos.[5]
In his antics, however, he both relieves the group from its own oppressive
conformity, and chastizes the deviant through his pranks. Hence the ambiguity of his nature, for he is both the outlaw of vicarious pleasure, and
the regulator of aberrant behaviour, an amoral figure who, in relation to
the group, vacillates between the incipient villain and the incipient cultural
benefactor.[6] We see in this how useful trickster can become as a point of
critical departure, for just such themes and paradoxical relationships play
themselves out again and again in the intrigue plays of the period in
question—which is still not to say that the play becomes what it is through
a projection of remembered archetypal essences, but that the very exploration
of such themes necessitates the recovery of the archetype. Jungians would,
in fact, claim that the very necessity for designing the intrigue plot arises
out of inherent conflicts in the human psyche that can be dealt with only
through the mediating powers of literature designed to answer to needs and
questions about freedom and conformity deep in the human psyche.

Yet, what is of interest here is that through a recognition of this
characterological principle, the animateur agent of the Renaissance comedy can be comparatively positioned amongst the other recognized forms
of trickster. Those most frequently discussed are coyote and crow of the
Amerindian, Br'er Rabbit of the American blacks, the Scandinavian Loki,
the Greek Hermes, the African Zande trickster.[7] Closer in time and place
to the plays in question are the Medieval tricksters: Merlin, Tristan, Reynard
the Fox, Tyl Eulenspiegel; and the Renaissance tricksters: Rabelais'
Panurge, Grimmelshausen's Courage, Pulcinella of the *commedia dell'arte*,
and the Spanish picaro in his many incarnations.[8] While such comparisons lie outside my present purposes, one can see how the appreciation

of such a play as Jonson's *Volpone* depends upon a recognition of the common denominators between a Venetian legacy hunter and the primordial trickster fox of European lore—the acquisitive machinations of the crafty, self-declared outlaw who tricks for pleasure as well as for survival; Jonson expects his readers to be comparative critics.

At the foundations of this incarnation of the generic trickster was a sense of the theatrical codes that, *de rigueur*, were observed by the playwright in the erudite tradition. Those codes entailed the formulation of an action artificially enhanced by a clever premeditated strategem on the part of a tool character within the play, thereby engineering a tightly structured and controlled fable and fulfilling expectations involving rigorously specified temporal and spatial restraints. There is a sense in which the codes of the erudite drama necessitated the development of the intriguer agent as the nearly exclusive means for extending the range and novelty of the genre without violating the spirit of the codes of the *commedia erudita*. Critical incentives had much to do, ironically, with the eventual breakdown of the Plautine servant-master formula, thereby liberating the trickster within the play society, granting him both greater latitude for self-expression and a greater capacity to distance himself from collective values by standing openly against them in nature and in purpose. If the basic genre was to have a future in the theatres it had to be expanded through such a process; "liberating" the trickster agent was the only possible means, and that is precisely what happened. That liberation, of course, gave him the chance for a destiny of his own as a true force character once his psychic motivations and will also come under examination. In this process, the trickster figure evolves in a way inviting analysis in historical terms. Each play offering a novel trick or disguise adds to the vocabulary of trickster devices and to the scope of the trickster's will. There is no sense in which this accumulation represents progress of the type manifested where a predetermined goal is all along in view. The historical approach risks lending a false intentionality to the reappearance of the archetype—an intentionality beyond probability, and certainly beyond demonstration. Yet there can be no doubt that a pragmatic process of borrowing, adapting and conflating trickster gestures provided the evolutionary dialectic that refitted the archetype through the selective processes of the Renaissance makers. While insisting upon that process, one can also point to the remarkable degree of correspondence between the trickster forms of the comedy and concurrent forms of the trickster incarnation.

What were the structural variants that contributed to the recovery of the type? There were at least four. The first was the development of the intriguer as an internal plotting agent. The erudite playwrights inherited a tradition of comedy that recognized the value of building the fable from the inside out through the offices of a witty agent able to project the fulfillment of desires through deception and social manipulation. Such procedures lent a degree of realism to the extent that the agent could be integrated into the social order of the play. The potential in that factor of design was not only to make the action an extension of character, with all the advantages of economy and purpose that gave, but to grant to that action the significance of the ideas that propel it. The prospect is thereby raised for the creation of an authorial persona, a surrogate maker in the place of the author himself, whose voice is heard through the order of the intrigue.

The second category was the extension of the trickster's personality and motivations, entailing a greater social diversification of the type, and a more innovative treatment of the relationship between the intriguer and the protagonist. Trickster as designer ultimately had to remain in the service of the new society in the process of formation throughout the play. Yet irony became increasingly prominent where the approved benefits came about in opposition to the trickster will, or as an accidental by-product of trickster machinations, as in the *Lena*, where an angry bawd seeks her revenge against an old man by pandering his daughter—but, as it turns out, straight into the arms of her beloved. Experimentation with characterological formats produced tricksters not only as slaves, but as bawds, marriage brokers, servants, meddling friends, and up the social ladder—the climbing courtier, and the duke-in-disguise.

A third area for development was the repertoire of ruses and devices through which the intriguer could structure and express his will. The basis for many such plots was the practical joke, as when the Duke in the *Marescalco* spends five acts gossiping his homosexual stablemaster into an unwanted marriage, or when a nephew in *Epicoene* imposes a chatterbox upon his morose uncle in the guise of a silent wife. Conditions for the scheme could be found in disguises, false rhetoric, deceptive jargon, fraudulent representations of merchandise, a cynical exploitation of misplaced greed or lust. This expanding repertoire also included the compounding of the trickster himself, giving rise to the double or even triple zanni-lackey plots. The competition between knaves, as a structural invention, had a spectacular future in the Renaissance comic theatre, particularly in France and England. Again the social status of the competitors could rise, thereby allowing for new possibilities as realized in the knave upon knave plot of *The Jew of Malta* and *Volpone*.

The final structural variant was the repositioning of the intrigue agent in the social order of the play, an innovation barred from full development without first raising the degree of consciousness of the trickster vocation within the character himself. The trickster cannot become hero without understanding his own nature as a thematic force, or at least without being designed by the author to function in accordance with that nature. In this phase, the play expresses the preoccupations of the animateur, identifies his ambiguities, and makes revelations about his morality. Often, it is the trickster's own temper which extends to the entire play world so that his lust, ambition, acquisitiveness reduces the social order to a reflection of himself. In the world of getting and spending, the arch-trickster is king. Only a step away is the rogue of dawning consciousness who turns upon the imperfections of his own nature and attempts to "improve" himself morally in the image of a more integrated psyche: Bosola's career as trickster in *The Duchess of Malfi* culminates in this way.

Only when the preoccupations of the trickster psyche are distinguished from the conventional desires seeking fulfillment through comic resolution—love, wealth, position—can his true nature be assessed. To the list of basic drives for food, sex, personal power must be added the drive for play, which is the trickster's distinguishing trait. Since the publication of Huizinga's *Homo Ludens*,[9] the structures of play have been superimposed upon the patterns of culture in a wide variety of ways suggesting how much the very dynamics of civilization have been influenced by the logistics of play. Definitions of the trickster archetype, however, have not yet profited from this body of writing. Yet, as a mediating force, trickster's primary means lie precisely in his command of the powers of play. His very essence, above his own interest in food, goods and sex, is his sheer love of waggery. Trickster is, to a very large extent, the archetypal embodiment of the impulse for play, and it is this "attitude" that preserves the integrity of the type, for when he abandons play as the presiding spirit behind his acts, he becomes easily confused with other related types.

The design of comedy depends largely upon the manner in which elements of play are introduced into the action. One strategy is to isolate the "play" character as a manipulating force from the characters seeking sexual gratification or social power, thereby necessitating an *entente* between, let us say, the love seeker and the play seeker. In this way the structure of the game can be amalgamated with the pursuit of love, wealth or status without forcing the lover or status seeker to author the fraud by which his ends are achieved, as in the *Mandragola* where Ligurio's intellect serves Callimaco's ends. This arrangement allows for an initial distinction between him who desires principally to possess and him who desires principally to play. This separation of interests is useful as a way of getting around the characterological incompatibility between the socially integrated figure seeking to strengthen that membership, and the marginal figure whose relationship to society is based on the ironic distance created by play. Through an endorsement of the spirit of play as an acceptable manifestation of the human spirit, the audience reconciles itself to the interference of the comic intriguer.[10]

In a conventional situation, the waggish valet comes to the rescue of his love-smitten master. The lady's reticence, an obstinate parent, a rival (including husbands), social incompatibility, prearranged contracts are a few of the conventional obstacles blocking the fruition of the lover's desires. In the cause of such love, the lackey exercises his wits as a go-between, an eavesdropper, an agent for delaying or drawing off unwanted presences, as a guard, a bluffer or schemer. His ability to think quickly in a pinch, invent lies, fool his superiors, his knowledge of the streets and alleys, his *passe partout* cunning, and his pragmatic understanding of human nature allow him to surmount circumstances against great odds. The lackey thereby gives shape to the action.

One of the most sparkling deployments of the servant-master formula is in Odet de Turnèbe's *Les Contens*.[11] Turnèbe, with seventy years of the erudite tradition to draw upon, offers no appreciable advancement of the trickster personality. His lackeys remain simple, earthy servants adapted only on the surface to look at home in a Parisian setting, but who are otherwise very like their Roman predecessors. Yet Turnèbe displays a mastery of the variables of intrigue by creating three such master-servant configurations with all three of the "gentlemen" in love with the same girl. The servants spy upon one another, eavesdrop on all who appear in order to gain

the advantage for their respective masters. Eustache, the lover champion-
ed by the girl's mother, is frightened away by a concocted tale of breast
cancer told him by a bawd in the employ of Basile, who enjoys the audience's approbation as the one sincere suitable mate for Geneviève and
the one she herself loves. The third is a blustering braggart in the *miles
gloriosus* tradition who stages a race with Basile to seduce the girl, disguised
in Eustache's suit, in order to present the mother with a *fait accompli* that
would force her to choose between scandal and a quick marriage. The name
of the play suggests not only that Basile and Geneviève are satisfied in accordance with the sacred rights of love, but that the plot devices of Basile's
lackey not only engineer the brilliant plot, but reconcile all the contenders
to their respective gains and losses. Turnèbe does not liberate his low life
intriguers, does not raise their social station or their consciousnesses, but
brings to its apogee the mechanically compound plot involving the servant-
lover formula.

At this level, the trickster signifies the cause of love and youth in opposition to age and materialism, yet as a "borrowed" voice he also serves
to draw off the residual opprobrium for the means employed to win the
girl. Antoine's marginal status makes excuses for the cynical solution he
urged upon Basile to enjoy the girl first in anticipation of marriage. The
lovers entertain at least some moral scruples and let themselves be persuaded
out of desperation, while the lackey speaks from his own purely physical
view of sexuality. In this way, the lackey creates a moment of license that
lies, nevertheless, at the heart of a play circumscribed by bourgeois standards and bourgeois ambitions including those of the lovers themselves.
Antoine, in a way far below his own consciousness, mediates between
freedom and conformity through his pragmatic strategems for getting Basile
into Geneviève's bed and for getting him out of a potentially disastrous
situation when the mother sees them in *flagrant delit* through the keyhole.
This was as far as the mechanical compounding of unmodified servant
characters could go.

More critical to our purposes, however, was the invention of the "free-
agent" intriguer who, through a deversification of his social status and identity, assumed a more personal impetus for his pranks. Throughout the era
in question, every guise and mentality, every profession and social type
harbouring the causes and techniques of a jokester or cheat gave themselves
up to theatrical exploitation. The Elizabethans were particularly ingenious
in forging intriguers out of their literary borrowings and through the mirrors they held up to their own society. George Chapman wrote a series
of difficult but genuinely original Elizabethan social comedies in which an
array of gentlemen socialites and meddlers amuse themselves and preen
their vanities by inventing witty solutions to the problems of associates,
and by holding up to ridicule those who offended their sense of fun. The
relationship between Piccolomini's *Alessandro* and Chapman's *May Day*
demonstrates the drift of Chapman's comic genius through the manner in
which he expands the rather shadowy and indeterminate role of the accomplice friend Alessandro into the pervasive machinations of Lodovico,
whose wit dominates the action and cements the diverse plots together. In
the magicians, necromancers and marriage brokers, right up to the knave

courtiers, usurers and dukes-in-disguise, the dramatists of the age discovered trickster faces, trickster duplicity and the social foundations for the urge to play. There was a sense in which the more the social fabric itself yielded up models for trickery, the more deception itself was identified as the leading denominator of the age.

Broadly speaking, two trickster types emerge from this laboratory of structural experimentation: the subservient agent who seeks his satisfaction largely through aid to another, serving love and marriage without more than a token threat to the collective order; and the more self-conscious, self-serving intriguer who is apt to achieve his ends by attacking social decency and morality, by violating the sanctity of private property, and by compromising the public image of those he confronts. Such tricksters need not be villains, since we may find ourselves in at least relative agreement with their attack upon greediness and arrogance, and with their *ad hoc* justice (such as arranging for wealth to pass from stingy fathers to impoverished sons). An attack upon possessions is often their means for punishing smugness and for tormenting miserliness. But where such tricksters exercise their cunning to excess, the trickster "morality" comes under examination.

An early instance of the morally ambiguous trickster appears in Ariosto's *Lena*, in which a desirable union comes about through the vituperative wiles of a wronged, but nevertheless unscrupulous bawd.[12] The romance structure, once carried out, makes her a benefactress to love, because she is a more personalized and professional *machinatore* figure, there is an ironic gap created between the will of the agent and the mores of the collectivity. The trickster as professional cheat inevitably forces reflection upon the dubiousness of the means. As the logistics of his profession assume responsibility for the social ethos of the play, the agent comes to dominate both means and substance; the question of public morality in a context of social realism takes precedence over the right of fertility and wish-fulfillment.

The moral ambiguity created by the trickster in Machiavelli's *Mandragola* has dominated the critical history of the play.[13] The plot, in overview, resembles more conventional love comedies in which the lovesick youth wins his lady through the aid of an accomplice. But there the resemblances end. First the lady is not the eligible and pragmatic young girl of *Les Contens*, but a married woman, pious almost to a fault and as unlikely a candidate for a casual liaison with a pining young man as any woman could be. Secondly, Ligurio the trickster is no faithful valet, but a parasite and marriage broker whose very profession bears the same relationship to love as Chaucer's pardoner does to true spirituality. Ligurio is one of the most amoral knaves the erudite comedy has to offer, since he is not only willing to play upon a sterile couple's desire for children with his mandrake fraud, by which means Callimaco will gain access to the lady's bed, but he is willing to enlist the help of Lucrezia's mother and her confessor in persuading her to the plot. That such an act would not be sin because a certain good (that children would follow) takes precedence over an uncertain evil (that the first man to sleep with her after the potion could die) is the epitome of his cynicism. Ligurio is brilliant in his device: he provides a surrogate father for Messer Nicia's family, and he cures the lovesick Callimaco of his potentially fatal disease. Structurally, his scheme for using the fraudulent potion shapes the entire action of the play: all that transpires emanates from his prevenient device. Quite revealing in terms of Ligurio's reading of human nature is the fact that his ruse comes off without hitch or hindrance. Ligurio is a professional who executes his plan with an astonishing degree of moral indifference, for money. The dénouement of this carnivalesque prank is the anticipated union and promised fertility, together with a "new society" in the form of a functional *ménage à trois*. As trickster, he has been a fertility force, considerate enough never to expose the folly, or to wound the reputations of his gulls. But he is, at the same time, a confidence game operator in search of the kinds of social situations where his skills can be sold; Ligurio straddles the world of "carnival romance" and the world of knavish materialism.

Ariosto's *Il Negromante*, employing a different balance of forces, likewise falls between the comedy of love and the comedy of the underworld. The magician Giacchelino plays doctor to a young "impotent" who, already married, merely assumes the infirmity in order to ward off a second marriage urged by his father. True to his opportunist nature, Giacchelino hires himself out to rival parties on the promise he will ignore his contracts with the others. With tactics far more transparent than Ligurio's, he nevertheless succeeds where gullible people in stressful situations are willing to support charlatans proposing the most ludicrous solutions, their judgements corrupted by their hopes. Irony lies in the fact that Giacchelino does nothing at all to advance the causes of his clients; his triple commission is entirely self-cancelling. The romantic plot thus resolves itself through confession to the father, a timely enhancement of the young wife's material status, and the acquiescence of the father to the secret marriage. There is, then, a curious discrepancy between the interventions of the intrigue and the resolution of the romance plot, leaving Giacchelino free to represent the ineffectual and ultimately defeated confidence game trickster. As such, he has no place in the terminal social order based on marriage, and banishes himself with haste. That inability to adapt to social normalcy is a mark of the trickster in Jonson's underworld plays, and ultimately a characteristic of the archetype.

Giacchelino not only preludes a long list of sorcerer and magician figures in Italian drama, but also the confidence man tradition culminating in Subtle of *The Alchemist*. By naming the play after the *machinatore* necromancer, Ariosto gives a small boost to the eventual centralizing of the charlatan character. *Il Negromante* is paradigmatic in several ways: it introduces the professional swindler to the theatre, it offers a sketch of the underworld mentality as a precondition to his exploits and it pioneers the comic action in which the intriguer becomes a theme character who is, in due course, brought down in a knave-out-knaved dénouement.

With the acquisitive trickster whose sense of play is oriented entirely towards material gain comes an entirely new context for theatrical exploration. The matrix for this new comic form can be traced both to literary models and to the social realities that such characters reflect. Once established as a theatrical "idea," the exploitation of gulls could pattern itself after all manner of fraudulent practices, featuring knaves who assume a multiplicity of guises, jargons and authority. The confidence operator could profess arcane knowledge and skills equal to the task of satisfying the most luxurious desires. They were quick-change artists and masters of the diversionary lie. Their traffic was based on keen wits, and on even keener appreciation of the exploitable dreams and aspirations of others and the price men would pay to have them fulfilled. Jonson measured the scope of those vulnerabilities in *The Alchemist* from Abel Drugger's simple desire for business success to Sir Epicure Mammon's perverse conflation of lust and luxury. In *Volpone* those opulent appetites become the motivating forces behind the most subtle of all the confidence game plays in Elizabethan drama. In Volpone, the trickster is hero. His feigned sickness is the device that gives the entire action its order so that the trickster will and mentality rule the ethos of the play.

The false face, the calculated prevarication is the characterizing gesture of the trickster and the basis of his gaming tactics. The lie, from the quibble to the sophistic assault, serves to bring the other characters into his sphere of power. It incorporates not only language but disguise, a misleading ambience, corroborating witnesses. Jonson's tricksters are masters of the professional jargon and arcane gibberish by which they impose themselves upon the credulous. Verbal misrepresentation assumes increasing importance over the shifting costumes of the farce, though impersonation never loses its appeal as a fundamental stage device.

The spectator becomes a part of the structure of play by the way in which he is granted knowledge of the lie. By one strategy, the audience is informed of the double dealing from the outset of the operation. By another, it is made a victim of the trickster's arts insofar as a penetration of the ruse is not granted to the spectator before it is granted to all the characters within the play. Finally, there is a game structure in the artistic statement whereby the audience is told the truth at the outset, yet refuses to believe it, as in Marlowe's *The Jew of Malta* where sympathy for a nobly spoken man, seemingly more sinned against than sinning, turns out to be misplaced sentiment for a culprit who uses the rhetoric of pity as a verbal smoke screen. Machiavel tells us in the Prologue that Barabas is one of his own. The trickster lie can be seconded in the control of the comic irony whereby the audience falls victim to the ruse along with the others in the play, as in Jonson's *Epicoene*. More often, however, the spectator is lured into collusion with the trickster, insofar as his fertile wit, his mental agility, his animal energy and audacity, his astonishing *savoir faire* invite irrepressible admiration. Even the trickster of the underworld, whose very ruseful mendacity forewarns of his heterodox ethics, nevertheless incites a willing indulgence of vicarious pleasure—an enactment of aberrant impulses. The trickster claims an enthusiastic tolerance and, in that paradoxical state, confirms his nature through his incorporation into the viewer's experience. What trickster becomes in his contract with the beholder is of the essence in determining his character.

Trickster meaning, then, is inherent in the way he makes himself perceived, a character entirely "unstable" because he typically arouses both attraction and repulsion: attraction in that he expresses deviant instincts, latent or active ambitions to prevail over one's enemies through craft, a desire to see the vain, fatuous and smug victimized and exposed; repulsion because he is an outlaw who, at the same time, goes beyond our sense of fair play, violates common morality, the sanctity of reputation and of private property. The trickster, even in the most static of representations, generates dynamic responses because what first allures by way of his knavery either exacerbates upon reflection, or in its drab sameness cloys; the reader abandons him either annoyed or bored. Barabas goes on a holiday rampage against the Maltese Christians in Marlowe's play, until his true arrant knavery is exposed beyond doubt. He is a character of seemingly endless cunning, but the work of art demands a finale and a clear "sense of an ending" as well. That sense demands that the trickster, unredeemed by his accomplishments in the eyes of a restored collective morality, must be banished. Only those who rid society of blocking characters, transfer wealth to deserving hands or champion birthright, fertility and right social order as a by-product of their machinations can be granted a place in the new society at the play's end. Chapman's gentleman meddlers are warned, pardoned in light of the good they manage according to the laws of comic justice, and find reintegration into society, while Jonson's incorrigible tricksters are often too intransigent for reintegration. Jonson took his audiences to heights of revelry in the dramatizing of the lie, but invariably "purged" them when the order of the quotidian reasserted itself, of drab necessity, against a deviancy surpassing collective tolerance. The approbation of Volpone's predacity upon the carrion hunters, Corvino, Voltore and Corbaccio, is called into doubt by his assault upon Celia. Volpone seeks fulfillment of his appetites with astonishing gusto, but with moral indifference, thereby alerting in the spectator a compound and dynamic response to the protagonist's nature. The first level of our recognition of that generic being is in the contours of response he raises in the spectator, a response which takes cognizance of his playful strategems, his insatiable appetites, his satiric voice, his suspicious advantages which are the product of the lie he has mastered.

Where trickster exposes the lies of others, he can become a culture hero. As satirist, he is the voice of the artist, the self-appointed social critic and the illegal legislator.[14] The Elizabethans mastered the logistics of satiric comedy by appointing the trickster to the task of executing that censuring from within the play. It was a formidable artistic invention whereby the artistry of the playful knave could be allowed full expression in a way that served the collective order. Trickster survives in nature through a cunning that gives him an advantage over his prey, often related in the beast fable in terms of the sophister and victim. Where folly persists, tricksters thrive. The trickster is reborn with the confidence man as hero, since every profit-raising ploy simultaneously exposes a gull, and where the gull is exposed, the satirist's voice can be heard in the transaction.

The trickster, as an outsider, could also exercise an unprecedented perspicacity in detecting folly—the petty foibles, the unchecked passions, the acquisitive manias that motivate others. The levelling powers of the itinerant prankster was a favourite topic of medieval and renaissance story tellers; the satiric potential produced by the clever opportunist is already apparent in Reynard the Fox, Tyl Eulenspiegel, Johann Faustus, Courage, Celestina and Lazarillo. The comic wit in search of human fallibilities, domestic strife, unguarded ambition, courtly corruption, bourgeois pretensions, finds precisely those circumstances that he can master through the lie, and thereby he dominates or explodes all manner of busybodies, bores, wet blankets, skinflints, gossips and boasters, old fools and dodderers, cowards and upstarts, the parvenu, snobs, the smug, the arrogant and pedantic, coxcombs, fops and dandies, poseurs, salon haunters, lechers, effeminates and viragoes, the falsely pious up and down the social ladder. The Elizabethans experimented at length with the variables of the trickster vocation that would lend themselves to the creation of the satiric agent. There was, of course, at the same time a sense in which the agent himself could become too shrill, too insistent, thereby imperilling the sense of the play as a valid mimetic action. That is a question of a different sort, and the satiric drama was to have its own rise and fall within the period. But what that drama could become at its best depended upon an accommodation of the intriguer to the process of comic exposure, which had to arise as a by-product of the trickster's own will to exploit human vulnerability in accordance with his own ambitions.

Elizabethans had relatively little of substance to add to the repertoire of gonadotropic artifice; they were inclined to pillage the *novelle* and the romances for their love plots, refurbishing them with contemporary detail and citizen respectability. It was the acquisitive theme that brought the trickster into his own as hero, rogue and satirist in their theatre. And finally, there was a third area of Elizabethan experimentation, relating the trickster to the imperial theme. There seems to have been no precedent for this in continental theatre; the issue of political power appears to fall entirely outside their perception of comedy. But the Tudors, through the history play, came to recognize a perplexing affinity between the arts of diplomacy and the logistics of deception, between *realpolitik*, hypocrisy in the name of the state and the lies of the confidence man. They came to see the associations between knavery in the streets and knavery at court, the dissembling that defended freedom and the dissembling that led to power. The arts by which the prince was served were the arts by which he could be overthrown. All that pertained to intrigue and the intriguer's will, to appetites and motives could be adapted to lessons of statecraft, tracts on tyranny and political ambition.

There is no accounting, in so brief a sketch, for the way that recognition came about in terms of structural experimentation. One unlikely matrix was the native farce tradition with its vice figures and side-slapping villains. Such Tudor ephemera as *The Blind Beggar of Bednal Green* illustrate the formula of the popular rogue in disguise who slips out of one scrape after another by shifting disguises with a virtuosic dexterity challenging all credence. Munday's *John à Kent and John à Cumber* featured a three-way disguise which *Look About You* increased to six. So much interest in multiple disguise trickery plots at the Rose in the years before 1600 depended upon the success of the formula as well as upon the skills of a lead actor in the Admiral's Men specializing in impersonation roles. Whatever the reasons, Chapman creates out of the formula a prototype play of political ambition. In *The Blind Beggar of Alexandria*, Irus, a "shepheardes sonne at *Memphis* borne," becomes King of Egypt through a series of disguises. His spectacular rise is made possible by a capacity to be several persons at once so that, as though by divine prescience, in one guise he was always able to astonish and manipulate those at court by accurately predicting what he would do in another. The play improves little upon the episodic opportunism of the switch-and-flee tactics of the rogue. There is a ludicrous high point when, being married to two women at once, the protagonist has the dubious pleasure of twice cuckolding himself by seducing each wife as the husband of the other. But the play *is* about the drive for power and rulership, and the multiplicity of faces as a mechanical device comes back a very few years later in more sophisticated ways in the historical duplicity of Sejanus, a story Jonson found half-dramatized in the pages of Tacitus, and in the psychology of political deceit that Shakespeare explores in *Macbeth*.

The study of trickster as ambitious courtier did not require the kind of legitimizing strait jacket of responsible historiography that Jonson thought essential in *Sejanus*. John Marston, in *The Malcontent*, provides one of the happier conflations of politics and formulaic stagecraft in which the duke-in-disguise motif allows for the trickery necessary to bring the kingdom back to the rightful duke. The strategies of diplomacy fascinated the Elizabethans for overtly political and historical reasons, and the playwrights made such virtue of that fascination as to reshape the views of man the political animal in the image of the effective dramatic representation of him. Theories concerning *realpolitik* shaped the arts of the political trickster, just as intrigue structures shaped the representation of the climbing courtier. Such a conjunction of values and structures was a concomitant avenue to the archetype. Duke Altofronto had been too politically good, too naive to withstand the wiles of ambitious statecraft: "I wanted those old instruments of state, / Dissemblance, and suspect . . . ," and because of it "the crowde: / (Still liqerous of untried novelties) / Impatient with severer government, / Made strong with *Florence*: banisht Altofront." (I.iv.9-17)[15] The legitimate duke returns to his own court disguised as Malvole the spitting critic, watching for all opportunities to wreak the havoc and turmoil that would allow him to leap back to power. His legitimacy is, of course, pardon for all his deviousness, and his abandonment of trickery comes at the moment in which he returns to his former rule, a wiser and more circumspect potentate. An interim life of trickery had been his belated apprenticeship in the right management of his kingdom which yet does not corrupt his sense of justice. Malvole is, therefore, no through-and-through outlaw, but the manners of the trickster now assume a rightful place in regulating the affairs of state. The logistics of theatrical trickery could come as close as the Elizabethan dared to asserting the Machiavellian doctrines that Elizabethan statesmen, not to mention the Queen herself, practised in their own ways. Marston creates an effective theatrical statement on the lies, flattery, gossip, the jealousy and political mayhem that plague the highest echelons of nation-states. At the same time, Malvole's choice of means as the trickster-intriguer in regulating his affairs shows how the tactics of comedy can steer a safe course between the deposed guerilla fighters of history and the lone revengers of tragedy. In this play the able and energetic wit accommodates himself to the logistics of *realpolitik*, perhaps in a way more wishful than possible. Whether the drive to make an effective play prevails over the desire to make an astute political statement is beyond demonstration in this case. The other side of the coin is, of course, that by these means the playwright also manages his intrigue entirely by bringing the techniques of comic intrigue to court through the franchising of the duke as trickster, and the satirist as prime mover rolled into one.

In these plays dealing with affairs of state, as in the plays of love and the plays of acquisitiveness and the underworld, the trickster mode experienced rapid development and diversification. In *The Fawn*, Duke Hercules goes in disguise as a scourge of decadent manners, now at his neighbour Gonzaga's court. But while he is there, he also arranges for the marriage of his timid son Tiberio to Gonzaga's daughter. In loose association, the two modes nevertheless go together, for the scourge of folly is a kind of gesture of banishment, at least in a symbolic sense, of those who should not belong to the new order. It is a holiday play in design, but no less concerned with the corruptions of court life. Marston had found a formula for his satire that also allows for the joining of the imperial and romance themes through the trickster as both duke and father.

Massinger, in *The Duke of Milan*, borrows from the same repertoire of statecraft trickery to design his own brand of court play built on the strategies of deception. His play is a *coup de théâtre* (though not otherwise a particularly brilliant play!) largely because he allows the audience to believe throughout that the scheming protagonist is driven by the lust for power in the tradition of Irus the blind beggar, whereas in fact he creates a hero in the tradition of Kyd, whose will to revenge escapes even the audience. In that ambivalence, the playwright gives a lesson *en passant* of the trickster denominator between these two favoured sub-genres of drama—whether pitched in the comic or tragic mode. The structure of the play is internally organized through the carefully planned machinations of the ostensible power-seeker who insinuates his way into Sforza's personal graces, emerges as the superintendent of the realm during the duke's absence and attempts his virtuous wife with offers of love and with plans to murder the returning ruler. Francisco's carefully crafted knavery is spectacular and melodramatic, and a thorough study of popularized views of the devious courtier. Massinger's trump is, as already mentioned, hiding from the audience all knowledge of the climber's true motivations, for while we all along assume ambition, Francisco is impelled by revenge against the duke for having taken liberties with his sister. There is the stuff of *Othello* in the making, and while it is a pale play by comparison, it openly illustrates the genre with its emphasis upon the old intrigue devices of the disguise, the lie and the underlying desire to plot through such craft a ''revenge-in-kind'' as a perverse form of trickster ''play''. Through contamination, the witty knave comedies had a good deal to do with the theatrical development of the Elizabethan revenge tragedy.

Shakespeare complicates infinitely the question of the political man as trickster in *Hamlet* because he is more interested in the innuendoes of the would-be trickster's mind than he is in the inflections of the actual deeds. Yet in that very fact, there is an entirely new consciousness in the trickster which turns upon the moral ambiguity of his innate nature. When the trickster becomes self-censuring, he comes to the last phase of his psychic development, perched at the edge of the light of common day that will destroy the essence of the type and for that same reason turn Hamlet into a trickster-*manqué*. The Teutonic tradition of feigned madness as the survival technique of a son forced to live at the court of his father's murderer is at the centre of the play. Saxo Grammaticus relates his version of the tradition in his account of the story of Amleth.[16] As a potential revenger, Hamlet belongs to the tradition launched by Kyd, but he is reticent about his role and turns to a sporadic and ineffectual kind of trickery in order to temporize, and in order to settle matters of guilt. Nevertheless, he knew moments of ruthlessness as when he employed a sustained duplicity in dispatching Rosencranz and Guildenstern. His story is that of a would-be trickster who lacks the means, the determination, or the circumstances to so conduct himself. In Prospero, Shakespeare gives the duke-in-disguise motif an extra dimension by conflating him with the benign sorcerer. As the banished duke, with his extended powers, he joins the politician's will with the warlock's means to regulate the ills of state. At the one extreme is the courtier-intriguer who proves himself a villain, and at the other is the ruler-trickster who employs the techniques of deception as a benefactor to his state.

So cursory a list of plays can barely relate the degree to which the Elizabethans were addicted to intrigue plotting in a way that entailed a thorough anatomization of the intriguer mentality as mover within the plays. For prototypes, they scoured the existing literatures at their disposal, both native and foreign, exploited nearly every convention of trickery and disguise, and raised as many models for the role as an imitation of contemporary society would yield. The ethos of carnival lay more or less outside Elizabethan sensibilities, but they learned how to build plots around the extended *lazzi* that could give shape to their plays. The Elizabethans brought low life roguery to a fine art, as in Marston's Cocledemoy in *The Dutch Courtesan*, who is surely one of the most deft sleight-of-hand characters in all of drama. They carried the rogue's logic and mentality into the fairs, the houses of citizens, into the towns and courts. The age was preoccupied with new influence and new money, with the contest between the old families and the parvenu; in the social transactions and transitions of the age, intrigue seemed to serve as the operative means and metaphor for such contests of power. The plays suggest, repeatedly, that deception was the tactic of the new man, his means to power, both licit and illicit, in a post-chivalric world. Trickster motifs become not only the design patterns for the compact character-motivated fable, but "tool-ideas" for analyzing society. The novelty and complexity of intrigue plotting in the Elizabethan theatre, together with an implicitly recognized sociology of the trickster, brought him as a dramatic agent to his fullest theatrical maturity.

To be sure, not every intriguer, as a mere mechanical strategist, contains in his personal motivations the archetypal attitudes associated with the folk type. Yet, the very act of deception illustrates his tactics, and out of such tactics comes intimations of the formative will—if the character has any personal substance at all. The lover can dabble with the harmless ruse for tricking the old one, but only the outsider can devote himself to the prank that reveals ironic essences. Love, status, material wealth, political power are universal movers, both tragically and comically, but only the trickster as hero plays these desires across the gap of irony that is signalled by his spleen, the satiric diatribe, his sporting misanthropy, his wagering and taste for risks, in short, his self-driven sense of play, whether cruel or gay, that prefigures his every gesture and his sense of self.

The trickster is, above all, a connoisseur of his own wit. Though Volpone is moved by greed and lust, his distinguishing feature is his conscious delight in turning the perfect ruse. He was a potential overreacher in his pursuit of Celia, but in point of fact, it was his desire to perfect his work as an artist of intrigue that prompted him to create a last testament in jest in order to torment his legacy hunters giving Mosca at the same time the ultimate means to betray him. Likewise, Mosca reveals the self-consciousness of a practising artist in his celebration of the parasite. His enthusiasm for the trade as the pinnacle of worldly achievements is, simultaneously, a celebration of his own expertise. Mosca is an avowed trickster whose very essence is his elegance of manner, his ability to match all moods, assume importance or stoop in humility, move with agility, alter plans to adjust to unforseen circumstances, process several clients at once or put on a new personality for any occasion in a trice. The primary trickster lives to test his wits on those about him. He delights in creating confusion and mayhem when it serves his ends. He is the eternal knave who can put on heroism and nobility at will. He is ready to suspend mores and public decency in order to turn society on its head, whether for fun or for profit. His advantages over others reside in his uncanny capacity to anticipate their foibles and weaknesses. The urge to win, dominate, compromise or expose by deception and the precalculated ploy, and to do it with ingenuity and panache is his defining complexion. The bare unaccommodated trickster is on perennial holiday from conformity. The will to play, superimposed upon the more pragmatic goals that compel the lackey, the bawd, the confidence man, the gentleman wit, the legacy hunter, the duke-in-disguise, the Machiavellian villain, the crafty revenger, the climbing courtier, the streetcorner wag—all faces granting trickster a characterological *modus* and a name— defines the archetype.

Inversely, where such faces emerge as the engineers of the action through premeditated scenarios in keeping with their respective natures and vocations, that characterological force, to the extent those scenarios are enacted according to expectation, not only gives shape to the dénouement, but also ambience and a moral tone. Such completed actions must be understood as expressions of the trickster's involvement, and thus of the trickster's will. Admittedly, there is room for irony—for the counterpointing of trickster ambitions with the principles of the new society. Yet it is the process of selection through the artificial scheme that determines the inclusion into or exclusion from the new order, and the moral quality of that order. The predation of knave upon knave at the end of *Il Negromante* banishes the trickster, whereas Ligurio creates a *ménage à trois* as the accepted *status quo* and thereby guarantees his own survival as a parasite. The trickster's will embraces the fertile union, the satiric exposure and the carnival diversion. He may not set out consciously to be the scourge or the shaman, yet his ambitions and his projects are precisely those that make the *Mandragola* a carnival play and *The Fawn* a rite of passage. There is little doubt that in pragmatic terms the intriguer is a by-product of structural and thematic experimentation. Yet the will behind the structures guides and controls the ethos of the action, and that avenue of assessment, together with the conscious exploitation of a motivating mentality amongst the Elizabethans, suggests that there was, in the theatre of the trickster as hero, some feedback from the characterological principles that had arisen from previous experimentation.

The trickster entered the final phase of this "incarnation" in the theatres when, in a way of speaking, he became cognizant of his own mission as social hammer and scourge. In *Gammer Gurton's Nedle*, Diccon of Bedlam, with his filching and gleeful lies, creates the circumstances that expose the pettiness and gullibility of an entire village. Diccon is a direct descendant of the folk farce hero who merely labours for his own appetites. Yet the play shows just how entire realms of exploitation and exposure can follow from that anarchic spirit. Thus, without any conscious effort, the prankster, in being himself, becomes the supreme interpreter of the social order. Where his mission becomes a conscious attack upon the excesses of that order, his voice threatens to become synonymous with that of the author. There is the danger then of a too devastating advantage. Shakespeare hints at that fault in his management of the few spitting critics in his own plays, and generally seeks other solutions to comedy than the trickster's. His gestures in that direction, such as the anti-Malvolio subplot in *Twelfth Night*, have incessantly troubled his more dewy-eyed critics. When Jonson is at his best and wittiest, when his prankster spokesmen, such as the triumvirate in *Epicoene*, are in control, we exult in the sweep of their trenchancy. Yet the trickster, unrestrained, spares no office or incumbent; nothing is sacred; all is play. Nothing escapes denigration or degradation. So viewed, the urbane life itself seems to pass beyond redemption. Comic order also necessitates the silencing of too much truth. While trickster is in the ascendancy, he serves society as leech and leveller. But the dénouement must also level the leveller, must make the architect of the social disorder within the play the victim of his own work—better done by cancelling knaves through an internecine struggle than by imposing an extraneous magistrature upon him at the end. The rise and fall of the trickster is inherent to his nature within the comic order, since trickster has no long-time abode and can prolong his survival in other more episodic forms of literature only by passing from village to village and from vignette to vignette. In his own search for power, food and sex he has a paradoxical capacity to keep the society with which he interacts from running to decadence and decline, though integration is beyond him. He is congenitally unable to come to terms with his own nature in light of collective standards.

Man is a ruseful creature, driven by appetites, hampered by the exigencies of civilization, a psychic malcontent, a competitive survivor. Trickster is an expression of the reverie of freedom whereby man gains advantage in these matters through deception. Just as the logistics of the psyche project themselves into the strategies of the trick, so the characteristic shapes of the trick reflect the will and intellect that creates them. Trickster thereby embodies an archetypal relationship of energies expressed in the encounter between the deceiver and the deceived. It is more useful, for our purposes, to see that nexus of character and act as a product of direct literary influence than to see the literary record as an upsurge of archetypal contents. Yet there is a particular satisfaction in seeing, retroactively, how the solutions to mechanical problems, reflections of contemporary society and the experimental contamination of structural modes and elements conspired to reproduce the universal type. The history of that process remains conjectural with regard to detail, for it involves the most intimate aspects of the creative process. Yet the leading features are clear: the general social elevation of the stock tool character; the adaptation of *novelle* plots to the Plautine formula; the integration of the carnival world order; the stylization and personalization of the intriguer's motivations; the gradual centralizing of the type as play protagonist; the development of the underworld and court settings. Above all, through a long apprenticeship, the power of the intriguer as a master intelligence capable of managing, often in *stretto*, the threads of a compound plot, was fully appreciated and developed. At the opposite extreme from fortune on the plot spectrum was the precast operation that prevails through its capacity to anticipate all responses to its manoeuvres and to mould the desires of others to its purposes.

The outcome of such structural procedures is not only the internally designed and controlled action, but also a generic presence. The realization that the play must also be concerned with the mind behind the deed led to reflection upon the role of the anarchic appetite and of deception in the context of society. When the lover, gentleman, courtier, revenger, legacy-seeker all become tricksters in order to reach their ends, the structural convenience of the tool character gives rise, simultaneously, to a trickster society characterized by conditions of survival for which only the trickster is equipped. For Jonson, Marston, Chapman, Webster, Marlowe and others there were very real reasons for believing this was the right mode for analyzing the conditions of their age. Put otherwise, the compounding of trickster elements and characterological formations alone made such a vision of society in the drama possible.

This essay has been speculative in nature, intending primarily to examine the relationship between a literary tool-figure whose generic personality comes to dominate a major sub-genre of Renaissance comedy and the archetypal figure called trickster. The high degree of correlation, the essential attributes and common cultural content suggest that the comedy of intrigue, in its growth throughout the sixteenth and early seventeenth centuries, had provided a matrix for the type and that, in turn, it must be viewed as one of the major artistic media expressing the archetype. The fast-paced plots of social competition master-minded by the privately motivated schemer express a pleasing and at the same time frightening anarchy. The road I have taken is to show how the figure generating such contents is a product of pragmatic artistic experimentation. The inverse of that argument is that the trickster protagonist, along with the forms that contain and feature him, is a product of the same psychic and social phenomena that have always generated trickster, at a point in history in which a new freedom for expression asserts itself against still fresh memories of oppression, whether of internal or external origins. Marlowe's Faustus is the most familiar case in point of the anthropocentric, self-defining Renaissance man assuming trickster attitudes against a pervasive and disciplining religious structure. The ambiguous issue of that contest perfectly expresses the ambiguities and ironies attached to the trickster nature. Following that approach, we see not only how the comic forms of the age reanimated the type in the specific characters, but also how the social and psychic climate revolutionalized the comic theatre in the image of the trickster. Thus two independent and yet entirely complementary principles seem clear as a result of the enquiry: one (the more fully explored in this paper) is that, to a very large extent, the entire potential for the growth of any new form of social comedy in the Renaissance depended upon the refitting and redeployment of the characterological formation here defined as the trickster; the other is that just as the Italian writers managed to create the ethos of carnival through the trickster intermediary, so the Elizabethans came to an analysis of the "new" political and acquisitive habits arising from their nation-state status and their vigorous bourgeois mercantilism only through their discovery of the means for projecting these new men of town and court into trickster roles through the theatre.

NOTES

1 Leo Salingar in *Shakespeare and the Traditions of Comedy* (Cambridge, 1974, rpt. 1976), 88-128 provides two formative chapters in which he traces the comic deceiver as trickster to the Old Comedy of Aristophanes, attempting a history of the type through Rome to the comedy of the sixteenth century. He concludes that "the trickster or the ironies that belong to his part reassume their importance, despite a long series of variations in detail, throughout the tradition of imitating or modernising New Comedy that was introduced by the Renaissance." "More than anything else, it is the invitation to the audience to enjoy an exhibition of some form of deceit that distinguishes comedy from romance in the theatre." 128.

2 There is room for a lengthy study on the sociology of trickster and the nature of carnival, since he has a large part to play in the knavery involving food, sex and violence that characterise carnival license. Carnival was also a festival of identities in which insiders and outsiders were clearly differentiated, as epitomized by the mock battles. The logic of charivari and the manifestations against officialdom and the rest invite trickster antics. For a survey of the circumstances of carnival see Peter Burke, *Popular Culture in Early Modern Europe* (London, 1978), 90ff. Also of related interest is the article by Natalie Z. Davis, "The Reasons of Misrule: Youth Groups and Charivaris in Sixteenth Century France," *Past and Present* 50 (1971), 41-75.

3 *Four Archetypes: Mother, Rebirth, Spirit, Trickster*, trans. R.E.C. Hull (Princeton, 1970), 135-52.

4 For a treatment of trickster as a product of folklore see Munro S. Edmonson, *Lore: An Introduction to the Science of Folklore* (New York, 1971). Edmonson points out the processes of transmission and the way they encourage improvisation, convergences and divergences in a single tradition. He shows how the patterns and characterological types are preserved by analogy (as they were in Renaissance comedy) from writer to writer and how such patterns lend them-

selves to transformational inversions (trickster may be young or old), yet how the content of the myth remains constant. With regard to trickster specifical-ly, Edmonson deals essentially with the ways in which trickster stories were collected into cycles around a central personality, and how those cycles of tales and the character type interacted to define each other. Yet he makes a number of suggestions about the type as a product of his relationship to society and to narrative structures. He outlines the extremes of cunning and foolishness that make up the type, his motiveless malignity, his craving for the satisfac-tion of basic drives including his need for deception and for playing pranks. As in all other forms of lore, trickster must have a high level of "communicabili-ty" (p. 27) and his "voice" in dealing metaphorically with experience must be a record of shared cultural experiences.

5 On the significance assigned to trickster as a violator of taboos see Laura Makarius, "Le Mythe du 'trickster'," *Revue de l'Histoire des Religions*, 175 (1966), 17-46. Her thesis is that the trickster is scapegoated after ritually break-ing certain taboos upon which civilization is, perforce, based, relating to sex-uality and to blood allegiances. A society profits psychologically from the viola-tion of such taboos through the liberation of certain magical powers, even though the transgressor must be punished. Occasionally, the trickster as hero is made to bear collective guilt, thereby transferring this pattern to the com-edy in question. But the pattern is not a universal one insofar as certain tricksters succeed without banishment or punishment, though the question of moral in-fractions often remains in the viewer's mind.

6 On the kaleidoscopic nature of trickster and his tendency to metamorphose into surrounding types with variant or different orientations, see O.E. Klapp, *Heroes, Villains, Fools: the Changing American Character* (Englewood Cliffs, N.J., 1962). This work is not about trickster *per se*, but its methodologies and treat-ment of related types clearly illustrate the governing principles involved.

7 Perhaps the most outstanding of the Amerindian tricksters is neither crow nor coyote, but Wakdjunkaga of the Winnebago, in a cycle of stories published and analyzed by Paul Radin in *The Trickster: A Study in American Indian Mythology* (New York, 1956). See also Gary Snyder, "The Incredible Survival of Coyote," in *The Old Ways* (San Francisco, 1977) and *Coyote the Trickster: Legends of the North American Indians*, ed. Gail Robinson and Douglas Hill (London, 1975). On Loki see Anna Booth, *Loki in Scandinavian Mythology* (Lund, 1961). Con-cerning Hermes see Norman O. Brown, *Hermes the Thief: The Evolution of a Myth* (New York, 1947, rpt., 1969). On the Zande trickster see E.E. Evans-Prichard ed., *The Zande Trickster* (Oxford, 1967).

8 For a survey of the Tyl Eulenspiegel cycle see the Introduction to the transla-tion by Paul Oppenheimer of *A Pleasant Vintage of Till Eulenspiegel . . . .* (Mid-dleton, Conn., 1972). For *Courage* see the Introduction by Hans Speier to the translation of Hans Jacob Christoffel von Grimmelshausen, *Courage, the Adven-turess & The False Messiah* (Princeton, 1964).

9 *Homo Ludens: A Study of the Play Element in Culture* (London, 1949). Huizinga does not discuss the elements of play in the theatre *per se*, but the patterns he identifies throughout society have their counterparts in art and correspond to the various levels of trickster behaviour.

10 Salingar points out how moralists have made many pronouncements about the didactic responsibility of art, but that even they assume "almost without question, that, within certain limits or on certain licensed occasions (such as Carnival), double dealing and practical jokes are permissible and even ad-mirable. This assumption, or something like it, goes far back into the origins of literary comedy; without it, most European comedy as we know it would disappear." *Shakespeare and the Traditions of Comedy*, 87.

11 The modern critical edition of this play is edited by Norman B. Spector (Paris, 1964); it is also in English translation as *Satisfaction All Around* (Ottawa, 1980).

12 For English texts of this and *The Necromancer* (*Il Negromante*) see *The Comedies of Ariosto*, trans. Edmond M. Beame and Leonard Sbrocchi (Chicago, 1975).

13 For a more extensive treatment of this play as a problem in trickste rethics see my article on "Machiavelli's *Mandragola* and the Emerging *Animateur*," *Quaderni d'Italianistica*, 5,2 (1984), 171-89.

14 There is a complex relationship between the trickster will and the satiric mood when the social advantages of the trickster can be placed in the service of the railer, misanthrope or social reformer. For insights into their common territory see Robert C. Elliott, *The Power of Satire: Magic, Ritual, Art* (Princeton, 1960, rpt. 1972).

15 John Marston, "The Malcontent," *The Plays of John Marston*, ed. H. Harvey Wood (Edinburgh, 1934), III, 151.

16 For a more thorough discussion see H.R. Ellis Davidson, "Loki and Saxo's Hamlet," *The Fool and the Trickster*, ed. Paul V.A. Williams (Totowa, N.J., 1979), 3-17. See also Theodore Lidz, *Hamlet's Enemy: Madness and Myth in "Hamlet"* (New York, 1975).

The Sorcerer
in Italian Renaissance Comedy

Douglas Radcliff-Umstead

Since Italian authors of comedies during the Renaissance intended their works to be mirrors of everyday life, the study of the leading character-types in their plays would constitute an ideal approach to understanding the nature of the erudite theatre which flourished throughout the sixteenth century. While some character-types, like the braggart warrior and the parasite, derived from the ancient Roman comedies of Plautus and Terence, other figures, like the pedant and the clergyman, reflected contemporary Italian society. A thorough investigation of all those character-types still awaits scholarly scrutiny: only the braggart warrior has received attention in a complete volume of study, while the pedant has occupied a preliminary essay of intent for further exploration.[1] Another character-type that appears in numerous plays throughout the Cinquecento is the sorcerer, who introduces the dark features of Italian renaissance society in relying on astrology, necromancy, and demonology. The prominence of the sorcerer in play after play illustrates the strong role of the magical arts in almost every social class in Italy, while the comico-satirical focus on the sorcerer's criminal behaviour and the credulity of his victims reveals the rational skepticism of intellectually inquisitive writers seeking to expose the ridiculous truth of daily existence. An appreciation of the sorcerer as a theatrical character-type will follow from a brief presentation of the importance of magic to late renaissance Italian society.

A sinister view of the supernatural, which occult arts could summon at the will of gifted practitioners, lasted throughout the Middle Ages and Renaissance well into the seventeenth century. Roman antiquity had given to modern Europe its own superstitions about ominous occurrences, prodigies, and auguries. In a Christian world with a strong fear of eternal damnation, belief in spirits betrayed a fear of Satan and his troops of diabolical demons. Workers of magic had to demonstrate to secular and ecclesiastical authorities their desire to avoid alliance with the spirits of condemned souls in favor of benevolent supernatural forces. The general willingness of society, even among members of the highest educated professions, to accept the existence of both evil and protective spirits often created situations for exploitation by unscrupulous workers of magic pretending to exercise power over the world of demons.

Magic in the Renaissance involved a total picture of the universe and the role of humankind in controlling all of Creation. Through occult arts one could command Nature. Witchcraft, astrology, divination, the Kabala, and alchemy all pointed the way to a mastery over the world with the ability to bring about physical transformations of reality. To prevent reliance upon evil demons, the Florentine Neo-Platonic philosopher Marsilio Ficino

(1433-1499) sought to create a purified, natural magic which would invoke the assistance of good spirits so that magic and religion might work together for the advancement of humankind. Although Ficino's younger contemporary, Pico Della Mirandola (1463-1494), resolutely opposed judicial astrology which foretold the future, he looked to the esoteric Hebrew tradition of the Kabala to decipher the angelic and divine names which would unlock the occult bonds holding together the entire animated universe. Both Ficino and Pico agreed that humans were special creatures intermediate to angels and beasts, with the capacity to elevate themselves to heavenly heights. This view of humans as possible demigods led to a general social acceptance of the *"magus,"* the "Arch-Magician" or "master sorcerer" endeavoring to manipulate those occult bonds unifying the whole of Creation. The Faustian aspirations of certain researchers into sorcery confirmed an optimistic belief in the divine powers of humankind to unite the spiritual and physical facets of reality in a search for perfection. A "magus" would be able to commune with celestial forces through non-diabolical ceremonies and the use of wondrous amulets. The master sorcerer excited popular imagination with the opportunity to possess power over Nature, material objects, and other persons. In the careers of some scholars into the occult, one could follow the stirring quest for lordship over the unknown forces in the heavens and the earth. To most Europeans in the sixteenth century, the German Heinrich Cornelius Agrippa von Nettesheim (1488-1535), briefly a lecturer on esoteric philosophy at the University of Pavia, symbolized the Arch-Magician with his impassioned struggle to discover the secrets controlling the universe as recorded in his influential text *De Occulta Philosophia* of 1533. The Swiss physician Paracelsus (1493-1541) rejected reliance on the writings of ancient sages in favor of an experimental alchemical approach to transmute reality with a medical chemistry. An alchemist could hold the secrets for unlocking Nature that would perfect humankind. Even though the authors of Italian erudite comedies in the sixteenth century would scoff at the Faustian pretensions of would-be master sorcerers, two of those comic playwrights—Giordano Bruno and Giambattista Della Porta—passionately investigated the mysteries of occult sciences.[2]

Renaissance fascination with magic far transcended a Hellenistic interest in performing miraculous acts. Plautus had reflected a serene Hellenistic interest in magic as the marvelous in his play *Mostellaria*, where the servant Tranio uses the ruse of a haunted house to rescue his young master Philolaches when the youth's father returns home unexpectedly just as his son is holding a drunken party. Ancient Latin comedy did not represent on stage the sinister aspects of magic which renaissance researchers into the magical found in the Hellenistic world of Ptolemaic Egypt through the esoteric writings attributed to the legendary sage Mercurius or Hermes Trismegistus. By 1463 Ficino completed a Latin translation of the extant *Corpus Hermeticum* to introduce to the European intellectual community magical notions about alchemy as a mysterious art, astrology as a study of planetary demons and earthly substances, and the use of talismans and figurines to invoke spirits. Hermetic literature seemed to offer a key to unleashing mankind's creative genius through knowledge of occult practices. The Hermetic tradition opened to Renaissance scholars of magical lore a philosophical vision of Nature as a system of mysterious signs that the sorcerer could interpret to gain power over the physical world.[3]

While astrology generally dominated the attention of occultists in the first half of the sixteenth century, the Paracelsan movement at mid-century shifted investigation toward alchemy. Judicial astrology functioned as a form of divination, claiming that the planets and stars controlled parts of the human body and influenced the course of months and days. The study of astrology led to sorcery, so that in the literature of Cinquecento Italy the terms *"astrologo,"* *"mago,"* and *"negromante"* (necromancer) are nearly interchangeable. Astrology enjoyed so much respectability in Italy that until the time of the Catholic Reformation it remained part of the curriculum of the universities. Popes like Julius II, Leo X, Adrian VI and Paul III employed astrologers to cast their horoscopes. In medicine, astrology joined with alchemy in the theory of transmutation to change disease into health. Through knowledge of the planets and the metals of the earth an alchemist might create life-enhancing tinctures to heal every illness. Leo X encouraged the publication of texts on the art of metallic transmutations. Along with the products of their distillation laboratories, alchemists resorted to using amulets, incantations, and magical rituals to call forth the unseen forces animating Nature. Through furnaces, alembics and other equipment alchemists sought to transform base metals into magical gold and to discover an elixir which would prolong life. Aged persons might regain their youth, and the poor would find unending riches from the pure quintessences extracted by alchemical researchers. Both holy prelates and secular rulers in Italy patronized the quest of alchemists after the divine gold of mysterious origin.[4]

In addition to the officially sanctioned arts of astrology and alchemy, on the popular level throughout Italy witchcraft thrived, since the Christian view of the universe which condemned souls working for Satan actually promoted that profession. Persons hoping to advance their schemes of greed, lust, or ambition would seek out witches and sorcerers. An entire colony of witches and enchanters operated during the fifteenth and sixteenth centuries at Norcia, the home of St. Benedict, in the very territories of the Church. In Bk. I ch. lxv of his *Autobiography*, Benvenuto Cellini comments how a priestly sorcerer of his acquaintance wanted to visit the hill country of Norcia to consecrate a magical text of his. Italian sorcerers and witches were on the whole very practical. The rather "romantic" type of witchcraft popular among the Germans flourished only among the Italian Alpine valleys. Financial profit, instead of knowledge of arcane mysteries, attracted the majority of magical workers whose claims to performing marvelous deeds merely served to win clients and increase their earnings. Italian practitioners of magic had to exercise great caution for fear of prosecution by magistrates and inquisitors. With a bull by Pope Innocent VIII in 1484, official harassment of sorcerers and witches on charges of pursuing black magic began to intensify, and in following years other bulls by pontiffs like Alexander VI, Leo X, and Adrian VI authorized German Dominican monks to carry out a campaign of persecution. If one wonders that those were some of the very same popes who supported astrologers and alchemists, the answer astrologers and alchemists, the answer lies in the distinction between respectable investigators of the occult and workaday warlocks or witches seeking their livelihoods in piazze from relatively humble clients. One of the major functions of witches was to inflict a disease on a person hated by a customer of theirs, often with a waxen image of the one to be injured. Clients turned to witches and warlocks to win back the affections of unfaithful lovers or to ruin the happy love-affairs of amorous rivals. Witches prepared love potions, performed abortions, and made foolish young women appear to be virgins.[5] Summoning the dead, of course, occupied the attention of necromancers like the Sicilian priest in Book I, ch. lxiv, of Cellini's *Autobiography* who met the goldsmith in the Roman Coliseum one night to hold a ceremony with precious incenses, incantations, and pentacles to fill the stadium with fiendish devils and four threatening giants. Magical spectacle fascinated Italians from every class and profession.

Because of the general acceptance of magical arts in Italy, charlatans easily took advantage of the greed and ambitious folly of clients eager to amass fortunes or to acquire political power. There existed a pseudo-magical criminal sub-culture of rogues as alchemists, mountebanks, enchanters, necromancers, and conjurors. The members of that magical underworld differed from the professional warlocks and witches in that the criminals intended to defraud their victims rather than render satisfying services.[6] As Italian playwrights were to portray them, the confidence-game charlatans became adept at distorting language with solemn phrases that sounded like Hebrew, Greek, or Latin to ignorant clients easily impressed by a display of occult knowledge. Falsifiers of language, coins, and currency, the charlatan magicians duped entire governments with their counterfeit erudition. Alchemists with claims of producing tinctures for gold and immortality especially succeeded in swindling rapacious patrons dreaming of riches and everlasting youth. One amazingly successful charlatan who won great prosperity in life and aesthetic immortality for himself was Tommaso Gianotti of Ravenna (or Rangone), who charmed the patricians of Venice with wondrous medications and used his earnings to glorify himself by commissioning the restoration of churches with statues of himself by famous sculptors.[7] Self-affirmation by sheer ego power, rather than knowledge of occult arts, led to the triumph of pseudo-magicians.

Although the Venetian government had forbidden the practice of alchemy as early as the last quarter of the fifteenth century, the rulers of the Most Serene Republic would fail to enforce their own laws when metallic transmutation seemed to promise unlimited revenues for the state. Particularly after 1570, with the loss of Cyprus and its maritime empire, the Venetian Senate looked to alchemy as a means of salvation to rescue the nation from decline. By 1589 the government of Venice was competing with the Duke of Mantua for the alchemical services of the Cypriot refugee "Mamugnà called il Bragadino," who had established himself in luxurious circumstances near Brescia, seemingly from his ability to fabricate gold. Late in 1589 Bragadino accepted the generous invitation of the Venetian Senate to move to their city to set up a laboratory at state expense. Wealthy patrons flocked to the alchemist in the hope of increasing their fortunes. Bragadino proved to be far more an extractor of other persons' money than of alchemically produced gold. Such a fierce gold fever seized citizens that the prices on chemical equipment rose enormously in Venice. But Bragadino's inevitable failure to deliver the miraculous tincture and write a detailed description of the process to transmute gold led to his hasty retreat out of Italy to the court of the Duke of Bavaria, who in 1591 ordered the swindler's execution for his crimes against the state and credulous private citizens.[8] Italian comic dramatists would depict the careers of fictive charlatans on an erratic course of frenzied welcome and enraged disappointment by gullible clients, to mirror the real-life misadventures of swindling alchemists and astrologers.

Contemporary life, rather than the ancient theatre of Plautus and Terence, provided dramatists in Italy with the models of magicians playing upon human desire for riches and eternal life. Throughout the sixteenth century classically structured erudite comedy would deride credulous individuals who patronized criminal magicians. Writers of comedies also could draw from the narrative tradition of novella collections whose authors derided magicians for claiming to perform the marvelous, or poked fun at the stupidity of those clients who permitted impostors to cheat them. The Latin humanistic comedy of the Quattrocento provided a major precedent for the figure of the mountebank magician in the play *Epirota*, published in 1483 in Venice by the patrician Tommaso de Mezzo. In one of the *Epirota*'s episodic scenes a charlatan holds a medicine show promising that his drugs will heal any number of illnesses. Astrology became the target of ridicule in the vernacular *sacra rappresentazione* called *Sant'Orsola* by the Tuscan Castellano de' Castellani, who labeled fortune-telling by the stars a "stupid affair." With the creation of an Italian erudite comedy on regular classical lines, playwrights could seek inspiration for their portraits of rogue magicians in true life and modern literary traditions to build a dramatic world about the temptations of occult pseudo-sciences.

During the carnival of 1513 at the court of the Duke of Urbino, the magician as a dramatic figure in the erudite comedy made his stage entrance in the play *La Calandria* by Cardinal Bernardo Dovizi da Bibbiena. An atmosphere of enchantment appears in the prologue Bibbiena composed for later performances of his comedy, where the actor delivering the prologue imagines he has found the fabled magic ring of Princess Angelica to make him invisible in order to fly through the city observing others in humourously compromising situations.[9] With its setting in contemporary Rome under papal rule, *La Calandria* presents a society of continual metamorphoses in the carnival masquerade of transvestite disguises where the Greek youth Lidio dresses as his lost sister Santilla in order to meet his lover the Roman lady Fulvia, while the actual Santilla, from her initial fear of Turkish invaders, has been disguised as the apprentice merchant Lidio. During the frenzied erotic course of this play Fulvia, for fear of losing Lidio, has to go out alone on the streets in male disguise. Those androgynous exchanges of identity contribute to the play's comic spirit of amorous confusion resulting from deceiving appearances. Rome becomes the centre for marvelous reversals in situation and sexual role.

Magical assistance enters into Bibbiena's play to assist the motivating power of love which holds all the major characters under its sway. Fulvia

hires Ruffo, described as a "*negromante*," to bewitch Lidio so that her lover
will never desert her. But Ruffo will remain a coldly isolated figure to the
charms of love, a force that in this comedy owes more to Boccaccio's
Decameron than to the plays of Plautus and Terence. Never once does the
sorcerer act as an agent of the drama's reversals. Ruffo falls to the play's
sidelines, very much like Lidio's pederastic preceptor Polinico, who attempts
in vain to dissuade his student from a passionate and adulterous involvement with Fulvia. In this early Italian Renaissance erudite comedy, Bibbiena was not only introducing new character-types, but his association
of the pedant and the sorcerer in function established a precedent for later
dramatists like Giordano Bruno. The sorcerer and the pedant both twist
language to their own purposes, relying on dead tongues to convince others
with their specious arguments. Culture works as a debased instrument for
those two professional purveyors of distorted knowledge. Ruffo continually fails to promote the aims of romance. The only Lidio that this magician
knows is the youth living at the home of the Florentine merchant Perillo:
in reality the twin Santilla, who on the advice of her servant Fannio takes
part in the illicit liaison with Fulvia. Whereas magicians ordinarily dupe
others, in this play Fannio deceives Ruffo by informing him that Santilla
is a hermaphrodite with the ability to appear male or female as the occasion demands. The claim to sexual transmutation then acts as one of the
comedy's themes in its confusing game of constantly altering appearances.
But when Fulvia thinks that her lover has been changed into a woman,
Calandro's wife assails Ruffo for irreparably ruining Lidio. Trusting in
Santilla's pretensions to a readily convertible androgyny, the sorcerer assures
Fulvia of his magical power to restore Lidio to his masculine identity. When
Lidio's servant Fessenio learns of the supposed sexual enchantment of his
young master by Ruffo, that wily attendant begins to admire the sorcerer's
illusory gifts of transformation. At no moment, however, does Bibbiena's
magician ever seem other than a marginal and exterior character to the
central force of love.[10] Forever relegated to the drama's periphery, beyond
its core of romantic intrigues, this ineffective charlatan cannot participate
in the new order of socially approved loving relationships to emerge at the
comedy's conclusion.

　　Ruffo neither enters actively into the world of Renaissance magic, nor
does he display the flair of a grand charlatan. With its inspiration in the
Decameron, this play exalts the force of intelligence that rises to every challenge
and transforms defeats into triumphs. The servant Fessenio possesses the
traits of resourcefulness and inventiveness lacking in the sorcerer. No matter
what the reverses caused by arbitrary fortune, whether through mistaken
identity, unexpected intervention by customs officials, or through the
jealousy and lechery of Fulvia's husband Calandro, and the suspicions of
family members, this servant will devise new stratagems to advance the
lovers. Fessenio, rather than Ruffo, has the superior intelligence needed
to save others in difficult situations. He uses magic far more enthusiastically
than Ruffo, as when, in Act II, Sc. 6, the servant pretends to teach the
stupid Calandro how a man's body can be taken apart limb by limb, placed in a chest, and later reassembled by saying the magic word "Am-
bracullac," which the doltish Roman citizen succeeds in verbally mangling.

Calandro, unable to repeat the spell, cries out in pain when the servant almost twists off his arm; and Fessenio scolds him for ruining the spell. Since Bibbiena's play lends itself to a farcical game where complications forever arise, Fessenio works to make every problem disappear, as in the final act after Calandro's brothers have discovered Fulvia and Lidio together at her home and have gone off to report to her husband. Fessenio achieves the comedy's supreme transformation by substituting Santilla for Lidio, thus preventing all charges of adultery against Fulvia. It is the servant's intelligence rather than the magician's occult arts that have conquered adverse circumstances to bring about the triumph of love. Santilla will wed Fulvia's son Flamminio, and Lidio will marry Verginia, the daughter of the merchant Perillo. The two motivating forces, love and intelligence, as inspired by the *Decameron*, achieve victory in this early erudite comedy. As the faithful servant of love and the agent of astute ruses, it is to Fessenio rather than the ineffective sorcerer Ruffo that the right falls to deliver the comedy's envoi. Honour goes out to him for overcoming all obstacles to romance.

With Ludovico Ariosto's comedy *Il Negromante*, first completed in 1519 and then performed in a second version at the ducal theatre of Ferrara in 1528, the sorcerer moves to the centre of dramatic attention. Cremona, the setting for this play, was one of the areas where, toward the close of the fifteenth century, the Dominicans were prosecuting cases of accused witchcraft. The play's prologue attributes the miraculous arrival of Cremona on stage in Ferrara to the necromancer's power to command devils to transport the Lombard city to the Emilian capital. In this play the title character is the magician Giacchelino, a Sephardic exile from Castile who travels about the Mediterranean world under a variety of assumed names and false nationalities represented by appropriate disguises. Leading a gypsy's life, he pretends to be a Greek in one town; in other places he passes as an Egyptian or an African. Although Giacchelino is nearly illiterate, he has acquired a considerable fortune from his skill at representing himself as a master of demons and a seer of coming events. In the play's first version the magician calls himself a *"fisico"* (a physician or worker of magical medicine); in the second version he refers to himself as an *"astrologo"* or a *"negromante."* This flamboyant necromancer amazes potential clients by claiming to be able to transform humans into beasts. But his chief occupation has been to seek out unhappy domestic situations where he could profit from promising to make barren wives fertile or to restore peace between spouses. Success has come to Ariosto's necromancer by discovering the vulnerability of his clients and exploiting their weaknesses.

All the threads of *Il Negromante*'s complicated plot will pass into Giacchelino's dexterous hands as the major characters confide their secrets to him. The well-to-do Cremonese citizen Massimo has retained the sorcerer to cure his adopted son Cintio of the impotence preventing him from consummating his marriage with Emilia. But Giacchelino knows that before the official wedding to the well-dowered Emilia, Massimo's son entered into a clandestine union with a young woman who did not possess a dowry. Fazio, the guardian of Cintio's secret bride, has offered to double Massimo's fee to the magician so that he will bring about an annulment of the marriage to Emilia. A young man with the ironical name of Camillo Pocosale ("Little-wit") has also engaged Giacchelino to bewitch Emilia so that she will succumb to his romantic advances. What is striking here is the reliance of Massimo, Cintio, Fazio, and Camillo upon the sorcerer from whom each client readily expects a miracle to solve every obstacle to happiness. Ariosto created, in his magician, the portrait of an ingenious scoundrel adept at winning the confidence of troubled individuals desperately seeking a saviour.

In this drama the author did not ridicule the central character's criminal nature so much as the credulity, folly, mercantile greed, bourgeois prejudice and lust of the many persons who accepted Giacchelino's pretensions to magical powers. Nibbio, the sorcerer's servant, points out the factor which favors his master's victories: "la sciocchezza, che al mondo è in abbondanzia" ("the stupidity, which abounds in the world"). Comic distortion results from stupidity, reducing both the older and younger generations of Cremonese citizens to pawns to be manipulated by the Castilian refugee. A man without a country, Giacchelino reveals a strong degree of malicious resentment, since he is a classless outsider taking advantage of individuals who enjoy secure roles in the bourgeois society of a northern Italian town. An outsider can operate with a freedom impossible to citizens bound by established codes of decorum and proper relationships. The price for Giacchelino's liberty of action is remaining without a place in any society. This rogue enviously rejoices in compromising and robbing the members of a bourgeois society where he can merely play the part of a servant hired to perform a task of limited duration. From Massimo, the sorcerer demands payment of a black calf (supposedly to perform a sacrifice but actually as a banquet for himself and Nibbio), expenses for his laboratory equipment, and use of the wealthy citizen's silverware to conduct magical rituals. When Giacchelino informs Camillo that Emilia (who is unaware of the youth's passionate interest in her) is about to melt in his embrace, Pocosale at once believes the sorcerer's talents have caused the girl to recognize his qualities. Camillo also entreats the necromancer to intensify Cintio's apparent impotence. Pocosale's vanity leads him to agree to Giacchelino's ruse to have the youth transported in a trunk to Emilia's quarters, without his ever questioning why the sorcerer does not exercise his miraculous arts to convey the youth by magical means. Understanding his victim's foolish self-confidence as an attractive lover, the astrologer plans to make Camillo a prisoner in the trunk in order to steal his valuable possessions and flee Cremona. Giacchelino's manipulation of his victim-clients serves to exemplify comic injustice where the magician aims to profit from the vices and prejudices of a mercantile society.

Within that world of abundant stupidity only one character stands apart from the crowd of the gullible: Cintio's servant Temolo. The third scene of Act I in the play's second version belongs to Temolo as he makes fun of the blind faith which Fazio and Cintio place in the magician. Both the old man and the youth marvel at Giacchelino's ability to go about invisible, but Temolo asks them if they have ever seen the astrologer when he was invisible. After they relate how Giacchelino darkens daytime and brightens the night, Temolo claims to possess similar powers over the forces of Nature: at night he lights a lamp, and during the day he shutters the windows. Cintio derides the servant, commenting how little experience of the world Temolo has known. When Cintio remarks that the sorcerer can change men into animals, Temolo replies that such transmutations are not miracles but daily occurrences in the careers of public officials like judges and notaries who abandon human traits to act like wolves, foxes, and vultures. Temolo, like the magician, comprehends the human capacity for the bestial behaviour to yield to temptation, as frequently befalls public officials. The sorcerer, unlike Temolo, exploits those tendencies to bestiality on the part of his clients. After Fazio and Cintio attempt to convince Temolo of the necromancer's control over the spirit world, the servant confesses to his skepticism:

> About these spirits, to tell you the truth,
> On my own I would have very little belief;
> But great men, both princes and prelates,
> Believe in them, and by their example
> They compel me, a most lowly servant,
> To share their faith. (Act I, Sc. 3, vv. 413-17)[11]

This humble servant functions here as the voice of intelligence criticizing the blind acceptance of nonexistent miraculous talents. Temolo, despite his humble social position, does not mimic the stupid mistakes of the "great." His questioning attitude opposes the universal stupidity predominating in the society of this play. Temolo displays the Boccaccian intelligence that Ariosto held up to praise in his first comedy, *La Cassaria* of 1508. In this drama cleverness centres in only three characters: the sorcerer, his attendant Nibbio, and Temolo. While Giacchelino and his servant battle for the tempting forces of corruption, Temolo represents the redemption of intelligent inquiry and challenge.

It is in the interplay of combat between the intelligent trio, Giacchelino, Nibbio, and Temolo, that *Il Negromante* comes to life artistically. Ariosto realized their essential importance to the comedy's intricate web of intrigues when he prepared the play's second version. In the drama's first working, Giacchelino makes his final stage appearance in the last scene of Act III, although Nibbio will refer to his master on a number of occasions in Acts IV and V. Recognizing the structural failure of relegating his title character off-stage during the last two acts, the playwright brought the magician into greater prominence than before in his second version. In the reworking, Giacchelino's criminal background is set forth in a soliloquy by Nibbio in the opening scene of Act II, while in the first version that unmasking speech takes place in the second scene. A conversation among the astrologer, Nibbio, and Cintio, that occurs in scene ii of the third act in the original version, also moves to scene i. These changes to structurally important opening scenes of Acts II and III demonstrate that Giacchelino is in no way a peripheral character like Bibbiena's necromancer Ruffo, but the central figure of this drama. For the second reworking, Ariosto also added three scenes to Act V so that the magician reappears at a crucial moment after all his schemes have failed. His stratagem to rob Camillo ends disastrously when the chest is intercepted and carried to the room of Cintio's true bride Lavinia, where Pocosale overhears a conversation between the lovers and learns the facts about their marriage which he later reveals to Massimo and Emilia's father Abondio. With the collapse of his charade of deceptions Giacchelino, the master of human psychology, twice falls victim in the new scenes. Temolo cheats the sorcerer of his cloak in the fourth scene while in the following scene Nibbio terrifies his master about the risk of imprisonment and directs him to the city's port on the pretext of his finding a boat for their escape. But in the envoi, Nibbio confesses that he intends to steal all the magician's goods from their room at an inn in order to end his wandering existence of one day travelling in Italy and then another day moving on to Picardy. By these new scenes, with the ironic close where the grand thief is twice robbed, Ariosto shifts dramatic attention away from the play's romantic intrigues to the vital misadventure of the defeated charlatan.[12]

Giacchelino's cynicism led to his downfall and deprived him of the right to claim any reward in the new social order forming at the comedy's close. This sorcerer was even prepared to destroy Emilia's chaste reputation by having Camillo transported to the innocent maiden's home. Arbitrary Fortune, instead of astrological prophecies or spiritual invocations, resolved the obstructions to romance after Massimo came to learn that Lavinia was his child by a woman he had married under an assumed name. Cintio could remain with his original bride, since both of the lovers would be Massimo's heirs. Camillo was to see his hazardous service to romance also rewarded by marriage with Emilia. The sorcerer proved to be an agent of evil corruption. Although the audience might admire the astrologer for his ability to manipulate the folly of his credulous clients, no one could sympathize with the wickedness that sought to profit from guiltless lovers. The demands of bourgeois society and youthful romance could at last come into accord with each other while the cynicism of an arch-criminal justified the degrading victimization practiced upon him by his own servant and by the socially humble character who alone resisted pretensions to magical talents. In Ariosto's comic design the manipulator of human weaknesses becomes the vulnerable pawn of Fortune that refuses to smile any longer upon him. An inner viciousness propels the once enchanting rogue sorcerer to a vastly humiliating catastrophe.

Magic contributes to the triad of socially disruptive forces in Agostino Ricchi's structurally unconventional comedy *I Tre Tiranni*, first performed at Bologna upon the state occasion of an alliance pact between the Holy Roman Emperor Charles V and Pope Clement VII in 1530. The title's three tyrants that will call for magical assistance are Love, Gold, and Fortune. This work's youthful author, who was a student at the University of Bologna, introduces a political dimension to his drama when one of his characters prophesies the new Augustan Age that the Emperor will establish for Europe.[13] Even with his optimism for a new social order, Ricchi acknowledges in this play the threat of chaos that erotic passion, greed, and unpredictable Fortune represent, whether in the lives of private citizens or in the affairs of state. Sorcery serves in the drama as a means to gain control over persons and circumstances in the playwright's symbolic design of human obsession with wealth and sensual domination.

Throughout this play Ricchi aims at creating an allegory of the three tyrannical forces. A contemporary scholar, Alessandro Vellutello, provided a commentary to explain the emblematic roles of the three major male characters who compete with each other for the young Bolognese maiden Lúcia: "in old Girifalco, Love; in young Filocrate, the harmful and severe persecutions of Fortune; and in the noble Crisaulo, the supernatural power of Gold." Those three rivals acquire emblematic value either because of their moral qualities or their dramatic circumstances. But although Love rules elderly Girifalco and Fortune brutally assails Filocrate, Gold is no more than an instrument of power for the wealthy Crisaulo.[14] The desire for riches, however, will predominate in some of the minor characters like the witch Artemona, the parasite Pilastrino, and his thieving confederate the false necromancer Listagiro. The sole tyrant who holds sway over the three main characters is Love that will debase Filocrate and bring about his year-long exile to Spain, that will cause the miserly Girifalco to fall victim to ferocious swindlers, and that will compel Crisaulo to marry beneath his social rank. Ricchi intends to portray the various strata of Bolognese society in his lifetime: the well-to-do nobility represented by the privileged Crisaulo with his retinue of servants; the bourgeois class of the financially cautious Girifalco; and the minor gentry of Filocrate with his countryside villa. Characters like Artemona, Pilastrino, and Listagiro belong to a parasitic periphery offering their fawning services as panders of sexual pleasure. Across that panorama of society the author depicts a predatory world where magic debases human relationships instead of ennobling them as the acquisitive characters seek to out-maneuver each other.

In that grasping society, gold works as a bewitching and animating force. The Hermetic text *The Emerald Table*, which alchemists regarded as their Bible, refers to gold as the source for acquiring the full glory of the entire world, the mightiest power of all powers. Even though Crisaulo's name derives from the Greek word for gold, the nobleman in his financial security lives beyond the hunger for immediate enrichment. Crisaulo considers greed to be a sin, but his own vice dwells in the power that wealth grants him over others, as represented by the large staff of servants who do not all approve their master's amorous assault on Lúcia. The young noble plays upon the devotion that other characters hold for money in order to manipulate them in his cause. To a great extent, Crisaulo succeeds over his rivals Filocrate and Girifalco through the eloquence of the procuress Artemona. That witch participates in a literary tradition with the classical Spanish *alcahueta* Celestina and the title character in the contemporary Italian Renaissance comedy *La Cortegiana* by Pietro Aretino. Artemona combines feigned religious piety with witchcraft to satisfy the erotic demands of generous clients like Crisaulo, winning entrance into respectable homes like those of Lúcia's mother Calonide. Behind the façade of sackcloth and the constant recitation of prayers, the witch has gathered around herself a horde of meretricious accomplices: young women that Artemona fattens like capons in order to sell them to the highest paying bidders. Those prostitutes also assist the procuress in the laboratory where she prepares love potions and elixirs for her anxious customers. Crisaulo's servant Fileno describes that magical establishment as a collective effort at producing counterfeit remedies:

> . . . There all the women have
> their own jobs: one pounds bones
> and other bizarre objects; one sifts
> powder and seeds; another puts herbs
> in a press and extracts their juice;
> this one makes medicines; another unguents,
> from crayfish (I believe) and similar creatures;
> one works on turpentine; and another
> falsifies metals and with nitre
> and sulphur she makes the house stink.
> All around you see a thousand kinds
> of alembics and distilling glasses,
> the most counterfeit decanters
> in the world. There you see furnaces,
> shelves, stoves, jugs, flasks, paint-pots,
> and cauldrons. Along the window sills
> you see flowers, herbs, and seeds,
> roots, gourds, squash, and saucepans,
> jars, cooking-pots, and tubes of chemicals
> and strange things. And there you will see
> limbs of birds and many flayed animals;
> and skin and fat and blood as black
> as ink, talons and dead hair. (Act I, Sc. 6)[15]

Throughout this passage the predominating impression is of the disgusting stench of corruption and falsification issuing from the witch's workshop. Although Calonide's maid-servant Fronesia will later (Act III, Sc.2) attempt to put Artemona in Lúcia's good graces by extolling the rare perfumes and cosmetics that the old woman's workshop produces, the repulsive odour of that laboratory prevails over every effort at dissimulation. No guise of piety will ever remove the stench of hypocrisy in the elderly seductress, whose magical establishment represents nauseating deceitfulness. It is not from unguents nor perfumes that Artemona triumphs over victims like Lúcia, but from her understanding of human psychology and the vulnerability of a young woman before the ardour of a wealthy and handsome nobleman. Upon her success in conveying Lúcia to Crisaulo, the witch receives the reward of a costly golden necklace. In her immense jubilation, Artemona delivers a speech (Act V, Sc. 6) on the godlike powers of gold: the force to camouflage every defect, the source of every pleasure, the cause of every kind of warfare, the supreme idol of all times, the splendour of the sun and stars. The witch's true object of religious worship is the gold for which she has prostituted the world about her.

Artemonas's chief enemy is the parasite Pilastrino. Ricchi broke from the conventional structure of the erudite comedy not only by violating the unity of time to make his drama last more than a year, but by departing from the traditional characteristics of figures like this parasite. The hunger that Pilastrino once directed toward fine foods turns into a gluttonous passion for gold—a trait rarely found in comic parasites, for whom money is usually just the means to satisfy their ravenous appetites. Pilastrino's deterioration from a *bon vivant gourmand* to a violent thief develops with the change in the object of his desire. Originally hoping to become the banquet guest of the miserly Girifalco, the parasite in time degenerates into a criminal after he enlists his fellow sychophant Listagiro to pose as the necromancer Maestro Abraham. In the third scene of Act II, Listagiro resorts to the typical Renaissance charlatanry of fusing astrology with chiromancy by reading Girifalco's hand in order to relate the lines of fortune with stars favourable to the old man's desire to marry Lúcia. Listagiro's ability to flatter the amorous pretensions of the elderly lover succeeds in securing a sumptuous dinner for the two parasites. Through the play's second act the two gourmands do not deviate to a great extent from the traditional portraits of voracious sycophants. But with the opening scene of Act III, the two will acquire a sinister nature as Listagiro pretends to be initiating Girifalco in a magical ritual that will permit the old man to seduce Lúcia that very evening. That false initiation will not only humiliate Girifalco, but abuse him physically after the confederates blindfold him and beat him declaring that devils are assaulting the elderly miser. As generally occurs with charlatans, Listagiro distorts language with an incomprehensible spell that resounds with Latinizing words and names of demons. Language functions to mislead and mystify through its very lack of significance. The theme of vision enters in that the accomplices do not allow their victim to behold the reality of their assault and theft as they reinforce his erotic obsession. Having deprived Girifalco of sight, the two criminals reinforce his delusion by reciting the meaningless incantation. The supreme affront comes in battering him as if a thousand fiends were upon the old man. With this act of violence, sorcery moves to a degrading stage that wounds its victim in body, goods, and dignity.

After this robbery, Pilastrino increasingly succumbs to the lure of gold. He closes the third act by going out to bury his sack of glittering coins, but afterward Crisaulo compels the thieves to return all but a third of the money to Girifalco. Pilastrino, still, can no longer renounce his fascination with gold, and he attempts to wrest the golden necklace from Artemona. Only by the play's close does this parasite revert to his original gluttony. Pilastrino differs from the conventional parasite by joining the criminal world, having his confederate play the same kind of impostor role as Giacchelino in *Il Negromante*. Greed is not the usual character trait of a parasite— especially not with the degree of violence occurring in this unorthodox drama. But the two truly magical forces working in Ricchi's play are the obsession with gold and the subjection to sensual desire. The transformation in the parasite arises in the demonic power of gold to enslave its ecstatic worshippers.

Here in Ricchi's drama the practitioners of sorcery do not have to flee society. Because Artemona worked as a sincere and successful advocate of Crisaulo's passion for Lúcia, she will retain her well-merited reward, although the necklace will continue to be a source of envy and possible theft. Pilastrino will deliver the envoi, hungrily anticipating the banquet to celebrate the triple wedding ceremony between Lúcia and Crisaulo, the maid Fronesia and Filocrate, Calonide and Girifalco. Even though society has once again re-formed, the chaotic might of Love and Gold remain operative while wilful Fortune ultimately determines the fate of all the contending parties. Witchcraft, astrology, necromancy, and chiromancy appear as ineffectual tools of fraud before the ferocity of Agostino Ricchi's three tyrants.

In the comedy *Lo Spirito* by the Florentine Giovan Maria Cecchi (1518-1587) a sorcerer not only escapes the destiny of the stereotypical outcast, but emerges as a victor against adverse Fortune. Cecchi was the most prolific playwright of the Italian Renaissance, borrowing freely from Plautus, Terence, the authors of fifteenth-century religious dramas, and the writers of erudite comedies. His secular comedies usually received their first performances at carnival time by the Florentine *brigate*, amateur associations who also mounted the elaborate allegorical floats for carnival processions. The Company of the Fantastichi originally produced *Lo Spirito* in 1549. While Cecchi took immense pride in being a Florentine, his comedies criticized the moral weaknesses and venality of a mercantile culture where a self-styled magician could profit from the ignorance and provinciality of the Tuscan bourgeoisie.

Pretense to occult powers, deception of the gullible, and false possession by spirits figure in Cecchi's complex play which finds unity in the central theme of the triumph of intelligence over Fortune. The work's prologue explains its title from the mad little spirits that invade persons' bodies, especially those of attractive young women, to take possession of them. Cecchi notes in the prologue how he intended his audience to gain a double benefit: the pleasure of laughter and the usefulness of seeing how spirits supposedly take sway and then depart, as well as viewing the lesson of the consequences of being duped by a fictitious story of possession. Within this stage work the author constructs an intricate series of multiple romantic attachments and the obstacles to their fulfilment. Only the intervention of a resourceful outsider with claims to magical talents and the timely discovery of unsuspected family relationships will rescue this drama from the impasse of its amorous intrigues.

In the figure of the fraudulent Greek magician-astrologer Aristone, Cecchi's audience could behold the gift of natural wit combating forever changing destiny. Ariosto's Giacchelino was the model for the characterization of Aristone as a swindler exploiting the tensions within middle-class households where he would succeed in making everyone pay him for miraculous acts that he merely promised to achieve. Aristone's greatest offense consists in betraying the trust that unhappy lovers place in him, but he differs from Giacchelino in not being a common thief. Cecchi's sorcerer excels by taking advantage of individuals whose rational faculties have yielded to amorous distress. Rather than actually practice magic, Aristone seeks to create the reputation of being a wondrous enchanter. To that end he endeavours to win the esteem of influential Florentine citizens like the merchant Anselmo, whose faith in his powers would draw still more clients for the false necromancer. To his servant Sollecito this supreme realist confesses his actual limitations:

> ˙ . . . . . Believe me that all
> these enchantments and the knowledge of Spirits
> are only jests today: that art which once
> existed (if indeed it ever did exist) is lost,

and whoever wants to make a show of it as a profession
has to be astute and stay alert so as to dupe everyone.
(Act III, Sc. 2)[16]

Fearing a summons from the Holy Inquisition on charges of practicing black
magic, this wily character officially calls himself an herbalist rather than
a necromancer or an astrologer. Aristone even fabricates credentials by
claiming to have studied logic and physics at the University of Padua, with
post-graduate training from a Calabrese alchemist. Since this charming
charlatan constantly quotes Aristotle, the unlettered Anselmo asks him if
he is related to that sage, and Aristone appropriates the great philosopher
as one of his ancestors. It is this trickster's dazzling use of language that
bewitches his clients hoping to find in the magician's artifice the solution
for their romantic involvements.

Three love-distressed characters seek out Aristone's talents: middle-
aged Anselmo for lady Laura who is subjected to the tyranny of her brother
Neri (the play's chief blocking character); Neri's young ward Napoleone
who has secretly married the former slave Emilia; and Emilia's official husband Aldobrando who actually adores the niece of the foreign physician
Maestro Antonio. The case of bigamy immediately recalls Ariosto's *Il
Negromante* with Cintio's two marriages. Like Giacchelino, the magician
in Cecchi's play decides to assist his romantic clients by having them
transported to their beloved ladies in chests, though never with the intention of robbing any of them of their possessions. Aristone prefers to persuade others to pay him high fees by playing on their superstitions and
their amorous predicaments. But just as customs agents intercept the trunk
bearing Calandro in Bibbiena's comedy, similar disaster befalls the three
incased lovers of *Lo Spirito*. Acting on Aristone's instructions via a servant-
woman, Emilia has been feigning possession by a spirit that causes her to
speak in Latin, so that the sorcerer was able to convince Emilia's guardian
Anselmo to quarantine the maiden in her bedchamber, to which Napoleone
came conveyed in a trunk. Aldobrando also holds trysts with the physician's niece thanks to a similar stratagem with a chest. In his desire to elude
the spies with whom Neri surrounds Laura, the gullible Anselmo agrees
to a plan for him to be carried to her room in a chest. By the end of Act
IV every one of Aristone's ruses with the coffers ends in failure, leaving
the sorcerer exposed to his public as a total fraud.

Throughout this comedy various characters accuse Fortune or Destiny
of acting as their enemy. In Act V, Sc. 5, Aristone blames Fortune for
the simultaneous collapse of his schemes with the three chests. At the time
that Cecchi composed *Lo Spirito*, the author still believed optimistically in
the power of human intelligence to alter destiny. Yet it is the chance recognition (in dramatic terms "agnition") of certain family relationships that saves
this play from absolute defeat for the lovers. Emilia and Aldobrando become
identified as noble refugees of the Turkish occupation of the Balkans. With
Aristone's revelation of the clandestine marriage between Napoleone and
Emilia, the magician secures parental approval for the public acknowledge-
ment of the match. Neri also discovers that Antonio's sister Maria is the
merchant's long-lost wife and that the physician's niece is none other than the

old man's daughter. Neri decides to permit Aldobrando to marry the girl. In the mood of peaceful resolution and family reunion, Neri at last agrees to Laura's marriage to Anselmo. It is Aristone's composure at a time of angry confrontations and his tactfulness in dealing with aggrieved parties that enables the false magician to reconcile the combattants and bring about the recognition of their family ties. That affirmation of intelligence and diplomatic skill is Aristone's true working of magic which gains for him an invitation to become Neri's guest during the rest of his stay in Florence. This ingratiating trickster also delivers the envoi since credit goes to him for mediating all disputes.[17]

In *Lo Spirito* Cecchi strives to create a vivid impression not just of the immediate scene on stage in Florence, but of the vast Mediterranean world from which his sorcerer has appeared in the Tuscan capital. Commercial voyages to the Levant, Neri's earlier political flight to Romania, diplomatic missions to France, and enslavement in North Africa and Sicily indicate the broad geographical bounds for this drama of antagonism between Fortune and intelligence. Several members of the cast are refugees from the fall of the Byzantine Empire. Contrasted to the cosmopolitan sophistication of this comedy's international characters is the parochialism prevailing in Florence and therefore promoting Aristone's success in impressing the Tuscans with his magical talents. Florence appears here as a constricting society dominated by mean-minded shopkeepers, scheming lawyers, and disgruntled physicians. Aristone's servant Sollecito views society with a scorn born of cynicism:

> In fact, in this world it is necessary to be
> a dissimulator and a cheat; you have to know
> how to pretend to be learned, wise, and holy . . . . (Act II, Sc. 2)

Sollecito and Antonio's errand-boy Rondine try to parody the vain masquerade of knowledge and respectability by the Florentine bourgeoisie and professional class. Aristone sees clearly through the faults of the societies through which he travels and takes advantage of petty-minded and poorly informed merchants. Giovan Maria Cecchi has fashioned in *Lo Spirito* a playworld moving across international frontiers to lead the sorcerer to the restricted social orders of a provincial centre.

Following the theatrical practice of his day, Cecchi included in his play a series of verse intermezzi that would announce the crucial developments of each act. The intermezzi work to engage the public in the drama by pointing out parallels between their condition and that of the dramatic characters. In the intermezzo preceding Act I, actors costumed as dreams, chimeras and spirits sing a madrigal proclaiming that their role is to cheer *The Spirit* which is coming to the audience in the form of a play that will demonstrate Love's might. The second intermezzo analyzes the state of lovers living between fragile hopes and certain pain. To prepare the public for Aristone's stratagems to assist the lovers, the third intermezzo urges the spectators to employ the gift of intellect to see through chimerical appearances and behold the danger of errors. By the fourth act, when the main plot devices are growing increasingly complicated, the errant spirits of the intermezzo declare that neither their nebulous form nor the illusions which they produce are as distorted and confusing as the experiences that befall the lovers in the audience. After the catastrophic close of Act IV, the final interlude sets the audience at ease by explaining how Love is often severe in testing the constancy of lovers, but that now a joyous time is about to arrive when Faith and Chastity will fulfil every amorous expectation. One can see from the intermezzi how the sorcerer Aristone played the role of a good servant of love by assisting the various sets of romantic parties. With his crystalline clarity of vision the counterfeit enchanter works genuine miracles to close the play with multiple weddings in a festive celebration of love's triumph over the hardships of international warfare and the prejudices of class and caste.

With his play *Il Candelaio*, Giordano Bruno (1548-1600) attempted to demolish the structures and myths of Renaissance literary and cultural traditions. Bruno enthusiastically studied magic in the Hermetic tradition, hoping to comprehend an infinity of worlds. Displaying an heroic fury in his search for truth, this rebel scornfully set aside old literary forms to affirm the creative supremacy of humankind. Eventually that quest to demonstrate a newly ordered universe led him before the Roman Inquisition, who sentenced him to death at the stake. In *Il Candelaio* this playwright and Hermetic magician exposed not just the charlatanry of false sorcerers but the counterfeit representatives of Renaissance culture.[18]

Constructed in seventy-five scenes over five acts, *Il Candelaio* explodes on stage like an alchemical experiment. With its nineteen characters in types like the courtesan, the procuress, the pedant, the alchemist, the necromancer, and a criminal variant of the braggart warrior, this drama becomes so crowded that its actions nearly burst through the restraints of classical regular theatre. Because of his grotesque view of life, the author casts on stage before the eyes of his spectators the criminal underworld of Naples around 1580 in all its blatant depravity. Bruno published the play at Paris in 1582. Beginning with the title, this comedy stuns the ears of its audience with vulgar erotic language expressing the grossness of its characters. The English translation of the title as *The Candle-bearer* does not convey its satirical thrust against the pederasty of the central character Bonifacio. Bruno might have entitled his work "The Three Victims" to refer to the harassed trio of the amorous Bonifacio, the alchemically obsessed Bartolomeo, and the pretentious pedant Manfurio.[19] Since a great deal of the play's action occurs at night when criminal gangs roamed the streets of Naples seeking to entrap unwary victims, the work's prevailing nocturnal quality makes of it a drama of masquerade with one disguise following another. The arch-rogue Sanguino and his band of cut-throat accomplices transform themselves in the Neapolitan nighttime as Captain Palma and the "official" street-patrol apprehending suspicious figures moving about the town. Manfurio, Bonifacio, and Bartolomeo all fall into the hands of those captors, have to endure humiliating punishments, and pay dearly for their release. Bruno creates a drama of illusion-transforming-reality where characters appear on scene wearing false beards and donning the garb customary to other persons. At the end of Act III, the pedant and a thief exchange clothes as the Latinizing Manfurio cooperates in what will prove a painful and expensive charade for him. In this play of imposture, Bonifacio disguises himself as the painter Giovan Bernardo in order to set off for what he expects to be a rendezvous with the courtesan Vittoria, but what turns out to be an ambush by his wife Carubina dressed as the courtesan. The drama moves to a ridiculous mirror confrontation between the true Giovan Bernardo and the costumed Bonifacio, whose efforts to persist in his fake identity end in victimization by Sanguino and his band. Bruno insists in his stage work that nothing is as it seems to be. This author establishes a hierarchy of deceitful intelligence between the triumphant impostors and their laughable victims.[20] Through their multiple roles the various characters move as agents of comic reversal in a world where bewilderment is normalcy.

To Bonifacio, magic seems to offer a relatively inexpensive way to achieve his romantic designs on the lovely Vittoria, who usually demands costly gifts from her clients. Four years before the time level of the play's actions, Bonifacio underwent a profound transformation from pederast to heterosexual when at the age of 42 he married the beautiful Carubina, who was half his age. From contented husband he has now changed into a would-be adulterous lover composing badly written sonnets in a Petrarchan tradition that Bruno savagely parodies. As an economy measure, he has engaged the astrologer Scaramuré to enchant the courtesan for him. Vittoria, in league with the procuress Lucia, originally hopes to practice alchemy on Bonifacio by extracting gold from him, but on discovering his miserliness she resents his scheme to have Scaramuré bewitch her. For this drama Bonifacio represents the exhaustion and perversion of an insipid love tradition supported by distorted imitations of Petrarch's amatory lyrics. In reality this lover, who imagines himself irresistible but requires the services of a magician to attract a woman, participates in a world of criminal corruption and prostitution. With Bonifacio, love's magic becomes debased by vanity, pettiness, and domestic betrayal. This character's attitude toward magic is a mockery of the current Renaissance faith in the occult arts to compensate for Nature's deficiencies and to enable humans to dominate the physical universe. But all that comes to Bonifacio from his perverted romantic longings, his miserliness, his ridiculously inflated self-image, and his cash-down recourse to magic is public exposure as a sham, the pain inflicted on him by the band of thieves and the extortion of his funds.

Scaramuré succeeds by making his clients believe that he has always been working to their advantage when in truth he has exploited their passions to his own profit. Speaking a rather incorrect Latin, the astrologer reckons Bonifacio's horoscope on the pretext of advancing his affair with Vittoria, but his astrological knowledge leaves almost as much to be desired as his mastery of ancient languages. Yet Scaramuré has accurately recognized how easily the ignorant Bonifacio can be impressed by a fake show of occult wisdom. This practitioner of sorcery claims to be using a relatively safe natural magic instead of the sinister black arts that summon evil demons. The false enchanter corrupts the long-standing theory of love as "fascinazione," ocular transfixion where the spirit of a lover enters through the eyes of the beloved to invade body, heart, and soul. On Scaramuré's lips love traditions are devalued and cheapened by his mercenary intentions to convince his customer of his ability to bewitch the courtesan. The magician

finally obtains his fee from Bonifacio by pleading the exaggerated costs of
the materials required to model a waxen image that, along with the incantation of a spell and the performance of special rites, will conquer all of
Vittoria's hesitations toward her new lover. After the false civic guard im-
prisons Bonifacio, Scaramuré explains to his client that the magic rites failed
when Bonifacio substituted Carubina's hair for Vittoria's in the waxen image. This wily sorcerer, who has allied himself with Sanguino, effects his
only transformation by arranging for Bonifacio's release from the gang of
thieves. Scaramuré's rhetorical skill consists of delivering long speeches with
extended digressions on topics like the situation of courtesans in Naples,
Rome, and Venice—merely to hold his anxious customer in suspenseful
despair over leaving his venal captors. Bonifacio becomes the foil for the
astrologer's astute ploys that make this comedy a farce of intrigues and
deceptions without the slightest trace of magical enchantment.

Just as in Ricchi's *I Tre Tiranni* a repulsive odour pervades the
laboratory of the witch Artemona, in this play smoke (*fumo*) darkens Bartolomeo's workshop while soot covers his face and hair. Smoke symbolizes
the lack of substance issuing from Bartolomeo's costly attempts to fabricate
gold according to the charlatan alchemist Cencio (whose name means "rag"
to indicate his worthlessness). Frequently in European literature, alchemists
appear as tattered, thread-worn figures whose merchandise is nothing but
smoke.[21] Error blackens the gullible clients of the ragged alchemists. The
forever belching furnace in Bartolomeo's workshop constantly menaces to
explode and destroy all his illusions of unlimited riches. While Bonifacio
has transferred the object of his sensual desire from males to attractive young
women, Bartolomeo's two loves are Lady Argenteria (Mme Silver) and
especially Lady Orelia (Mme Gold), whom he adores with religious fer-
vour. His obsession with the alchemical production of gold arouses the
jealousy and anguish of his wife Marta, who laments how Bartolomeo has
imprisoned himself behind smoking glasses and rows of retorts. Marta comments (Act IV, Sc. 9) on a basic principle of economics, how the acquisi-
tion of wealth generates a need for still more income: Bartolomeo lived in
easy circumstances without excessively preoccupying himself over finances
until he received an inheritance and then began his frenzied alchemical
pursuits to the complete neglect of his wife. Both Marta and Carubina will
betray their husbands out of revenge for the way the deluded men aban-
doned them. At the play's strategic mid-point, in the opening scene of Act
III, Bartolomeo rhapsodizes over the alchemical virtues of Gold and Silver,
comparing them to the Sun and the Moon governing the world, while he
remains oblivious to the destruction of his domestic life. In his perverse
worship of precious metals Bartolomeo has permitted alchemy to act as the
spiritual force of his life.

Sustaining Bartolomeo's manic vision of existence in alchemical principles is the cunning Cencio, one of the supreme confidence men of Italian
Renaissance literature. This thieving exponent of metallic powers illustrates
how alchemy in the sixteenth century thrived upon human greed with promises of untold wealth and worldly might. Cencio has mastered the jargon
of alchemy to create a linguistics of swindling where he refers to Hermes
Trismegistus, Arabic alchemists, and Albertus Magnus on the planetary

signs for major metals and the secret of transmuting base minerals into gold. That mastery of technical and mystical terminology so convinced Bartolomeo that he has paid Cencio hundreds of scudi for the formula to achieve transmutation. In the experiments that the two have conducted together, Cencio's legerdemain proves to be his one magical talent when he conceals gold inside a hollowed piece of wood that he inserts into the furnace to demonstrate his power of extraction. Cencio truly belongs to the criminal world of this play, like the shake-down members of Sanguino's gang in their disguise as the night patrol. This swindler adroitly practices the tricks of confidence men of all ages and countries: making a "switch" to substitute one item for another before his unwary client, and finally working the "boarding-house deceiver's ploy" by leaving a package with the apothecary Consalvo that supposedly contains *"pulvis Christi"* (the secret substance to transmute other metals into gold) but actually holds rocks.[22] It is through knowledge of his clients' greedy vulnerability that Cencio the manipulator has profited.

As the motto for this comedy Bruno employed the Latin phrase "In tristitia hilaris, in hilaritate tristis" ("Cheerful in sadness, sad in cheerfulness"). This writer of paradoxes always sought to expose the vulgarity behind corrupt pretensions to loving affections, alchemical expertise, and academic erudition. As this play's language moves from ecstatic rhapsody to obscene derision, the drama juxtaposes the realm of the deluded triad of Bonifacio, Bartolomeo, and Manfurio with the predatory underworld that eventually degrades, judges, torments, and robs them. In a society dominated by lust, hypocrisy, avarice, and vainglory the only bonds that become stable are those holding together a fraternity of criminals. The attempt at alchemical purification or the recourse to amatory enchantment never achieve genuine metamorphoses, but merely disguise individual and collective corruptibility. For Bruno, as for Elizabethan playwrights, all the world was indeed a stage, one where the actors were always concealing their base intentions. In the subculture of the night, what is illegal becomes judicial in its authority to pass sentence upon transgressors of authentic human values.[23] Magic functions in the playworld of *Il Candelaio* as a projection of a vitiated and doomed striving for dominance in erotic and financial fortune.

Bruno's occult research, his clash with the Inquisition and his activity as a comic playwright all have parallels in the career of his Neapolitan contemporary Giambattista Della Porta (1535-1615), who was to gain European-wide renown from the repeated publication (in revised and enlarged editions) of his text *Magiae naturalis* (*Of Natural Magic*). Della Porta's fervent investigations into such diverse realms as the supernatural, optics, botany, biology, and chemistry won for him the fame of being called a *"Mago"* (*"magus"*) or an *"Indovino"* ("Diviner of Enigmas"). Della Porta issued the first version of his *Magiae naturalis* in 1558 to bring together the results of his experiments with plants, herbs, magnets, and minerals. His type of "natural magic" consisted of a very practical use of alchemical, astrological, and botanical knowledge. Like Bruno, this writer also hoped to perfect the field of mnemonics as expressed in his treatise *L'Arte del Ricordare* (*The Art of Remembering*, 1566) on his methods for organizing areas of knowledge.

Believing that there existed an essential oneness throughout all of physical Nature, Della Porta began his studies in comparative morphology and physiognomy with the text *Phytognomonica* (printed 1583) to trace the formal similarity between sections of plants and their analogues in animals. With his *De Humana Physiognomonica* (published 1586) he extended that study of resemblances to the level of humans and other animals to note anatomical and moral traits in common such as asinine and simian features—observations that the author extended to the characters in his comedies. Just as Della Porta accepted a unity across Nature, a thematic unity pervades his scientific, occult, and dramatic writings.

Although for Della Porta anatomical structure did indicate major facets of human personality, he asserted that free will allowed for overcoming any pre-determined traits. Following upon the standard Roman Catholic assertion of free will, he attempted in the treatise *Coelestis physiognomoniae* (issued 1601) to move on a heavenly plane of astral influences, terrestrial revolutions, and human actions. A researcher into natural magic could foretell the future by recognizing key signs in the stars, the earth, and humans. During those same years Della Porta was writing a treatise on palmistry, *Chirofisonomia*, to be published posthumously in 1677. To gather information on personality features as shown by signs on hands and feet, the author examined cadavers of executed criminals and of persons who died violently. He frequented Naples' jails to observe the hands and feet of prisoners to make sketches and plaster impressions. In his various texts of comparative physiognomy, Della Porta displayed his skill at meticulously cataloguing minute details—a skill that appears prominently in his plays when he describes the moral tendencies of his characters, especially the criminals of his comedies. With his text *De Distillatione* (1608) the writer produced a concise treatise on chemistry and alchemy. Throughout the final years of his life Della Porta pursued his interest in demonology and tried to receive official sanction to publish his study *Della Taumatologia*, to no avail; only its index remains. His desire in the *Taumatologia* was to produce an encyclopedia of occult secrets, where, like Ficino before him, he would demonstrate how to summon the aid of benevolent demons. Always considering himself a natural philosopher, Giambattisa Della Porta regarded the whole universe of humankind, animals, plants, and stars as his realm of inquiry.[24]

This writer's impassioned fascination with magic brought him such notoriety as a sorcerer that in 1579 and 1592 Della Porta had to render an account of his research to the Holy Inquisition. Because of his tactful submission to ecclesiastical authorities he escaped torture, prolonged imprisonment or execution, unlike Bruno. But he had to consent to abandon study of unnatural magic and to submit his writings to approval for publication by the Roman High Tribunal. The Inquisitors of 1579 also recommended that Della Porta turn his energies to composing comedies. As proof of his repentance, Della Porta wrote the comedy *L'Astrologo* (published in 1606 but finished decades before) to ridicule belief in the arts of a thieving magician.

With *L'Astrologo* the author directly represents the criminal underworld of Naples that he came to know from conducting his research on palmistry.

At its start the comedy introduces the magician Albumazar and his gang of accomplices Ronca (Weed-hook), Arpione (Grappling-hook), and Gramigna (Weed), all habitués of the Cerriglio, an inn-tavern of criminal infamy during the Renaissance. Albumazar calls himself a "meteoroscopio," a diviner of human character and future fortune through reading the signs upon the features of the face and forehead. Like most of the charlatans in Renaissance comedy, this rogue also resorts to astrology, necromancy, and the art of divination to hook his easily befuddled clients.

In contrast to other dramatists who used the character-type of the magician to deride greed, Della Porta concentrates in *L'Astrologo* upon the classical conflict of authority between generations and rivalry in romantic aspirations. The playwright constructs the drama upon double sets of marital alliances: the one false and destined to disaster; the other naturally authentic and eventually triumphant. Two elderly citizens, Pandolfo and Guglielmo, both widowers, at some moment before the opening of the play's action agree to the respective exchange of their daughters Sulpizia and Artemia as their future wives. Opposed to those marriages are Guglielmo's son Lelio (who loves Sulpizia) and Pandolfo's son Eugenio (who adores Artemia). Guglielmo's disappearance at sea during a commercial voyage so favours the young generation that Pandolfo enlists the sorcery of Albumazar to certify Guglielmo's actual death and to resurrect him for one day to bring about Pandolfo's marriage to Artemia. Prepared to take advantage of Pandolfo's romantic folly, Albumazar plans on disguising the vine-dresser Vignarolo to pass himself as Guglielmo in order to arrange the marital alliance while the magician and his henchmen will rob Pandolfo's home. Guglielmo's sudden return home leads to the customary mirror confrontation with the disguised Vignarolo. In time, Guglielmo establishes the authenticity of his identity and, in repenting his past foolishness, agrees to aid the youths by pretending before Pandolfo that he is the false "Guglielmo," tricking his friend by stipulating the terms of the weddings among the four children. While the playwright exposes the rapacity of the thieves, with his other characters the recourse to magic derives from romantic vanity rather than avarice.

In this satire on occultism and parental oppression, Della Porta points out the tie between sorcery and crime in the practices of the central character and his trio of confederates. Albumazar's rhetorical powers can stun his listeners with his litanies of Latinizing phrases. But the rogue expresses scorn for all occult pseudo-sciences and the clients like Pandolfo who trust in magic: ". . . That's what matters: he believes in astrology and necromancy. What more can you say? Even if he were a Solomon, believing in such nonsense would suffice to make him the greatest simpleton on earth. See to what extent human curiosity, or rather asininity, will reach." (Act I, Sc. 1).[25] Throughout the play character traits like asininity will surface as the author explores resemblances in physical and moral features between beasts and his human characters. Out of deference to his orthodox Catholic readers and spectators the author dismisses belief in the occult as superstitious foolishness.

Although Bruno's *Il Candelaio* reveals the bonds between thieves, this play stresses the disruptive tensions in the fraternity of criminals. Not only do Albumazar's henchmen succeed in stealing all the silver utensils that Pandolfo borrowed from friends to make possible the transformation of Vignarolo into Guglielmo, but the rogues flee with the goods for themselves after denouncing Albumazar to civic authorities. Treachery is the ethics of the magical underworld explored here by Della Porta. Because of the play's comic nature where society must re-emerge in a stable order, Pandolfo will recover his property while the sorcerer has to take to flight. The character trait common to Albumazar and his accomplices is their delight in being actors, constantly pretending to be what they are not in reality. Just as the sorcerer knows how to speak in a commanding voice that convinces dolts like Pandolfo of his talents over the spirit world, the trio of thieves perform charades to prove even to the most intelligent and doubting characters, like the servant Cricca, the magician's power to foresee the future, as when in Act I, Scs. 5 and 6, Ronca and Arpione act out a show of street murder for Cricca's benefit and then cause a heavy stone to fall from a building at Pandolfo's feet. Joy in performance becomes the sole magical art of this treacherous band of criminals as they transform reality with the intrigues that carry out comic reversals.

Calling himself a German Indian from Trebizond at the end of the world, Albumazar displays a cynicism that is almost as destructive as that of Ariosto's title character from *Il Negromante*. This sorcerer seems to thrive on contempt for the merchant class that hires him to resolve romantic entanglements. The author does indicate that Albumazar's contempt is somewhat justified, for in Act III, Sc. 1, Pandolfo regrets his impulsive offer of a valuable gold necklace as a reward to the sorcerer, and Cricca suggests that the merchant feign anger over missing gold and silver utensils with the threat of accusing Albumazar before the municipal court. Della Porta here reveals a common line of falseness and betrayal across classes, demonstrating with his social satire that what separates Albumazar's group from that of Pandolfo is merely the accident of circumstances. But the play makes its moral point in Albumazar's being duped by his confederates and forced into exile. The figures in mainline society, like Guglielmo and Pandolfo, can correct their follies and restore order by renouncing their tyranny, while the criminals who relied on the jargon of magical arts and their histrionic talents end in defeat over their treacherous performance before the public. Della Porta's morally enlightening drama must result in the sorcerer's exposure and banishment.

Through Vignarolo's disguise as Guglielmo, this comedy questions the reality of social roles. The lowly but non-criminal vine-dresser consented to the charade when Pandolfo his landlord promised to remit a portion of his rents and to provide him with a dowry to permit marriage to the servant-girl Armellina. Vignarolo feels socially insufficient as a rural share-cropper and hopes to discover in his masquerade as a gentleman the confidence to win Armellina's affections. But the transformation leads merely to a series of misadventures: victimization by a pick-pocket, solicitation by a prostitute, concealment in a barrel that is almost filled with scalding water, and then his being rolled down to the shore. Believing the transformation to be the genuine result of true magic, Vignarolo comes to feel trapped in an identity that brings him humiliation and physical suffering. Brutally rejected by his son and servants, Guglielmo upon his encounter with the transformed Vignarolo begins to doubt his identity and to consider (Act IV, Sc. 7) whether he is the victim of a Pythagorean transmigration of souls. But in time that carnival confusion of roles will end as Guglielmo re-asserts his parental role and renounces his undignified marital demands. By participating in the disguise-within-a-disguise as "Vignarolo" playing "Guglielmo," the actual merchant will end all false metamorphoses and establish solid relationships for the future with the double wedding ceremony. Here the farce of social roles yields to the one authentic transformation where youthful romance triumphs.

With the restoration of proper social and moral values, Della Porta's comedy can close with an envoi by the servant Cricca, the sole character who ever questioned the magical skills of Albumazar. By writing this play about false transformations, the author attempted to redeem himself before his critics. For he produced an ethical comedy in the spirit of the Catholic Reformation that aimed through satire to attack occultism by its treacherous practitioners, to expose the credulity of vain dupes who enlist the assistance of sorcerers, and to unmask ridiculous social pretensions. This comedy also contributed to Della Porta's fame throughout Europe. Travelling troupes of *Commedia dell' 'Arte* actors performed this drama according to a condensed scenario as they wandered across the continent to England. Then on March 9, 1614, students at Trinity College of Cambridge University enacted the English adaptation of this play as *Albumazar* by Thomas Tomkis. By that time, Ben Jonson had already created his scathing comedy of greed, deception and false transmutation with *The Alchemist* of 1610. Consequently Della Porta's work as a playwright enjoyed a European vogue similar to that of his occult publications.[26] Through *L'Astrologo*, the writer who was among the most famous exponents of magic showed to the world the bestiality of the criminal recourse to occult pseudo-sciences.

Examples of the practice of magic, by sorcerers or witches, occur in numerous dramas of the Italian Renaissance by writers like Pietro Aretino, Anton Francesco Grazzini, Francesco D'Ambra, and Bernardino Lombardi—to cite only a few playwrights beyond the six studied in this essay. Although one might regard the prevalence of enchanters as character-types in erudite comedies as evidence of a Counter-Renaissance perpetuating a sinister view of the supernatural,[27] the theme of magic in drama actually reflects the mainstream of Italian Renaissance intellectual endeavour where humankind aspired to achieve angelic greatness in dominating the cosmos. Italian comic playwrights attacked the betrayal of that Faustian striving by deceitful rogues just as they ridiculed the gullibility of the vain and greedy clients who permitted themselves to be duped by promises of erotic conquest or alchemical wealth. Charlatanry and credulity undermined the faith in magic as a way to glorify humanity. More trenchantly than any other Italian dramatist, Giordano Bruno portrayed the prostitution of the sublime dream of Renaissance occultism. Both Bruno and Della Porta had to face persecution by the religious authorities who required them to sacrifice their quests into the unknown: the first by death, the second by unceasing censorship. Pretensions to visionary powers had to give way to the mocking scorn of satirical farce. All of the comic playwrights studied in this article project their stage fictions onto a world where swindling deceit corrupts intellectual inquiry. Through the character-type of the sorcerer, Italian authors of learned comedies in the Renaissance represent the universal folly of the irrational attempt to dominate reality with demonic, alchemical, and astrological wizardry.

NOTES

1 For the examination of the braggart see Daniel C. Boughner, *The Braggart in Renaissance Comedy* (Minneapolis, 1954). Antonio Stäuble, "Una ricerca in corso: il personaggio del pedante nella commedia cinquecentesca," *Il teatro Italiano Del Rinascimento*, ed. Maristella Lorch (Milan, 1980), 85-101, sketches some of the traits of the pedant as a figure representing a crisis in Renaissance Humanism and concentrates on the pedant Manfurio in giordano Bruno's comedy *Il Candelaio*.

2 Charles G. Nauert, Jr., *Agrippa and the Crisis of Renaissance Thought* (Urbana, 1965), passim, traces Agrippa's all-pervading influence over late Renaissance magical inquiry. Daniel P. Walker, *Spiritual and Demonic Magic from Ficino to Campanella* (London, 1958), 3-4, explains the role of "*spiritus*" in ficino's cosmic system.

3 Lynn Thorndike, *The Place of Magic in the Intellectual History of Europe* (New York, 1905), 84-87, describes the wide-spread influence of the Hermetic texts on European occult research.

4 John M. Stillman, *The Story of Alchemy and Early Chemistry* (1924; rpt. New York, 1960), 300-19, considers the Paracelsan revolution in alchemy.

5 Gene Brucker, "Sorcery in Early Renaissance Florence," *Studies in the Renaissance*, 10 (1963), 7-24, details the function of workaday witches in Tuscan urban society.

6 Cf. Charles Nicholl, *The Chemical Theatre* (London, 1980), 8, on the magical underworld of Shakespearean times.

7 Grete de Francesco, *The Power of the Charlatan*, trans. M. Beard (New Haven, 1939), 136, describes Rangone's lucrative practices.

8 Ibid., 42-82, on Bragadino's career as a gold-maker.

9 Nino Borsellino, *Commedie del Cinquecento* (MIlan, 1967), II, 11-12, contends that this prologue was written for a play by an author other than Bibbiena, probably for performance in Florence. I am using Borsellino's edition of the comedy.

10 Luigi Russo, *Commedie Fiorentine del Cinquecento* (Florence, 1939), 185-88, compares the magical mood of the play to scenes of hallucination and near surrealism in the writings of Ariosto, Boccaccio, and Cellini.

11 Text in *Commedie*, ed. Aldo Borlenghi (Milan: 1962). Although the translation is my own, readers can find complete translations of the dramas in *The Comedies of Ariosto*, trans. E. Beame and Leonard Sbrocchi (Chicago, 1975).

12 Carlo Grabher, *Sul Teatro dell'Ariosto* (Rome, 1946), 95-108, compares the two versions of the comedy.

13 Ricchi's political opportunism becomes apparent from another version of the play in the municipal library of Lucca where praise for Charles V and Clement VII are replaced with compliments about Francis I and Sultan Soliman.

14 Ireneo Sanesi, *La Commedia* (Milan, 1954), I, 190, n. 63, cites Vellutello's commentary.

15 My translation from *Commedie del Cinquecento*, ed. I. Sanesi (Bari, 1912), I.

16 My translation from the Italian text in *Commedie di Giovan Maria Cecchi*, ed.

L. Fiacchi (Milan, 1850), II.

17 Bruno Ferraro, "Giovanni Maria Cecchi, the *Commedie Osservate* and the *Commedia Erudita* in Sixteenth-century Italy," Diss. Flinders Univ. S. Australia (1974), 453-59, analyzes this drama stressing Aristone's change from a necromancer to a mediator of disputes.

18 Frances Yates, *Giordano Bruno and the Hermetic Tradition* (Chicago, 1964), 144-56, describes Giordano as a Hermetic-style *"magus."*

19 There is a fourth victim, the apothecary Consalvo.

20 Paul Goodman, "Comic Plots: *The Alchemist*," *Ben Jonson*, ed. Jonas Barish (Englewood Cliffs, N.J., 1963), 110, studies how Ben Jonson in his drama *The Alchemist* presents a hierarchy of malicious intelligence.

21 Nicholl, *Chemical Theatre*, 7-8, speaks of tattered itinerant sellers of smoke in satirical English literature of the Middle Ages and Renaissance.

22 For a glossary of confidence-game terms consult David W. Maurer, *The Big Con* (Indianapolis, 1940).

23 A. Stäuble, "Il Personaggio del pedante," 97, cites the disruptive force of the irrational in Bruno's comedy that demolishes every certainty and value. The edition of the play used here is that by Borsellino, *Commedie del Cinquecento*, II. There is an English translation as *The Candle Bearer* by J.R. Hale in *The Genius of the Italian Theater*, ed. E. Bentley (New York, 1964).

24 Louise George Clubb, *Giambattista Della Porta, Dramatist* (Princeton, 1965), 10-55, sketches the background of Della Porta's non-dramatic writings. Casey Wood, "Johannes Baptista Porta' Neapolitan Oculist and Natural Philosopher," *Charaka Club Proceedings*, 8 (1935), 118-34, provides illustrations of the physical analogues between plants and animals, humans and animals in Della Porta's treatises on comparative physiognomy. Antonio Corsano, "Per la storia del pensiero del tardo Rinascimento: G.B. Della Porta," *Giornale Critico della Filosofia italiana*, 13, n. 1 (January-March 1965), 76-97, places Della Porta in the tradition of Agrippa's magical inquiries.

25 My translation from the Italian text in *Teatro italiano*, ed. Silvio D'Amico (Milan, 1955).

26 Marvin Herrick, *Italian Comedy in the Renaissance* (Urbana, 1960), 216, discusses the Commedia dell'Arte scenario of *L'Astrologo*. For a critical edition of *Albumazar* with an excellent introduction detailing the Renaissance attitude toward various magical practices consult Thomas Tomkis, *Albumazar, A Comedy*, ed. Hugh Dick (Barkeley, 1944)). The year of the first performance of *Albumazar* may have been 1615.

27 Stäuble, "Il pedante," 96, n. 32, cites H. Haydn's *The Counter-Renaissance* (New York, 1950), for a dialectical view of the development of European intellectual inquiry as being immersed in skepticism during the sixteenth century that moved in either the direction of empiricism or occultism.

Prefacing Renaissance Comedy: The Double, Laughter and Comic Structure

Francesco Loriggio
Carleton University

The simplest statement that can be made about comedy today will sound very much like a boutade or a gratuitous witticism. Yet to say that comedy must be taken seriously is merely to show awareness of historical facts, to voice one of the truths, perhaps one of the truisms, of the age. Literarily, what distinguishes modernity from previous, more traditional periods is the attention it has bestowed on lower forms of discourse, on those genres once considered secondary literature or popular entertainment rather than art or art at its best. Certainly comedy has not only survived the various reorganizations the literary system has gone through during the last hundred years or so, but has gained greater and greater prominence. From Bergson to Freud to Bakhtin to Bataille, more important writers and thinkers have concerned themselves with the issues it raises than with those emanating from other types of drama.

Common critical wisdom has usually compacted the rationale it has invoked for this reversal of fortune into a perfunctory allusion to the advent of times unfavourable to the heroic and those structures aspiring to command both fear and pity—to, in short, the changing relation between the social and the aesthetic. Banal and questionable as the stenography may be (it rests its case on the notion of homology, implies that the present is a fall from grace, from the perfection of the past), it has kept intact the advantage it has for us: it still discloses, without too much ado, the associations which define comedy.

What do we mean, exactly, when we speak of the decline of the sublime and make it synonymous with the modern? Surely not that the sublime has suddenly vanished from literature: the poetry of a Rilke, the aesthetic writings of a Nietzsche or a Heidegger or a Derrida, all expressions of sensitivities heavily metaphysical in intent and ambition, would be enough to convince us of the contrary. We mean, more probably, that the sublime is no longer the measure of taste, that it no longer constitutes the most direct or the most typical response to the conditions art must, through assent or dissent, come to grips with. To rephrase it in terms derived from Walter Benjamin, whose works have provided the most luminous answer to our question, the one tell-tale sign of modernity in art has been the loss of aura of text and author, a loss, a deficiency proportional to the diffusion of techniques of reproduction, to the degree of presence of the copy.[1] Industrial serialization decontextualizes the aesthetic object no less than other objects. Portable, no longer unique, and therefore no longer demanding a ritualized fruition, as when it consisted of originals or of more elitistic features (leather bound volumes etc.), a painting, a musical performance, a book is deprived of its distance, of its aloofness: it becomes familiar, something to be used, not to be admired or venerated. The rhythm of its existence is the rhythm of consumption, the rhythm of the machine. In the new culture, analogy, repetition, duplication, authenticity and inauthenticity are key concepts.

Comedy, it is easy to see, comes into the picture willy nilly. Its rehabilitation begins in circumstances that are also one of the real *bona fide* anticipations of the century. In Bergson's seminal essay on the comic, *Le Rire*, the first edition of which dates back to 1899, laughter arises whenever someone's behaviour seems robot-like, when an action, a gesture gives "the illusion of life and the impression of mechanical arrangement."[2]

Of course, today, a hundred years later, a philosophy that finds mechanization so irrevocably funny will appear to be either too optimistic or too blatantly pre-emptive, something akin to exorcism. The Futurists exalted the new environment's capacity for acceleration, for movement, for increasing speed beyond organic tolerance and, by that same token, for reducing reliance on consecution, on syntactic structures. Marinetti's aspiration, it is well known, was to write without conjugated verbs, in a language that would be the equivalent of the simultaneity, the communication without wires that technology had just made possible.[3] The Futurist machine annexes further territories to aesthetic experience by enlarging the sensorium. Its impact on the relation between culture and literature is totally unlike that of the machine described by Benjamin (who, by the way, was not unaware of the Futurists. *Das Kunstwerk in Zeitalter seiner technischen Reproduzierbarkeit* contains a celebrated gloss of Marinetti's remarks about the beauty of war.)[4]

The Futurists' insistence on purely technical qualities, their disregard for the ethical dimension, encourages us to discern in their paean to modernity vestiges of the epic, archetypes now demotic (the equipment does not share the limelight as it did when it was customary to sing both of arms and great men) but quite recognizable beneath the heavy camouflage. Nevertheless, preference for the machine-reproduction sequence as co-ordinating principle seems more than justified. Literarily, Futurism is a *cul de sac*. It has left no tangible legacy, no thought or style for posterity to latch on to. And it could not because it was an essentially polemical movement, because its members were under the illusion that they could burn all bridges with the past. For it to be more than it was, Marinetti and his friends would have had to realize that in culture no-one starts from the beginning, that the institution, the "before," always impinges on the individual talent, on the "after"—which they could not do without contradicting themselves and never did.

By contrast, the view of the machine as recorder-reproducer has developed into an ontology. In Jean Baudrillard's recent updating of Benjamin's reflections, written with the advent of home computers and of videogames clearly in mind, modernity is that fraction of cultural history in which the replica, the duplicate, the simulacrum are ubiquitous, fill every moment and every space of life: spray gun messages, political polls, even biology (the DNA code turning us all into genetic combinations of a single alphabet) confront us daily with the capillary, physical, saturating intrusiveness of the sign.[5] And this view, while preserving modernity's originality, does not repudiate the past, whether it be the machine's or the past of the other items, cultural and literary, the machine connects with. One need only think of Pirandello. A writer of self-avowed philosophical bent and himself an author of memorable pages on technology and the *Zeitgeist* (Benjamin's essay mentions and comments a scene of *Si gira*, a novel on cinema Pirandello had published in 1915),[6] the Italian dramatist is the literary figure who best illustrates the valence of the double in the twentieth century. The problematics of representation, the opposition between art and life, between that which is free-flowing and that which is fixed by machines and technique, underpins most of his work. But it is a problematics which, even as it explodes the motif of the double by expanding it into the more general notion of duplication, can be embodied by images not exclusively modern. In Pirandello's theatre or fiction the pre-industrial, artisanal paraphernalia of the double have their place too. Mirrors, disguises, resemblances, symmetries, split personalities recur over and over: they are to the individual what media are to the group, and, together with the long and partly historical study on humour Pirandello produced early in his career, attest to his debt to and understanding of tradition.

Indeed, this view, wherein the machine is the purveyor of doubleness, will suggest to us the only credible criteria on which to found a system of genres, of the sort, at any rate, necessarily sketchy and fuzzy, that the age will permit. For modern taste, the sublime, the tragic has been substituted by the horror story, the narrative without any reassuring pity to allay the scariness, the fear. More specifically, it is not to Futurism but to the Freudian concept of the uncanny that we must look to re-establish contact with the high cultural past. The *heimlich-unheimlich*, sameness-difference, familiar-unfamiliar dichotomies, which were inspired to Freud by a reading of Hoffman's *Der Sandmann*, one of the classics of Romantic fiction on the double, situate in the domain of the sentiments a phenomenon that comedy has, instead, always made social, visible.[7] Interiorized, repetition kills; in the philosophical, metapsychological re-elaborations of the essay on the uncanny, it is the avatar of Thanatos and must be shrouded in the right atmosphere.[8] Externalized by machinery, its function as multiplicator of sign accentuated, the same process will cause laughter.

The modern repositioning of comedy cannot but affect the way we approach the genre's manifestations in other periods and, in particular, of the period that interests us here, the Renaissance. Not just, or not so much, because, as always in any endeavour involving history, the present must be conceded some prerogatives (twenty-five years ago many of the texts of sixteenth or seventeenth century Italian comedy were unavailable except in rare or very expensive editions, and without the stimulus coming from the publication of the works of Frye, Bakhtin, Bataille etc. would probably have remained so). With comedy the present has an irreplaceable critical function. No other century is sufficiently beyond tradition to guarantee the chiaroscuro that is required by true comparisons. The status acquired in the twentieth century, the network of convergences and divergences in which it fits, put comedy in touch with some of the great philosophical questions of modernity. To ponder the nature of laughter may be, today, to meditate on the human condition, to reflect on the fate of such notions as those of uniqueness, identity, person, communication under technology. Unless we stipulate that critics should close their eyes to historical developments we cannot ignore these contiguities and their impact on our perception of other periods. When we examine the collusions between the more figural antecedents of the modern double and comedy, we are bound, *by logic*, to check for parallels, to see whether the relations that obtain to-day also obtain in the past. On the other hand, the double, the co-existences it nurtures, do not eliminate historical gaps. They alter some of the priorities of assessment. Reproduction being one of the methods by which society deploys signs, quantity, more than speed, is now the basic factor in deter-mining chronology. Twins, portraits, mirror images display a similarity that is dyadic, finite, closed. Robots, serialized objects can be duplicated *ad infinitum*, are open-ended doubleness. The kind of semiotic economy they belong to, that we live with today, was unimaginable in the cultural system of pre-modern centuries.

Retrieved to be then pushed back, the comedy of the past becomes as refractory, as ambiguous as the periods in which it was written. Tradi-tion is not, for us, an innocently transparent discourse. Those of its entries that do appear to go by themselves are often the ones we must most urgently account for. Preambles are, today, an act of intellectual hygiene as historical-ly necessary (why else would we indulge in so much theorizing?) as they have always been in all periods, the Renaissance not excluded, which have found themselves cogently distant from pasts whose language they speak but must also redefine. The era we are concentrating on here has been too self-evident too long in its many roles as "cradle" of Western civilization, as codifier of modern literariness for its legibility not to be suspect. Con-cepts such as humanism, the most durable and most comprehensive of the ideals it has bequeathed to us, provoke an uneasiness second perhaps only to the one we labour under with words such as "Enlightenment" or "reason." In an age that has proclaimed the "death of man," taking them literally, at face value, would be impossible without either extreme critical nonchalance or extreme critical naiveté.

The paragraphs that follow will be adequately prefatory, will, that is, seek to confront some of the hesitations, the scruples the double has instill-ed in us. To this end, however, indirection will have to continue to be our virtue. For the different history, the sensitivity towards the cultural, the anthropological in literature, are nothing but a part of the preamble that the Renaissance demands from us. The double, its pre-eminence in the twentieth century, force us to look anew at the *form* of comedy no less than at its content. And if the thematic continuities of the motif convince us to rethink the affinities between comedy and the intellectual climate in which it has circulated, in the present and in the past, we cannot deny structure the same treatment. To be able to retrace all of our steps, to be able to deal with the Renaissance-ness of Renaissance comedy, we must also be able to deal with the comic-ness of the genre.

Structurally, the first generic feature we are obliged to notice in ac-costing comic drama *sub-specie* of the double has to do not with symmetry—as we might expect from the specularity in *mise en abyme*, the proximity of that notion to some of the turn-of-the-century authors we have discussed[9]

—but with the other category underlying the motif, polarity. There is a mixedness to comedy, additional to and quite aside from the quality inherent to it as theatre and according to which it will appear to us now as a fixed, written text, now as an audiovisual text changing with each adaptation or performance. This quality, typical of the genre whether it is read or listened to and watched, is perhaps most immediately brought home to us by the language: comedy has always been polyphonic, has always allowed contrasting stylistic registers, contrasting vernaculars to cohabit. But the aspect is no less conspicuous on other levels of the structure. In our century criticism has been quick to spot (and on occasion to theorize) the antinomies of the plot and its elements. One recalls Pirandello's famous illustration in his essay on humour. The comic character is by definition ambivalent and, together with laughter, must elicit reflection, with distance, participation, empathy. An old lady "smeared with some kind of horrible ointment," "dolled-up like a young lady" will cause hilarity, if we believe that she is the contrary of what she should be; should we realize that she finds "no pleasure in dressing up like an exotic parrot," that she may be "someone who does it to hold on to the love of her younger husband," for instance, we would no longer react in that manner; analysis, speculation have brought us from the perception of the opposite to the feeling of the opposite.[10] From another angle, British, American and Canadian critics, often harking back directly to the Cambridge School of Anthropology and its research on ritual, have pointed out that the plot-pattern of comedy would be entirely similar to that of tragedy were it not for the *Komos*, the marriage feast occurring at the end. In his early but still useful book on the origin of comic theatre, F.M. Cornford goes so far as to suggest that within this structure laughter does not begin until the arrival on the scene, during the celebrations, of the *Alazon*, an impostor character soon unmasked and duly reviled by the protagonist.[11]

On the co-presence of tragic and comic features, tradition is in general agreement with modernity. A Giambattista Della Porta or a Giordano Bruno will warn his audience in the prologue of his plays—that it might have to shed some tears as well as rejoice and revel.[12] For classical criticism the issue is a fixed topos: from Plato's *Phylebus* to the Renaissance and beyond, the ludicrous, one of the principal sources of laughter, will contain an element of pain. The impression one receives from the whole traditional debate on comedy is that comicness is a price specific characters must pay, a symbolic punishment for an equally symbolic hubris. Somewhat paradoxically, Lodovico Castelvetro, one of the most influential of Renaissance theoreticians, feels even compelled to urge playwrights not to exaggerate with the laughter-arousing devices, with the retribution, lest the disproportion between ridicule and guilt generate sympathy for the victim, as the comic character was suggestively called, thereby blurring generic distinctions.[13] In classical criticism, a comedy which did not contemplate the possibility of a brief downward turn in the protagonist's luck was not quite in line with the standards of the genre.

To begin with, then, we have mixture in comedy because the comic spills on to areas that are not, strictly speaking, literary. No less a figure than Croce berated Pirandello for championing a version of humour associated with reflection and analysis and ended the polemic by relegating the phenomenon in question outside the ken of art and artist and into the realm of the practical, hence of the sciences.[14] Aesthetic misgivings about the more happy side of the comic can perhaps be understood by just going over the data: on laughter, ethologists, physiologists, besides rhetoricians, philosophers and psychologists, have made significant contributions.[15] There is in laughter something organic or something social that is never fully redeemed by art. We do not react to the tragic with the same readiness: if we do at all we do it discreetly or privately (sobs are not easily produced, and are not a marketable commodity, as television producers—who will instead punctuate situation comedies with recorded laughter—know very well). Modern theorists and writers have been corroborating this obliquely, by reversing usual motivations. In Mikhail Bakhtin's influential study of Rabelais' works, laughter retains a liberating function precisely for the kinks it throws in aesthetic harmoniousness, insofar as it gives expression to the corporal, the scatological, to that which rejects authority, form, the artificial.[16] For Georges Bataille laughter is the most common experience of transcendence: it momentarily puts the individual beyond rule, beyond the system that encapsulates him.[17]

Retranslating the aesthetic into the structural, we could say that comedy is heterogeneous to the degree to which it is a story and a story that must make us laugh. The discrepancy would thus echo quite neatly the classical discrimination between the character who is ludicrous and the character who runs and avoids risks. The protagonist is endowed with a trajectory: he will change in the course of the action. The victim cannot: movement is not for him, as at least one Renaissance playwright-critic admonishes (Ben Jonson's theory of the humours is Bergsonism minus the parallel with the machine; it highlights genesis rather than effect: the character possessed by one "peculiar quality"[18] is condemned to repetition and funniness by chemistry and metabolism).

But on this score we can go further. Story and laughter rest on frames of different consistency. One, narrative, encompasses the whole text; the other is triggered by local structures, is therefore plural. Contrasting operations, and aptitudes, are required from the reader. Whether the term *fabula* (or story-line) is understood in the classical sense of argument of the play or in the more recent Russian Formalist sense,[19] as the reorganization, in logical and chronological order, of the events narrated, it refers to an intervention on and a manipulation of the textual. The object we keep after we have reconstructed the plot and with which we identify the narration, is an abstract, mental, ersatz entity: it is a reduction of the content of the action. Converted back into textual coin, each of the propositions of this summary would cover a lot of dialogue and stage time. The sentence: "Dopo molti scambiamenti Lidio e Santilla lietamente si riconoscono,"[20] ("After many changes of identity, Lidio and Santilla happily recognize each other") from Bibbiena's prologue to *La Calandria*, condenses more than half of that play. When we work on the narrative structure, we are dealing with the salient facts, the macrosequences. From this optic the comic component is not indispensible: leaving out the jokes, as we do when we tell someone what happens in a comedy, does not harm the story-line. Yet, on its own, the occurrence of laughter reaffirms, valorizes textuality. For the authors of the classical tradition the comic was rooted in the diction or the situation. Modern narratology would ascribe it to the discourse or to the plot, the events as they are presented by the play itself—to surface structures. As such, the comic calls for a more concentrated kind of attention. Whatever its embodiment, be it the joke, the pun, the repartee, the gag, the vignette, it partakes of the simple form: its unit is the microsequence. Little or no memorization is demanded of the reader or listener or viewer, no inferences about events to come, no recapitulation of events past. Laughter presupposes an almost unmediated consumption. Episodic, anecdotic, the comic introduces the present in the flow of the action. Whereas the narrative recontextualizes information, it isolates gestures, faces, narrative sequences from their chronological ambiance. At its most vitriolic and corrosive, laughter disrupts the continuity of the story, undoes the very fabric, the very logic of form. Central to comedy as a genre is a slippage, a non-coincidence of durations, procedures of fruition, structures.

Let us stop here. Comic heterogeneity obviously offers us criteria with which to carry out taxonomies. For example, on strictly narrative grounds we could assimilate some comedies to those texts whose task it is to reach a happy ending by traversing the pathetic. Female virtue is constantly threatened in pre-romantic fiction; families are dispersed by fate, reunited in the last minute, just as fortuitous agnitions in nineteenth century *feuilletons*; disguises and metamorphoses are staple material of detective novels and science fiction (not to speak of the characters: though less shady, the Renaissance necromancer does prefigure the scientist of modern mythology). Affinities such as these not only tell us of comedy's ambiguous participation in the unfolding of Western *Stoffgeschichte*; the preserving of certain themes by the very act which aims at eroding their authority, which sets them up as objects of laughter, helps us better appreciate the dynamics of single works and single periods. The protagonists of Annibal Caro's *Gli Straccioni*, written in 1543, are two brothers involved in a long law suit and now fallen on hard times. The tone of the story, which otherwise abides by all stock-in-trade rules of Renaissance comedy, always verges on the maudlin. In Shakespeare's *Love's Labour's Lost*, the witty bantering, the thrust and parry play-acting of the King of Navarre or his courtiers and the visiting princess of France is abruptly stopped before it comes to issue by the news of the death of the princess' father. In both of these plays, rather than outright deviation, we have a slightly different and probably not unexpected dosage of ingredients also present in the reigning models of the period.

But, more fundamentally yet, the conflicts inherent to comic heterogeneity alert us to a question that precedes taxonomy, though taxonomic ventures can hardly afford to overlook it. The logical functions that anthropomorphic doubleness narrates (symmetry, polarity and, when a character impersonates someone of a different sex, complementarity) interact with each other, often across textual levels. It is at this juncture that notions such as that of *mise en abyme* come in. One does not have to accept the prescriptions of Jean Ricardou and view all stylistic repetitions as instances of doubleness to believe that heterogeneity is aided and abetted by (and aids and abets) devices which steer the text towards symmetry.[21] Historically, textual reflexivity has always been with comedy. The *Alazon* and the *Alazoneia*, the character and the episode giving rise to laughter in Attic theatre, are, in Cornford's opinion, duplications of figures already on stage or of events presented earlier in the play.[22] The cornerstone of Renaissance comedy, the ruse, has as its structural offshoot the plot within the plot, the illusion within the illusion. In the twentieth century the processes are several and of diverse temper. Plays à la Marx Brothers are hotbeds of repetition. The massive recurrence of gags, of those abbreviated, instant little narratives which are the jokes, all but nullifies plot progression: at the end, with the actors relentless in their pace, in their rapid-fire delivery, we remember only the high points in the laughter. At the opposite end is Pirandello. Humour, the kind of laughter he advocates, is more analytical: it decomposes appearances, surface properties, by letting emerge ulterior motives, by enlisting the help of larger units. A Pirandellian story—the comments to the made-up old lady demonstrate it perfectly—will conceal a second or third story. In such trademark texts as *Liolà*, *Cosí è, se vi pare*, *Enrico IV*, the plot is undermined by narrative excess: because the plays contain the promise of other plays, are ready to become theatre about theatre, the truth-value of framing and framed tales is never fixed, must be continuously doubted.

The upshot is a prospect of the genre whose implications for criticism are still to be fully explored. The comedy heterogeneity depicts for us is always deconstructing and reconstructing itself, permitting the text to fragment but never relinquishing coherence. It is a strategy quite unique in literature. With comic works the term "structure" must be granted a latitude, a dictionary range greater than usual: it also designates influences that in other genres are the antithesis of structure. That the same notion should be responsible for the thematic patterning of the play and of its divisions is, thus, less preposterous than it may seem. Without some element cutting across both content and form, narration and laughter, there would be no sense. The double may induce a loosening of the plot's unity (through laughter, the multiplication of plots within the plot) and is the sponsor of that unity: either way it is the organizing agency of the text, since with comedy form is the contamination of order by disorder.

To properly describe the comedy of a period we must first, then, be able to identify and correlate the components of the textual structure. How does a period "use" the heterogeneity of the genre? Does it accent centrifugal or centripetal tendencies? Is the centrifugalness sustained, formally, by the repetition of small units, by the quasi-autonomous, surface or discourse items (jokes, gags, double meanings, word distortions and the like) or by the repetition of larger units belonging to the deeper, narrative plot levels? And what about the content? How does it interlock with the form? Which characters are the victims and which the creators of laughter? Whose story takes place in the plot within the plot? Secondly, we must be able to correlate the structural doubleness to the doubleness in the culture. Within the social thought of a period does symmetry or polarity prevail? Is the symmetry anthropomorphic, dyadic, or the unfettered repetition of mechanization?.

Set against the background of these parameters, the Renaissance will

confirm all that we expect from it: it is a period whose aim in theatre is
a judicious distribution of the elements. Balance being, by and large, its
objective, its poetics will take a middle course, will attempt to safeguard,
through the auspices of the double, at once laughter and story. Thus, even
in the most intricate structurations, the strategy will consist in multiplying
some of the items: prologues (Giordano Bruno's *Candelaio*), the subplots
(Giambattista Della Porta's *La Fantesca*) or characters (Shakespeare's *Comedy of Errors*). Like other less conspicuous but similar devices (the scene in
which a servant comes back from an errand and mistakingly gives what
he has brought back to his master's twin rather than his master, who will
then mistakingly ask the servant's double to perform the same errand again,
or the scene in which a servant parodies someone else's speech patterns
or vocabulary),[23] such features smuggle repetition and stasis into the action but do not jeopardize the integrity of the plot: they are bravura theatre,
convolutions which will let better stand out the neatness of the dénouement.
With some things the Renaissance author will not, cannot take chances.
While he will have some of the more enterprising servants name the name
of the game, blurt out to the audience that the prank they have just pulled
is not much different than a play,[24] he will stop short of disobeying the
precepts of mimesis, of questioning, Pirandello-style, the ontology of the
events enacted by the actors or the reality of the spectators.

As for the mediating role of the double, it is probably in greater evidence
in the Renaissance than in any other period. This, due, to be sure, to the
imperatives of classicist ideology, occurs on every level of the text and on
every scale, macro and micro. More often than not the refractions that
discourse structures send back at narration also strengthen local cohesiveness.
Stylistic figures of a certain type—double entendres, mostly—become more
frequent in those episodes in which a character is obliged to simulate another
sex. In *La Calandria* the servant Samia and the necromancer Ruffo distort
"ambiguo" into "anghibuo" and "ermafrodito" into "merdafiorito" when
the subterfuge of Lidio, who had planned to enter his lover's house, goes
momentarily awry (unbeknownst to our hero, and much to the dismay of
his lover, his sister had taken his place).[25] The errors gloss somewhat
ironically the situation.

In the single but wider context of narration, the double assembles and
reconciles with each other the elements out of which will emerge the gist
of Renaissance comedy. Until recently literary criticism had associated the
genre with the vicissitudes of the character who, love-stricken, achieves his
ends by ruse, usually impersonation. That story-line substantiated the values
of the Renaissance, and in a manner fully attractive: assenting to passion,
and being able to satisfy it through cunning and intelligence, by the creation of illusion and without damage to the self, is an indication of consummate humanity, a humanity the posterity of the Enlightenment could not and
dared not pay homage to. The approach via the double amends such a view.
For the optic it promotes, "the efforts of a young man to get possession
of a young woman,"[26] as it has been put, may be, statistically, and
especially in the English tradition, the "argument" of Renaissance comedy; it is not the only "argument" nor the final "content" of the genre
in that period. Side by side with the love-and-trickery fabula, with the

story of desire and cleverness and power, usually intertwined with it in the same work, is the fabula of pathos, the story of the character searching for the look-alike brother or sister he has been separated from and whom he will find at the end of the play. Family reunions, the double as symmetry, analogy, equivocation are perhaps of less official, less visible diffusion but they are not objectives the Renaissance would disclaim. Superimposed to the others—sexual union, the double as polarity, as complementarity, as intelligence—they shift structural emphasis. Since a second *telos*, culminating in the recognition, can be envisaged, since what the two plots have in common is the double, the issues emanating from that thematic cluster take precedence over anything else: comedy is above all about a dialectic.

The divergences between the two plot types are, at first sight, more striking than the convergences. Ruses and disguises arise out of an individual act of will: they are a contrivance, an instrument. Narratologically, the devices they insinuate into the form contribute to the syntagmatic scansion of the events: in spite of the *mise en abyme*, of the specularity that attaches to them, plots within plots initiate the process whose precipitate will be the ending. The double of symmetry intensifies the refractions without ever transcending them. The relation it holds with the *telos* increases the casuality rather that the causality of the events. Twinship is a natural phenomenon. Different from disguise, which must remain a private affair, with a precise, limited range (no-one but the protagonist and his entourage must know that the illusion created is an illusion, only some characters must be victimized), it engulfs all characters. The equivocations it induces, not guided by intention, by any perceivable logic, are public, collective: the play cannot end until everybody on the stage has had an opportunity to err, to add to the entropy that will be keeping events static, without consecution for a good part of the story.

These staple antinomies between nature and culture, casuality and causality, public and private, the paradigmatic and the syntagmatic, can be rounded out with a series of other oppositions. In Shakespeare's *Comedy of Errors*, the play which best expands and completes the Plautine model it derives from, the characters fall prey to some very primitive anxieties. The protagonist, Antipholus of Syracuse, does not know that his long-lost twin and namesake lives in the town he has just set foot in and is accompanied by a servant who is the mirror image of his own servant and, like him, also called Dromio. Unsure about the familiarity with which they are addressed by the individuals that they encounter, the two characters suspect witchcraft, "Dark-working sorcerers" that "change the mind,"[27] produce enchantments, a dream-like reality, and "steal"[28] names. For the citizens of Ephesus, who, confusing the two brothers, are surprised by the sudden strangeness of people they thought they knew well, Antipholos and his servant are "possessed."[29] It is a behaviour in quite open contradiction with the *sprezzatura* idealized in the first plot-type. The characters who disguise themselves believe only in the "magic" they create themselves by means of their rhetorical skills. When they engage the services of a necromancer, they are aware that they are dealing with small-time confidence men trying to eek out a living by expediency. The allusions to the black arts or to possession and madness thrust the characters of the second plot-type, virtually all the *dramatis personae*, outside of rationality, of civility. For a while the entire city is infected space. Only ritual will salvage it. In comedy the recognition which cures, which cancels out the errors, re-socializes, returns traveler and citizen to normality, to his own identity, must be as collective as the damage, that is, sanctioned by law (in Shakespeare's play it is the Duke).

The naturalness of twinship, the universality of the error and the corresponding magnitude of the emendation put us face to face with the sense of this fabula. In Shakespeare's play, in the Renaissance comedies that have variations of the same plot incorporated into their narrative structure, the undetected arrival of a double compromises the stability of the semantic reality of the characters. The traveling twin carries with him a world of specific, precise contours. Not for nothing the list of the *dramatis personae* and the stage directions distinguish between one master/servant duo and the other only through geographic labeling: Antipholus and Dromio of Syracuse are pitted against Antipholus and Dromio of Ephesus. Up to the time of the recognition the two worlds overlap. The characters inhabit an in-between, mixed, perplexing domain, one in which qualities are burdened with too many contrasting secondary qualifications, and is therefore ontologically not adequately founded. In Syracuse the name Antipholus refers to an individual whose main trait is, from the information we have about him, that he is unmarried; in Ephesus it refers to someone who is married, has a sister-in-law, lives at an address known to the Ephesian citizenry, enjoys a good reputation with friends and acquaintances. The *trompe l'oeil* that the physical and anagraphic doubleness induces abolishes the congruences between person and world. Some qualities can be ascribed to the wrong individual. As each of the brothers refuses some of the properties with which he is being charged (and Shakespeare quite rightly, semantically, makes the loss of the proper name, of the "designator" of identity, as specialists have called it,[30] one of the major sub-themes of the play), the citizens suffer: their own well-being depends on the correctness of their attributions. In comedy symmetry is funny, but it had better be counterbalanced by the difference recognition affords. Again, the imagery and the allusions in Shakespeare's play drive this home more forcefully than most Renaissance works, usually content with presenting events and their consequences. Nonetheless, in all cases (the anonymous Italian comedy entitled *Gl'Ingannati* or Bibbiena's *La Calandria* come to mind) what is being performed on the stage when an equivocation, an error, is being acted out is a drama of the mind. The doubling in the form is, with comedy, repeated in the content, which has, it too, a metalinguistic role to fulfil, is meaning about how meaning functions.

Needless to say, it is when we turn to this, the representation of the semantics of everyday life, that the two plot-types of comedy draw most closely together, reduce their oppositions. With the double as disguise probability does win over randomness and possibility over necessity. Events do, at least ostensibly, have an origin. Strongly agonistic, the reality of the characters will seem to us spectators or readers to be much like a crisscrossing of desires, of intentions. We are in the realm of the social sciences

rather than philosophy. But, though the plot tends to highlight human ingenuity, to promote the intervention of man in the conduct of his own affairs, the many worlds tossing about on the stage operate on a common
principle. To act, in the context of this plot, is to simulate action. One goes
with the other: the pretending is no less significant than the doing (the
English language wisely conflates the two into the verb "to act"). From
what happens on the stage, deceit could be defined as hyperbolic language,
communication with a second order, undeclared meaning level. It consists
of a pragmatic and cognitive element, each variable according to the role
of the individuals concerned. The perpetrator of the illusion must persuade,
and in persuading must bring to bear on his interlocutor's reception of his
actions or discourse a number of semantic procedures: events that for him
are signs are the hallmark of truth and factuality, are endowed with no
wilful purpose for the other person. To carry out his very usual but very
complex prestidigitation he must master premises (i.e. the belief that reality can be imitated) he himself would be oblivious to were he to be in his
victim's shoes. Whence the paradox of this plot: privately implemented,
the ruse is collectively practised; individually, imaginatively conceived, it
is subject to general rules. The character who is on the passive, negative
end of some design, prank or joke, dreams of his day of deviousness, of
being the manipulator of interlocutors who will equate the true with the
false. In this plot everyone is deceiving or is ready to deceive everyone else,
with perhaps the exclusion of blood relatives. In Machiavelli's *La Mandragola*,
the play which best grasps the socio-political implications of simulation and
how they apply to the very social ambiance comedy thrives on, even the
virtuous Lucrezia agrees to support the subterfuges that will give her aspiring
lover continued access to her household. And she does so when she learns
from him about the way in which he had managed to outscheme her scheming husband. Whether a character is a "knower" or a "not-knower," deceitful communication presupposes, along with a compatible system of values,
a certain semantic competence, notions similar to those at work in the plot
that proceeds in the other direction, towards disentanglement, instead of,
as here, towards successful entanglement.

Control can therefore never be absolute. Although illusionists are very
cautious and manage to co-opt and co-ordinate the ruses of their adversaries (husbands about to be cuckolded are regularly sent on long wild-
goose chases or convinced to don transparent disguises in obviously ill-
conceived plans), they too may be the targets of illusion. Since secrecy is
of the essence with such exercises, it is not uncommon that the hero and
his group become aware of the manipulation they have been subjected to
late in the story. Full ignorance is the only unkindness comedy will spare
them to separate them from the crowd. The title of *Gl' Ingannati* is, on this,
most explicit: it is a past participle of the passive voice and in the plural
(roughly translated it means "the deceived-ones"). In the play no-one is
exempt from error and credulity, least of all the protagonist: Flaminio en-
trusts messages for his lover to a page without knowing that he is actually
a she in love with him and in the process of casting her own net. As well
as with the designs of other characters the hero of Renaissance comedy must
always contend with chance. The irruption of a twin, in the plays in which

the two plot-types coexist, will always throw the most ingenious simulations in disarray. In *La Calandria*, Lidio, who has been dressing as a woman in order to meet with Fulvia undetected, has an unwitting competitor in his look-alike sister. When Fessenio, servant and orchestrator of the stratagem, learns that the necromancer hired by the impatient Fulvia to expedite the unfolding of the project may have outdone himself and really transformed his master into a woman, he will for some time have to resign himself to the prospect of defeat: unable by simple reasoning to imagine that there may have been an exchange of bodies, he cannot realize, until the *deus ex machina* of recognition rushes to the rescue, that the person he has frisked, while a woman, is not Lidio. Unexpected grief may also be brought on by the very efficiency of the protagonist's illusion. The Renaissance comic characters wishing to attain sexual satisfaction must first experience the travails of the opposite sex.[31] Those who imitate a woman or a man *are* the mask they have adopted: in *La Fantesca, La Calandria, Gl' Ingannati* they will be the object of the amorous attentions of the wrong people, of the father or husband or wife or lover or son or daughter or relative of the woman or man sought after. Other occasions of embarrassment for the hero will have the individuals whose identity he has borrowed appear suddenly and unannounced on the scene (*La Fantesca*). Or, the clearest instance of its power, casuality may interfere with events, with human affairs, through a *force majeure* (the death of the King of France in *Love's Labour's Lost*).

This is why any approach to Renaissance comedy which focuses on the protagonist and his intelligence alone will seem partial and tautological. Enlarging the love fabula and its dénouement into a global, overall paradigm would not only level the genre or isolate it from the narrative stock—the romance, "pathetic," *feuilleton* genealogy—to which it also belongs. Such a response would also be entirely subservient to the official image of itself the Renaissance has proposed, would be to espouse that which should be explained. As H.R. Jauss has indicated, the collaboration that comedy demands, which is its *sine qua non* condition (where there is no laughter, there is no comedy), is a highly specialized one: the third party, who with his laughter must bear witness to the comic effect, laughs with the teller of the joke or the creator of the prank and at the victim.[32] With Renaissance comedy the mechanics of reception activates a whole set of devices: the victim is generally the character who repeats himself or the character on whom illusion is being inflicted and who is always in one of the plots within the plot. Most significantly, with Renaissance comedy collaboration activates all the options that identification has programmed into its structure. The immediate spectators, the on-stage witnesses, cannot laugh at the hero: if they know that the illusion is an illusion they are the hero's servants or his confidants and cannot distance themselves from him or be superior to him. We, the off-stage, outer ring of spectator-witnesses can laugh and are superior. While we laugh primarily *with* the hero, we sometimes laugh *at* him, when he errs as all other characters do, or when he corners himself into situations to rectify which he will have to expend further uncalculated energy, or when he is the victim of chance. We cannot disregard this alternation and the constraints it imposes on our analysis of the texts and on us as participants in the comic process: with our laughter we surreptitiously ratify the incidence and function of chaos on and in the structure of comedy. Nor is it an alternation that is merely the by-product of a rhythm, that owes its existence to the highs and lows in the hero's trajectory. It is the stuff out of which heterogeneity is made. In the text we run across it everywhere (for example: the distribution of roles. The middle class character is the beneficiary of the comic story, the character with whom we should and to a large extent do identify; yet it is the servants who do the work, come up with the ideas and with whom we often in practice really identify). And the texts, the plays, are symptomatic. With only slight prodding we can find a similar ambiguity in the touchstone writings of the period. Didn't Machiavelli, in *The Prince*, warn his contemporaries that they presided over their destiny in tandem with Fortune, on a fifty-fifty basis?[33]

The fact is that when one moves from theocentrism to anthropocentrism, to resuscitate an old platitude but one which is, in this case, the proper resounding board, one is bound to experience inconveniences and to try to compensate. Spectators or readers, what we witness with comedy is the dramatization of an intellectual sleight of hand, a now-you-see-it-now-you-don't rhetoric that embellishes survivorship into heroism, presents as possible something that events have already shown to be of precarious feasibility. Both the initiating impulse and the shaping of comic reality are, when it comes down to it, beyond individual dominion. In all plot-types the initial impetus for any enterprise is a force—the instincts—whose calling is, for the characters, irresistible.[34] The counterweight to the compulsion towards union, familial or sexual, should be the constructiveness of illusion, human ingenuity, human history. But history, reason are also subordinate to codes, to protocols which depend on the suprapersonal. And they also breed disorder. In a plot teeming with simulations, in which everyone is busy conspiring, planning his or her brand of trickery, no design is capable of subsuming the others, of injecting enough sense into the non-sense that the contiguity of contrasting intentions generates. The disjunction the opposition deceived/deceiver must rest on to work is unjustified. The persuasiveness of the comic story notwithstanding, man's freedom, the theme of the genre, seems, rather than affirmed, postulated. As we leave the hero united with his lover on the threshhold of perpetual happiness we are tempted to diagnose an aftermath, a sequel. Considering that in comedy events are cyclical, that Cupid will be forever armed behind the scenes, that sharp-minded servants will be waiting for an opportunity to lend a sympathetic ear, that humanity will always be charmed by invention, the future in store for our couple cannot be too bright. Musings such as these are not completely legitimate, but they are not altogether off the mark. Renaissance comedy continuously reinstalls at the origin, at the centre of meaning the subject, the "I" the action decentres. It is not the glorification of triumphant spirit that we, the only "characters" in traditional comedy not laughed at, might wish it to be: it is an act of faith.

Typologically and historically our survey of comic heterogeneity anticipates—and validates—conclusions we would have reached had we confined our analysis to the cultural pertinence of the notion of the double. The ambiguity in and of the structure of the texts leaves Renaissance comedy in a relation to modernity as equivocal as the one implied by the comparison between twinship and industrialized repetition. Such an outcome concords with the views of those critics who have maintained that the non-disjunctiveness of the hero vis-à-vis his opponents allies the comedy of chronologically pre-modern periods to the culture of the sign, but departs from them in some vital respects.[35] In our version of things, the main trait of the hero—his being at once doer and done unto, maker and victim of reality—is a constant of the genre. That admitted, non-disjunctiveness, the liaison with the culture of the sign can hardly, for us, epitomize modernity and its episteme, as they have been thought to do: modernity would have to encompass every comic text from Aristophanes and Plautus on.[36] Together with sign circulation, a more judicious gauge for epistemic dating would be, one would have to believe, the attitudes with which non-disjunctiveness and its extensions have been met by the various periods. Beyond the features which predispose comedy towards the modern are the occultations. In Renaissance texts contradictions emerge from a deconstruction of the harmony, of the appearances the play is bent on saving against its better judgment. For all its Machiavellisms, the history acted out on the stage is too unsoiled, too pure: it refuses any contact with the intimations its hero, *homo faber*, is continuously colliding with. The dénouements of comedy restore the characters to privileges that are patently false, that do not quite square with the data and are, hence, ideological.

We have, with this, edged into the real theoretical centre of the Renaissance. The inconsistencies of the hero's story are matched by the inconsistencies of the period's criticism. In the works of the Castelvetros or the Robortellos or the Trissinos there is some cognizance of mixedness, be it linguistic or structural or otherwise. But the subject seems broached only to give vent to a vague intellectual discomfort. Each of the authors feels compelled to dispel the confusion laughter introduces into the play (by heaping too much ridicule or by lampooning the wrong person) with protestations about comedy's ultimately moral aims. The more intense polemic that later in the sixteenth century was to greet the birth of tragicomedy is only an outgrowth of this unsureness.[37] Nowhere in the Renaissance is any attempt made to collate all the issues, to connect the tragic hero's overt struggle with cosmic forces to tragedy's prestige (it is the genre which, with the epic, establishes reputations) or comedy's "lowliness"—its standing within the literary system—to the limitations of its protagonist's vicissitudes.

To put such ambiguity, such discomfort, in perspective, to see how a more acute intelligence of comedy's materials, how less evasive decisions about the hero's non-disjunctiveness redistribute the roles and functions of laughter and history, one last comparison with the twentieth century will suffice.

In Pirandello's *Così è, se vi pare* a freshly arrived family of three, composed of husband, wife and mother-in-law, arouses the curiosity of the inhabitants and the authorities of a small town. It seems that the younger woman never leaves the apartment she lives in and that the elderly lady, who is housed in a separate building, is not allowed to visit her. The problem soon snowballs. The younger woman is attributed a different identity by each of the two other members of the family. The husband, Ponza, claims that she is his second wife. For the elderly lady, signora Frola, she is his first wife and her daughter. Each character lets understand that he or she is adapting himself or herself to the circumstances to avoid causing anybody unendurable pain: according to Ponza the lady's daughter has been dead without the lady ever having been able to accept the event; according to Frola, Ponza, who has been gravely ill, suffers from delusions. As in Renaissance comedy, in this play, which a semanticist has labelled a play "about reference,"[38] identity straddles two worlds, impairs the characters' semantic competence. Meaning being at stake, here too the dénouement must be public, must take place before the law (the town's Prefect conducts an investigation of the family, finally orders Ponza to bring the woman before the townspeople, who are impatient to hear the truth.)

Who is right? Ponza or Frola? When she is asked the young woman answers by saying that she is Frola's daughter for Frola, Ponza's wife for Ponza and no-one for herself. The reply, however it is interpreted (in the twentieth century surrendering one's identity to let stand that of others may be the simplest, most concrete expression of altruism), is based on a negation, a denial that repudiates the key requisites of the traditional comic story. The grand finale of Pirandello's play does not recognize identity but, acknowledging instead its impermanence, its precariousness, dismisses it as a criterion for determining whatsoever in human affairs. In the Renaissance each sign has one referent. Surpluses or shortages of either referents (as when one quality is shared by two individuals) or signs (as when an individual appropriates himself of two qualities) are aberrations and must be censured and removed if they become perceivable. Comic dénouement underscores the singularity of each twin; illusion which does remain secret, which is unsuccessful, exacts a legal cost. More laissez-fairist and pessimistic, twentieth century semiosis can tolerate the entire spectrum of hypotheses: signs may be overabundant (Benjamin, Baudrillard), may refer to two entities or, the most scandalous alternative, to no entity at all.

The hierarchy of roles collapses, and with it the traditional system of response to the comic story. No character can now boast of privileges that would permit him the luxury of laughing at others and would secure for him the sympathy of the spectators. In Pirandello's plays the margin of freedom has greatly dwindled. History, which in Renaissance comedy is the everyday business of influencing other people, here is imbued with the elusive. The autonomy that some of the characters may enjoy has some cruel strings attached to it. The first of them is awareness. Laudisi, one of the townspeople and the only figure in *Così è, se vi pare* comparable to the manipulator-type of the Renaissance, takes pleasure in instigating the other characters' quest for truth, but knows full well where it will lead and that the result will apply to him. In the scene in which he is most sincere he is in front of a mirror amusingly addressing his image. The "I" that he soliloquizes to is a "phantom," somebody else's construct.[39] When at the end of the play, with everyone still dazed by the young woman's revelation, he will not be able to hold back his sarcasm ("There, my friends, you have the truth!" is his comment to the crowd),[40] the reverberations of the earlier scene will transform the boisterous laughter with which he accompanies his remarks. In *Così è, se vi pare*, as in all of Pirandello's theatre, humour is reflexive, self-inflicted, the humour of an individual whose only superiority over his counterparts is a lucidity about himself and the limits of reason that will always keep him hovering on the borderline between sanity and madness.

The fall of the reader/spectator is as momentous. Pirandello's play deprives us of the values that underwrite our role. The logic of the plot, its sense, unravel before our very eyes. Without characters properly defined, without a proper slate of identities there can be no identification, without identification no laughing *with*. *Così è, se vi pare* is a formally straightforward prelude to those other Pirandellian works, the theatre on the theatre, in which the spectator will be absorbed by the representation, so that, become audience and actor, no longer separated from the action on the stage, he will, if he dare laugh at anyone, be laughing at himself.

The twentieth century will not always be as radical. Other theorists or playwrights dissociate the object of laughter (its demise) from the subjectivity (or lack thereof) of the hero or the spectator. For Bergson, when we laugh at machine-like behaviour we cut artificiality down to size. Bakhtin's carnival is the feast of reversal, the dethroning of the powers that be. Both these authors, by refusing ontology, by staying within history, can preserve the object of laughter and some residual space between it and the subject. Judged on this by itself, outside of any context, they could be quoted in support of the contention that there is epistemic, in addition to generic, continuity with the past: laughing is conceivable and it offends. A return to the context, however, will quickly reconstitute temporal sequencing. When we compare Bergson's or Bakhtin's laughter to Pirandello's humour, what we note is not its vitalism but its effect on subjectivity. More than the individual, in Bergson or Bakhtin or Bataille, it is a collective essence, an historical or biological or metaphysical subject—the populace, the colloidal inman, Being—that is laughing. The occurrence may be positive or negative, depending on taste, on how one regards individuality: it does, in varying degrees, more in Bataille than in Bergson or Bakhtin, transcend the "I". In the texts the difficulties awaiting the subject are no different. As they forge chaos out of the order, the linearity of the plot and leave us aching from the laughter, the gags of the Marx Brothers annul the rules of normal participation in the comic process: they weaken identification, prevent us from realizing what it is that we are doing and, therefore, from asserting our superiority. We must not forget that the Renaissance suspends sense only on behalf of a greater logic, and the greatest logic of all, in sixteenth century comedy, is that of the spectator, who gets off scot free.

NOTES

1 W. Benjamin, "The Work of Art in the Age of Mechanical Reproduction," in *Illuminations*, trans. Harry Zohn (Glasgow, 1979), 244 ff. Though I have kept original titles in my text, for purposes of quotation I have, when they have been readily available, used translations.

2   H. Bergson, "Laughter," in W. Sypher ed., *Comedy* (Baltimore, 1980), 105.
3   See F.T. Marinetti, "Manifesto tecnico della letteratura futurista," in L. De Maria ed., *Teoria e invenzione futurista* (Milano, 1968), 40-48.
4   Benjamin, "The Work of Art in the Age of Mechanical Reproduction," 244.
5   By J. Baudrillard see especially the section entitled "L'ordre des simulacres" in his *L'Echange symbolique et la mort* (Paris, 1976), 77-128.
6   Benjamin, "The Work of Art in the Age of Mechanical Reproduction," 231 ff.
7   S. Freud, "The 'Uncanny'," *Standard Edition of the Complete Psychological Works of Sigmund Freud*. Vol. XVII (1917-1919), trans. J. Strachey (London, 1955), 219-52.
8   S. Freud, "Beyond the Pleasure Principle," *Standard Edition*. Vol. XVIII (1920-22). See 18-23, 44-61.
9   The term "en abyme" (whence "mise en abyme") was first used in a literary context by André Gide in 1893. See his *Journal 1889-1939* (Paris, 1948). Critically the canonical text on the subject is L. Dallenbach's *Le Récit speculaire* (Paris, 1977).
10 L. Pirandello, *On Humor*, trans. A. Illiano and D.P. Testa (Chapel Hill, 1974, 113.
11 F.M. Cornford, *The Origin of Attic Comedy* (London, 1974), 133, 136.
12 See the prologues of G. Della Porta's *La Fantesca* and Bruno's *Il Candelaio*, in *Il Teatro italiano. La commedia del Cinquecento*, Tomo III, G. Davico Bonino ed. (Torino, 1978), 152 and 299.
13 L. Castelvetro, *Commentary on Aristotle's "Poetics,"* in P. Lauter ed., *Theories of Comedy* (N.Y., 1964), 94 ff.
14 B. Croce, *Conversazioni critiche* (Bari, 1950), 44-46. But of Croce see also "L'umorismo," in *Problemi di Estetica* (Bari, 1966), 279.
15 An example is J.A.R.A.M. van Hooff's "Analisi comparata della filogenesi del riso e del sorriso," in R.A. Hinde ed. *"La comunicazione non-verbale* (Bari, 1974), 277-318.
16 M. Bakhtin, *Rabelais and His World*. trans. H. Iswolsky (Cambridge, 1968), 82. But see also the chapters on "The Grotesque Image of the Body," 303-67 and on the "Images of the Material Bodily Lower Stratum," 368-436.
17 Georges Bataille's aphoristic comments on laughter are dispersed throughout his works. Particularly à propos are those in *L'Expérience intérieure. Oeuvres Complètes*. Vol. V, Tome I (Paris, 1973), 106-08, 113 and the sections entitled "La divinité du rire" and "Deux fragments sur le rire" of *Le Coupable*, respectively 333-66 and 388-92 of the same volume of the *Oeuvres Complètes*.
18 B. Jonson, "Every Man out of his Humour," in *B. Jonson*, vol. III, C.H. Herford and P. Simpson eds. (Oxford, 1927), 432.
19 A good source for the notion of "fabula" is B. Tomachevsky, "Thématique," in T. Todorov ed., *Théorie de la littérature: Textes des formalistes russes* (Paris, 1965), 263-307.
20 *La Calandria*, 11.
21 J. Ricardou, "L'Escalade de l'autoreprésentation," *Texte*, I (1982), 15.
22 Cornford, *The Origin of Attic Comedy*, 141-42, 148.
23 Good instances are Fessenio's parody of lovers' language, as usual of Stilnovista-Petrarchan derivation, in *La Calandria*, 24-25, and Corcovizzo's Barra's and Sanguino's parody of the Pedant Manfurio's Latin in *Il candelaio*, *Teatro italiano* Tomo III, 240 ff. Very common are the servants' distortions of terms often associated with specific trades or professions. They are not always malapropistic. See the parasite Morfeo's transformation of "bucolica," which defines a literary genre, into "buccolica," which plays on the assonance with "bocca," ("mouth"), in *La Fantesca*, *Teatro italiano*. Tomo III, 329.
24 See the various allusions to theatre in Bruno's *Il Candelaio*, 262, 280, 291. Of some relevance is the fact that in Italian Renaissance comedy the term "trama" ("plot"), is also used to mean "trickery," "prank." The best example is in *La Calandria*, 60, 80.

25 *La Calandria*, 48, 60.

26 N. Frye, *A Natural Perspective* (New York, 1965), 72.

27 W. Shakespeare, "The Comedy of Errors," in *The Complete Shakespeare*, ed. by G.B. Harrison (New York, 1952), 274.

28 Ibid., 280.

29 Ibid., 288.

30 What I have kept in mind here is the philosophy of Saul Kripke and, specifically, his "Identity and Necessity," in M.K. Munitz ed., *Identity and Individuation* (New York, 1971), 135-63. The term "rigid designator" occurs on p. 145. As for the importance of names in Shakespeare's *Comedy of Errors*, that it is considerable is evident from Aegeon's speech in the first scene, when he explains how his lost sons "could not be distinguished but by names," 272.

31 This is a point that deserves more in-depth attention than it has received in this paper. I have emphasized the element of surprise, the relation between the circumstances –wholly unexpected– and the hero's project. Those interested in the psychoanalysis of Renaissance comedy are certain to find the result of the disguise suggestive in other ways. But, apart from this, two aspects, should, I think, be noted. The symbolical bisexuality of the disguised hero or heroine, with its Platonic reminiscences, is one of the features that bring the two plot-types closer together. When they are brother and sister, the twins form a set, are the androgynous whole which in Plato's myth humankind has lost. The disguised hero or heroine, who is biologically of one sex and symbolically of another, experiences that condition individually. Finally, the sexual disguise heightens, usually, the heroine's plight. She chooses the masculine identity to avoid problems but adds to them. In the comparison between the genders woman comes off the worst, since she must either reveal her true identity or fully act out her disguise and do things she cannot do. See Lidia's comment on this, when Perillo asks her to marry his daughter, in *La Calandria*, 28.

32 H.R. Jauss, "On Why the Comic Hero Amuses," in *Aesthetic Experience and Literary Hermeneutics*, trans. M. Shaw (Minneapolis, 1983), 195.

33 N. Machiavelli, *The Prince*, trans. G. Bull (Penguin Books, 1981), 130 ff.

34 Practically every play in which sexual satisfaction is the hero's objective contains passages attesting of love's powers. See for example, in Tomo I of *Teatro italiano. La Commedia del Cinquecento*, 15 (*La Calandria*), 108 (Machiavelli's *La Mandragola*); 161 (L. Ariosto's *La Lena*); in Tomo II: 17 (F. Belo's *Il Pedante*); 347 (Caro's *Gli Strraccioni*); in Tomo III: 168 (*Il Candelaio*); 307 (*La Fantesca*). In the other plot-type twinship, a biological anomaly, is itself an indication of the non-rational motivation of the hero's search.

35 I am thinking especially of Donald Maddox and his remarkable *The Semiotics of Deceit* (London and Toronto, 1984). Maddox reaches by other routes, by relying on the work of authors as diverse as A-J. Greimas, J. Kristeva, M. Foucault, conclusions about the structure of *Maistre Pathelin* not dissimilar from those espoused here about the structure of Renaissance comedy. On p. 162 he states: "*Pathelin* features a nondisjunctive axiology whereby the actors are normally devious and the deceived struggle to exchange roles with the deceived. Consequently, the closure of *Pathelin*, like that of the deceiver-deceived story, contains a latent disequilibrium: for every deceiver there is necessarily a deceived party, whence the potential for a renewed struggle between the actors who occupy these two roles." For me the latency of the disequilibrium, the fact that officially Renaissance culture does not recognize it, is as much a part of the data as the existence of the disequilibrium.

36 I am referring, again, to Maddox's study. This is not the place to carry out a full length analysis of the notion of *episteme* and of Kristeva's reading of Bakhtin's notion of carnival, both of which underlie, in Maddox's reasoning, the idea that the modern begins, epistemically, in the Renaissance. For the moment I will only say this: if non-disjunctiveness is, as I feel it is, built-in to comedy, then, with comedy at least, also other criteria must apply.

37 A discussion of tragicomedy and linguistic mixture can be found in G. Folena, "La mistione tragicomica e la metamorfosi dello stile nella poetica del Guarini," in *La critica stilistica e il Barocco letterario* (Firenze, 1958), 344-59. For the moral preoccupations that accompany the Renaissance's treatment of the ludicrous; the pages by L. Castelvetro or A.S. Minturno anthologized by Lauter are eloquent enough. See his *Theories of Comedy*, 77 ff. and 86 ff.
38 O. Ducrot, "Referente," in *Enciclopedia Einaudi*, Vol. XI (Torino, 1980), 705.
39 L. Pirandello, *It Is So! (If you Think So)*, in *Naked Masks*, ed. by E. Bentley (New York, 1952), 102.
40 Ibid., 138.

Green Plots and Hawthorn Brakes: Towards a Definition of Performance Space in the Renaissance

Leanore Lieblein
McGill University

The space that a play occupies cannot be defined by the playhouse in which it is performed or contained by the stage on which it is acted. Though the Renaissance was an age that witnessed the construction of permanent playing places and the revival of theatres in the classical sense, plays continued to be played, then as now, in a variety of settings, informal and official. Glynne Wickham's use of the word "stages" in his monumental study of early English theatre draws attention to a historical flexibility in the definition of performance places which survives into the Renaissance and beyond.[1]

But a play not only takes up or "fills" space; it also generates and redefines it. In order to examine the nature of the space occupied by the Renaissance play in performance it is necessary to look beyond the boards both to the play itself and to the context of its performance. This paper takes a preliminary look at some of the factors other than the stage —factors such as the language of the play, the physical and social contexts of the performance, and the relationship between the play and its audience— which help to create the space occupied by a Renaissance play.

I

When Shakespeare's mechanicals come together in the wood near Athens to rehearse their interlude, they are quick to adapt the available space to their needs:

> Here's a marvellous convenient place for our rehearsal. This green plot shall be our stage, this hawthorn brake our tiring house, and we will do it in action as we will do it before the Duke. (*MND*, III, i, 2-5)[2]

For all the innovation and advances in the construction of theatres in the Renaissance, Peter Quince is quite right to recognize that it does not take much to make a theatre. The simple act of naming makes possible the transformation of a green plot into a stage and of a hawthorn brake into a dressing room. Language is the instrument of the actor's as of the poet's imagination:

> And as imagination bodies forth
> The forms of things unknown, the poet's pen

Turns them to shapes, and gives to airy nothing
A local habitation and a name. (*MND*, V, i, 14-17)

Words in dramatic discourse designate; they turn a space into a place:
a clearing becomes a stage and a stage a given location. Nouns, pronouns
(especially demonstratives), spatial and temporal adverbs—all contribute
to the creating, through the process of deixis on the stage, the sense of time
and place.[3] It is naming that creates the fiction of place,[4] and even though
Quince is a carpenter, it is his only tool.

The dramatic language does its job whether the stage is backed by
the screen of a Tudor Hall, the unadorned facade of an Elizabethan public
theatre or a Spanish Golden Age *corral*, the painted hanging of a booth stage,
the mansions of the *Mémoire de Mahelot*, or the elaborate perspective designs
of a Serlio and their three-dimensional realizations in the wing and shutter
stagings of the late Renaissance. No matter how stylized or "realistic,"
the sense of place in the Renaissance, as on other stages, transforms its
space. It is a fiction created by the discourse as much as by the decor and
acceded to by the audience.

This sense of the stage as fluid is underscored by its metaphoric
reverberations in the Renaissance. Because all the world is thought to be
a stage and the stage represents the world—it is not irrelevant that
Shakespeare's theatre is called the Globe, one must look beyond the boards
for a sense of the stage in the Renaissance.[5]

Thus, though the discourse may be supplemented by such material
extension as a set, it does not necessarily require it:

How sweet the moonlight sleeps upon this bank!
.   .   .   Look how the floor of heaven
Is thick inlaid with patens of bright gold. (*Merch. V*, V, i. 54; 58-59)

The moonlight, the bank, and the star-studded heavens are a creation of
the language, which extends the theatre's space. That space can be enlarged, in fact, to include not only that which is imagined to be present, but
also that which is imagined to be absent:[6]

I know a bank where the wild thyme blows,
Where the oxlips and the nodding violet grows,
Quite over-canopied with luscious woodbine,
With sweet musk-roses, and with eglantine. (*MND*, II, i, 249-52)

Often, in the Renaissance, the sense of place, whether in the daylight
of an Elizabethan public theatre or in the candlelight of a private one, resides
in the language. It is suggested in the poetic image and completed in the
imagination of the spectator. In fact, to provide a material equivalent for
the language is to undercut it. When the mechanicals call for a calendar
and look in the almanac to "find out moonshine," (*MND*, III, i, 46), they
destroy the metaphor of "the silver bow/ New-bent in heaven" (*MND*,
I, i, 9-10) which is to preside over the marriage of Theseus and Hippolyta.
When they bring the moon onto the stage, the audience cannot imagine

it, for the very presence of the moon makes such participatory imaginative activity redundant:

> Sweet moon, I thank thee for thy sunny beams;
>   I thank thee, moon, for shining now so bright;
> For by thy gracious, golden, glittering gleams,
>   I trust to take of truest Thisby sight. (*MND*, V, i, 265-68)

The presence of Robin Starveling the Tailor with his lantern, thornbush and dog interferes with whatever the "gracious, golden, glittering gleams" might have suggested to a listener.

Viewed this way, dramatic language is a transaction that requires the participation of the audience to complete the creation of the play's sense of place. Hence traditional separations between the space of the actors and that of the audience are misleading. As we shall see, Renaissance plays and their conditions of performance make it impossible to maintain such separation.

II

Relatively little is known about the stage history of *A Midsummer Night's Dream*. If, as is often supposed, it was commissioned for a wedding celebration at Whitehall or in some great house,[7] it might have been presented in precisely the same circumstances as the "tedious brief scene of young Pyramus/ And his love Thisby" enacted within the play.

Performance in a great house would have been more intimate than in a public theatre, but both *Pyramus and Thisby* and *A Midsummer Night's Dream* can readily be made to work—though differently—in a clearing in a wood or in the "round" of an English public theatre with its apron stage as well as in the hall of a great house. Indeed, though it is true that the Banqueting House in Whitehall differs from, say, the Theatre or the Curtain, just as the pageants on which the *autos sacramentales* were performed differ from the *corrales*, we know that plays from one kind of theatre were readily transferable to another. The King's Men moved easily between the Second Blackfriars and the Globe, and Shergold cites numerous examples of *autos* performed in varying venues.[8]

One of the most fruitful activities of recent theatre historians has been the attempt to reconstruct Renaissance playing places.[9] We now have in many cases quite concrete information on the shape of the stage, the dimensions of the theatre, the location of the audience, the nature (or absence) of the scenery. On the whole, such activity has reinforced a number of polarities that have proven immensely suggestive over the years: indoor versus outdoor, fixed versus moving, court or private versus public, proscenium versus apron or arena, single versus multiple or successive locations, and so on. But polarization encourages, as well, a perception of actors as separate from audience and of national literatures as separate from one another.

I believe that such oppositions are helpful to our understanding of Renaissance drama and useful to our teaching of it. However, the refinements in our knowledge of different Renaissance stages have made it easy to overlook their similarities. The raised stage which was essential to the old scaffold and booth staging remained a feature of English, French, Italian and Spanish theatres, indoor and out. The proscenium arch which framed the stage picture was essential to the development of perspective sets which travelled from Italy to elsewhere, and there is evidence in more than one country for the informal arena staging of the theatrically unmodified domestic hall. In other words, the basic configurations of playing space transcend national boundaries.

There is undoubtedly a reciprocal relationship between a play and the playing space for which it is destined and in which it is performed.[10] Nevertheless, Richard Southern's suggestion that in England at least there is continuity between the trestle and scaffold of the outdoor booth stage of the medieval mysteries, moralities and farces, the Tudor dining hall performances of interludes, the wooden "O's" of the public theatres with their apron stages, and the indoor staging of the private playhouses should make us wary of oversimplifying the differences.[11]

Southern's reminder of the interconnectedness of the many forms of English theatre in the Renaissance is related to Cesare Molinari's caution that the Italian theatre of the sixteenth century was not so different from its predecessors as might seem. Similarly, Brian Jeffery argues for a reconciliation of the stage conceptions of Mahelot, Serlio, and the Valenciennes Passion. And for all the differences, John J. Allen proposes numerous similarities between the Corral del Príncipe in Madrid and the London Playhouses of the same period.[12]

In exploring the similarities and differences between theatres and the plays performed in them, we must consider more than the dimensions of the structure or the shape of the space. The space occupied by a dramatic performance is not only nor always material and measurable. It is an exclusive property neither of the *scène* nor of the *salle*, but a product of the interaction between them. Thus its boundaries are fluid and shifting and difficult to define.

Take the example of the booth stage which survived from the middle ages and earlier well into the modern period in Europe. In paintings of outdoor performances from the sixteenth and seventeenth centuries several things become apparent. The first is that no depiction of the stage is possible apart from its context. We see not only the auditors, the actors and the stage, but the square in which they stand and the buildings that surround them. The actors, as one might expect, are posturing and gesturing. (Often one can make surmises about the play they are meant to be performing.) But so are the spectators. A number have their eyes fixed on the stage or on the actors who may have descended from the stage to the place below, but others are looking elsewhere and doing other things. Children play and fight; adults chastise them. Conversational groupings suggest that gossip, courtship, and business are being carried on.

In such a situation, what are the boundaries of the "theatre"? Are they the dimensions of the stage? Or of the market place? Or, since in every illustration some spectators are more attentive than others, are the boundaries the limits of the auditors' attention, whatever their distance from the stage?[13]

The theatre does not exist apart from its context, its community, and its occasion. For example, attempts to reconstruct theatrical spaces in the Renaissance must rely on contextual evidence—information about the outside— in order to get some sense of the inside. Thus Richard Hosley in his discussion of the Swan Playhouse reproduces no fewer than half a dozen seventeenth-century views of the theatre in order to sift through the conflicting evidence for the shape of the structure.[14] However, regardless of the theatre's shape in any given illustration, again and again one sees not only the theatre but its surroundings: the houses, shops, churches, parks, and of course the river, which make up its neighbourhood.[15] Similarly when John J. Allen reconstructs the Corral del Príncipe, he must reconstruct the architecture and ownership of adjacent buildings as well in order to resolve questions of access, seating, and sight lines.[16]

III

If the boundaries of the theatre are difficult to define, the same can be said for the boundaries of the "stage" which are violated every time a character addresses the audience. Such violation of the stage boundary is institutionalized in the Prologue which, in a Renaissance comedy, frequently addresses the audience, whether to invite them to enjoy themselves or to tell about the play. We find this in numerous plays, among them *Les Corrivaus* by Jean de la Taille, *Les Contens* by Odet de Turnèbe, *L'Assiuolo* by Cecchi, and *L'Alessandro* by Piccolomini, just to take examples from plays that have appeared in the Carleton Renaissance Plays in Translation Series.[17] By doing so the play concedes its dependence on the presence and appreciation of the audience in the theatre. The Prologue in these cases acknowledges the separate worlds of play and audience, but mediates between them, insisting upon their interaction.[18]

It is also common for the audience to be coextensive with the world of the play: "Most of you out there must have known the scruffy scoundrels, the two brothers from Chios, Giovanni and Battista," begins Caro's *Gli Straccioni*.[19] "But I must ask you to be quiet if you want to be let in on it, for I see Master Josse coming up behind me; don't let him suspect anything," warns the Prologue of *Les Esbahis* by Jacques Grévin.[20] In this case it is not just the stage, but implicitly the space occupied by the audience as well, which is embraced by the play's fiction, since the spectators are addressed as neighbours and acquaintances of the protagonists. That the play's fiction spills over into the experience of the audience is visually implied as well in Serlio's 1540 perspective designs for the comic and tragic scenes. The front of the stage platform, which is decorated to form part of the scenic facade (a city wall?), contains steps that lead down into the audience, suggesting the continuity of the two spaces.[21]

In fact the spectator may typically not only share the world and the space of the play, but be an actor in it. For example, epilogues which invite applause may be detachable from their plays, but they may also make the audience instrumental in the play's resolution. When at the end of *The Tempest* Prospero asks the audience to "release me from my bands/ With the help of your good hands," (*Tmp.*, Epil. 9-10) and send him back to Naples, he makes the ending of the play depend on the collaboration of the spectators. Prospero remains a prisoner until the audience's indulgence "set[s him] free" (Epil. 20).[22]

As you see, I agree with Jan Mukarovský that "the stage and the auditorium [are] a single whole from the standpoint of dramatic space . . . [which] takes over the entire theater and is created in the spectator's consciousness during the production."[23] Thus in the notion of dramatic space the material and imaginative aspects of drama meet.

This is especially true of Renaissance theatres where, though the demarcation of the stage is usually very clear, it is at least as easy for the spectators to see each other as it is for them to see the actors and the stage, especially in outdoor daylight performances, but also indoors, since I know of no evidence for different light levels for stage and hall. Indeed spectators are known to have shared the stage with the actors in some situations. There are numerous satiric allusions to conspicuously distracting gallants seated on the Elizabethan and Jacobean stage. John J. Allen argues that spectators were also seated on the stage of the Corral del Príncipe. And the oldest surviving depiction of the interior of an English public theatre, the De Witt drawing of the Swan, has produced contention about whether the boxes behind the stage, because they are visually so much a part of the play, are seating for spectators or acting space for performers.[24]

As we have seen, a play does not exist apart from the space it both creates and occupies, in other words, apart from the theatre in its community and a potential or actual performance. Playing space is as much a function of the dramatic discourse as it is of the size and shape of the stage. It depends as much on the context of a performance and the attention of an audience as it does on the dimensions of a theatre. It resides, therefore, in the interaction of all of these.

NOTES

1 Glynne Wickham, *Early English Stages 1300 to 1600*, I (London and New York, 1963), passim.
2 All Shakespeare quotations are from *The Complete Pelican Shakespeare*, gen. ed. Alfred Harbage (Baltimore, 1969). Act, scene, and line numbers will be given in parentheses in the text.
3 Keir Elam, *The Semiotics of Theatre and Drama* (London and New York, 1980), 138-48 and passim.
4 Albert Einstein, "Forward," *Concepts of Space: The History of Theories of Space in Physics* (Cambridge, Mass., 1954), xiii-xiv. I am grateful to Darko Suvin for directing me to this and to other theoretical materials and for allowing me to benefit from his own work on dramaturgical space.
5 Anne Righter, *Shakespeare and the Idea of the Play* (1962, rpt. Harmondsworth, Middlesex, 1967), 59-78. I also wish to thank Leslie T. Duer for discussion of this and related points.
6 Alluded to by Jan Mukarovský, "On the Current State of the Theory of the

Theatre," *Structure, Sign, and Function* (New Haven, 1978), 214.

7   Anne Barton, Introduction to *A Midsummer Night's Dream*, The Riverside Shakespeare, gen. ed. G. Blakemore Evans (Boston, 1974), 217.

8   N.D. Shergold, *A History of the Spanish Stage from Medieval Times Until the End of the Seventeenth Century* (Oxford, 1967), 360 and passim.

9   For a bibliographical summary see J. Leeds Barroll, Alexander Leggatt, Richard Hosley, Alvin Kernan, *The "Revels" History of Drama in English, Vol. III, 1576-1613* (London, 1975), 482-87.

10 It is fruitful to examine Renaissance plays of different countries from the perspective of their different conditions of performance. The difference between the *Architettura* of Serlio and the *Mémoire* of Mahelot, which, despite the years that separate them, are a repository of sustained theatrical traditions, can illuminate the development of Italian and French drama respectively. Or recent attempts to reconstruct the Swan and other theatres in London and the Corral del Príncipe in Madrid can similarly shed light on the plays that were performed there.

11 Richard Hosley in Vol. III of *The "Revels" History of Drama in English*, op. cit., 124-35; See also Richard Southern, "The technique of play presentation," *The "Revels" History of Drama in English, Vol. II, 1500-1576* by Norman Sanders, Richard Southern, T.W. Craik, Lois Potter (London, 1980), 72 ff.

12 Cesare Molinari, "Les Rapports entre la scène et les spectateurs dans le théâtre italien du XVIe siècle," *Le Lieu théâtral à la Renaissance*, ed. Jean Jacquot (Paris, 1964), 63; Brian Jeffery, *French Renaissance Comedy 1552-1630* (Oxford, 1969), 64-73; John J. Allen, *The Reconstruction of a Spanish Golden Age Playhouse: El Corral del Príncipe 1583-1744* (Gainesville, 1983), 111-17.

13 Richard Schechner argues for what he calls "selective inattention," as an important feature of the audience's role in performances. His approach accounts for differences in the attentiveness of individual spectators and different degrees of collective attention at different points in the performance. "Selective Inattention," *Essays on Performance Theory 1970-1976* (New York, 1977), 140-56.

14 Hosley, op. cit., 137-41.

15 For an interesting study of a Renaissance theatre in its community, see William Ingram, " 'Neere the Playe Howse': The Swan Theater and Community Blight," *Renaissance Drama*, n.s. 4 (1971), 53-68.

16 Allen, op. cit., 52-69.

17 Jean de La Taille, *The Rivals (Les Corrivaus)*, trans. H. Peter Clive (Waterloo, Ontario, 1981); Odet de Turnèbe, *Satisfaction All Around (Les Contens)*, trans. D.A. Beecher (Ottawa, 1979); Giovan Maria Cecchi, *The Horned Owl (L'Assiuolo)*, trans. Konrad Eisenbichler (Waterloo, Ontario, 1981); Alessandro Piccolomini, *Alessandro (L'Alessandro)*, trans. Rita Belladonna (Ottawa, 1984).

18 Donald K. Hedrick, in an unpublished essay, "Risking Audience: Shakespeare and the Ideology of Epilogue," explores the ideological force of such mediation in his discussion of Shakespeare's epilogues which he analyzes for what they reveal about "the rhetorical and cultural situation of [the play's] production, significance, and strategies of thought."

19 Annibal Caro, *The Scruffy Scoundrels (Gli Straccioni)*, trans. Massimo Ciavolella and Donald Beecher, Carleton Renaissance Plays in Translation (Waterloo, Ontario, 1980), 3.

20 Jacques Grévin, *Taken By Surprise (Les Esbahis)*, trans. Leanore Lieblein and Russell McGillivray, Carleton Renaissance Plays in Translation (Ottawa, 1985).

21 Molinari, op. cit., 67.

22 The difference between a Renaissance and modern production was brought home in a 1975 performance of this play in a London West End theatre. Paul Scofield as Prospero put himself at the mercy of the audience but they did not

applaud, in spite of the seemingly endless wait, until the stage was darkened. Then the applause was deafening, but it was a technician, and not the spectators, who had ended the play.

23 Mukarovský, op. cit., 214-15.

24 Richard Hosley, "The Gallery over the Stage in the Public Playhouse of Shakespeare's Time," *Shakespeare Quarterly*, VIII (1957), 15-31, argues that they were used for both.

The Search for a Formula: Spanish Theatre at the End of the 16th Century

Louise Fothergill-Payne
University of Calgary

In all of Europe, but especially in Spain, the last quarter of the 16th century sees immense development and change in the theatre. It is a time of experimenting with new techniques and ways of expression, of establishing literary theories and seeking theatrical formulas. Poets from all walks of life try their hand at writing comedies and tragedies, the Jesuit schoolmasters produce countless plays in their colleges, and the church stages sumptuous morality plays at its Corpus Christi festivities. Meanwhile troupes go from village to village with their varied repertoire of comedies, religious plays and interludes, and the city's *intelligentsia* recite their poems and plays in the newly established literary *academias*.[1]

Although Spain's nobility continued a tradition of staging private performances in their great halls, the austere court of Philip II was adverse to the theatre; in fact, the King actively discouraged and, at one time, banned public performances. However, the absence of royal patronage, rather than stifling the growth of a national theatre, encouraged playwrights to seek a new way of expression eminently suited to the demands of the man in the street. And here, we see two seemingly opposing forces at work: the church and the municipalities, who, employing the same playwrights and the same actors, would eventually produce two uniquely Spanish art-forms: the *auto sacramental* and the *comedia nueva*.

Before the secular stage had come into its own, the church, inspired by counter-reformationary zeal and responding to public demand, had made live theatre the centrepiece of its Corpus Christi procession. Originally, the plays written for these occasions were simple, one-act compositions, Renaissance descendants of the medieval mystery and morality play. Towards the end of the 16th century, however, these plays gradually grew in dramatic impact, until, in the 17th century, they would become intricate philosophical allegorizations of man's struggle for salvation, comparable to Milton's *Paradise Lost* and *Paradise Regained*. For this religious stage, playwrights at first experimented with some full-fledged tragedy such as the semi-allegorical presentation of the Judas story, conceived along authentic Senecan lines of violence and bloodshed. But more popular and efficient proved to be a development of the morality play which more and more focused on the tragi-comic figure of man—man as fool, but also as victim of conflicting passions and battlefield of his own inner struggle. The constrictions of time and space imposed by the occasion of the religious procession and the necessity to cater to the tastes of different levels of reception and comprehension in the audience, would, in the end, create an ingenious mix of entertainment and sermon, of comedy and tragedy: the *auto sacramental.*[2]

In this entirely allegorical, one-act, play, the comedy of "Man the fool" turns into the tragedy of his hopeless struggle against himself only to end on a joyful note with the intervention of an all-forgiving Grace. Obviously Spanish audiences enjoyed comedy mixed with tragedy resolving in comedy; they expected, and found, a serious conflict portrayed in the *chiaroscuro* of a tragicomedy: they came for a laugh and a tear, suspense, relief and finally a deeply religious sense of order restored.

The plots go back to the medieval prototype of everyman and elkerlijk, often abstracted as the soul, a composite protagonist of body and soul or simply humankind. The great antagonist, of course, is the devil in all his tempting disguises and manifestations whose role, at times, reaches truly tragic dimension: as that of the suitor whose love will ultimately be rejected or the salesman who is bound to lose his business. Most interesting in these plays, however, is the development of the plot, the temptation itself, which becomes a complex interplay of psychological tensions, doubts and depressions pertaining to man's relentless pursuit of wordly delights and rewards.

What caught the audiences' attention most in these short plays was perhaps the conscious or unconscious sensation that in the protagonist each spectator recognized himself. Thus, the portrayal of the *psychomachia* brought home some everyday concerns such as the honour question, the problem of infidelity and revenge, simple vanity or hidden ambition, and all this presented in a contemporary setting of easily recognizable circumstances.

The formula was a happy one as it relied heavily on the spectator's own frame of reference. Making the audience his target, the playwright portrayed each spectator's personal experience of the inner struggle in vivid and often scary detail, but, like the priest in a sermon, sent him away with a message of hope and forgiveness. The protagonist was still, essentially, Everyman; his world, however, was darkened by anxieties and desires set against a background of Ptolemaean cosmology. In keeping with this view, man was the centre of the universe and solely responsible for the proper order and functioning of all its parts and elements. Needless to say, man invariably failed to fulfil this sublime mission, but, rather than portraying his fall from grace in bitterly sombre colours, the playwrights exemplified man's weaknesses in satirical and always comical scenes enlivened by song and dance. However, desperation soon takes over which, in turn, dissolves in the final apotheosis of the church triumphant.

In accordance with this grandiose conception, which at times encompasses the creation and destruction of the universe, the staging of these plays would reach unprecedented levels of ingenuity and technology. Multi-story towers framed the movable platforms that flanked the centre-stage, and revolving globes indicated the heavenly spheres while mountains, lakes and caves represented the world and its infernal consequences.[3] As the platforms were moved from district to district, each segment of the population would get its share of the spectacle. In solemn procession the "carros," as the platforms were known, would start in front of the palace to finish in the poorer quarters of the town. But whether the performance was for kings or paupers, the message was the same, while the allegory allowed several interpretations according to each spectator's level of comprehension.

In short, the *auto sacramental* was able to come up with a successful formula thanks to the well-defined role it played in the life of, literally, everyman. Following the religious theatre and often profiting from its advanced stage-craft, the secular plays rapidly grew in importance and scope as well. One major factor in the development of the stage was the arrival, in 1574, of the Italian *commedia dell'arte* player Alberto Ganassa who, sensing the enormous potential of a bourgeois public, concentrated all his attention on the urban scene. Within a few years he managed to convert the primitive patios, leased by hospitals for charitable purposes, into full scale commercial play-houses with a permanent stage for the actors and seats for the audience.[4] Ganassa's enterprising spirit was more than matched by the public's enthusiasm. Documents of the time show a staggering number of plays produced in the *corrales* as the playhouses were called. It is said that dramatic productions in Spain, at that time, exceeded the total of performances in all other European countries combined. Obviously, drama in Spain was taken seriously and the theatre-going public was to play a decisive role in its development. But the search for a formula in the secular drama did not come to a happy ending quite so soon, due in part to the mistaken idea the playwrights had of their role and that of the audience. Essentially, they viewed the public as a passive recipient that had to be instructed rather than delighted or moved. Pathos, sprung from the literary academies of Valencia, Seville and Madrid, would set the tone in the eighties, and tragedy was the favourite form chosen.[5] Preoccupied with the current *ars poetica* and faced with classical models, the poets of the time hovered between accepting and rejecting Aristotelian precepts. Choruses and allegorical figures would comment on situations, messengers speeded up the action, magic, dreams and ghosts prophesied disaster and gods interfered in the affairs of man. Each of the playwrights experimented with poetic precepts and each claimed to be an innovator in points of detail. But their efforts soon faded in the presence of the newcomer, Lope de Vega (1562-1635), who proposed a revolutionary albeit simplified style. Even so, Lope could not have come up with the ultimate formula without the experiments of the so-called *pre-lopescos*. Of this group three names stand out: the Valencian Cristobal De Virués (1550?-1614), the Sevillian Juan de la Cueva (1543-1610) and the Castillian Miguel de Cervantes (1547-1616).

Virués mainly wrote tragedies in which he portrays strong women either as rulers or as victims of complicated political intrigue. What is interesting in these plays is the author's attempt to justify his approach. In more than one tragedy Virués theorizes on his craft, especially where he challenges Aristotle's unities or explains the need to reduce the five acts to three. Also representative of his generation is the mention of the exemplary nature of his plays. For Virués, what is portrayed on stage should be understood as "an exaggerated image of reality" ("lo vivo se entienda ser en término excesivo"). This line has prompted some critics to look for a political message in late 16th-century plays and, indeed, this certainly seems to be true in the case of the Sevillian playwright Juan de la Cueva who, in his fourteen *comedias* and *tragedias*, sets out to convey a deeper, political message. Perhaps the most famous of his works is the *Comedia del infamador*, which presents the figure of a tyrannical and perverse youth, a character sharply contrasted with the nobility and innocence of his female victim. A detailed study of the play has brought to light that Juan de la Cueva consciously wanted to dramatize the controversial and much criticized invasion of Portugal by Philip II.[6]

Juan de la Cueva also theorized on his art and wrote down his ideas in a poetic treatise written twenty years after his dramatic compositions. In his *Poet's Guide* (the *Ejemplar poético*) he takes his stand in the controversy that was raging through Europe on the question of whether art was conceivable without rules. Like the *anciens et modernes* in France, in Spain the neo-Aristotelians, headed by El Pinciano, upheld classical models in the face of the opposing camp who advocated a free style in tune with modern times and modern audiences.[7] Juan de la Cueva, aware of Lope de Vega's success as a new man, did not want to seem old-fashioned. In fact, he claims to have been an innovator himself in blending comedy and tragedy, presenting kings and gods in comedies and using national rather than classical themes as subject-matter. On the other hand, his ideas on the superiority of the poet still make him a member of that 16th-century humanist élite that wrote to instruct the ignorant layman. However, it would be wrong to assume that Juan de la Cueva, looking down from the heights of his ivory tower, disregarded his public.

On the contrary, he defines the *comedia* as "a poem full of action, cheerful and made to give pleasure" (un poema activo, risueño y hecho para dar contento"). Even so, his definition shows how he still considered drama as part of poetry —"un poema activo"— an attitude he shared with most humanist playwrights in Europe. As such, he gave all his attention to words, stressing the importance of *decoro*, that is to say, the appropriateness of the spoken word to the character portrayed, the fluidity of the lyrics and the didactic content of the verse. Most significant in his attitude to his public, however, is his insistence that the mode of expression should be different in every way from common speech "since poets speak a tongue that differs from the peasant folk" ("pues hablan los poetas en otra lengua que la ruda gente"). Thus distancing himself from his audience, he again brands himself as an *ancien* in spite of his innovations and plea for freedom.

Cervantes, equally, failed to grasp the true nature of drama as a performance aimed at an audience. But then, drama had not been defined as a separate genre in Cervantes' days. If most literary theories distinguished between the epic, lyric and dramatic parts of the *ars poetica*, it was more to designate moods than techniques. In his plays, Cervantes clearly leans towards the epic mood of poetic expression, in itself not so surprising considering that the distinguishing feature of the epic form is the narrative, an art in which Cervantes was finally to excel. Unaware of his talents in that direction though, the young Cervantes set out to make his fortune out of the theatre boom that was sweeping the capitals of Spain.[8] Of his early plays, two still remain that have much to offer the reader, but which are lacking in dramatic know-how. In *The Siege of Numantia* (*El cerco de Numancia*) Cervantes records the events leading up to the population's decision to commit mass suicide rather than surrender to Roman occupation. In *The Algerian Dealings* (*Los tratos de Argel*) he describes the captives' plight in a Moorish concentration camp, an account that is largely autobiographical.

Both are moving plays. The first ends in sacrifice and, therefore, could be called a "tragedy" were it not for the allegorical representation of Spain prophesying the country's ultimate (16th-century) greatness. *The Algerian Dealings*, on the other hand, ends like a *comedia* with the captives' jubilant departure for home, but the tone is tragic, as accounts of death and torture are followed by scenes of separation, betrayal, temptation and agonizing soul-searching presented in allegorical form. In both plays, the main plot disappears behind the long moral and political *exposés* and the action is cut up in loosely related episodes. In fact, the structure of Cervantes' plays foreshadows his technique employed in the *Don Quijote* where an ever greater number of characters appear on the scene, each with a story to tell. That, as would become clear, works for a long novel, but not for the stage with its constrictions of time and space.

It took a born actor to see that there is more to writing plays than to telling stories or composing poetry, and this, more than anything else, explains why Cervantes failed and Lope de Vega succeeded in coming up with the ultimate formula.[9] Cervantes, at first, despised Lope's new style and did not hesitate to voice his contempt for it. In chapter 48 of *Don Quijote* Part I for instance, he calls the plays "mirrors of nonsense, examples of stupidity and images of lasciviousness," because, he says, "they do not obey the law of Art but the whims of the crowd [el vulgo]." In the end his animosity towards his rival would subside somewhat. In fact, Cervantes, later on, was to write eight *comedies* and *interludes* in the lopesque style himself. In the prologue to these plays he evokes his early days when, in his own words, he wrote "almost 20 or 30 plays which were all performed without any rotten tomatoes or other projectiles being hurled at them . . . but, I had other things to do and I stopped writing comedies. Besides, this monstrosity of Nature ["Monstruo de la naturaleza"], the great Lope de Vega came along and walked away with the crown of comedy ["la monarquía cómica"]."

And what, precisely, is this *comedia nueva*—Lope's creation and Cervantes' nemesis? Much has been said about the nature of this art form, especially in the last twenty years, when, under the impact of literary theory, new aspects and unexpected depths have been discovered in it.[10] The latest discussions on the *comedia*'s nature centre upon questions of whether it is a true *metatheatre* or *psychodrama* or both, whether it is a mere political tool or a theatre of ideas, whether some *comedias* are really tragedies or in what way, if at all, the *comedia* is "comic" since it seldom is very funny.

Lope himself had definite ideas on his craft which the Literary Academy of Madrid wanted him to make known to its members. He chose to answer the challenge in verse and called his long poem "The new art of crafting plays in this day and age." It is a masterpiece of insolence and mock humility, of defiance and self-defense. After showing due respect for the academic hero-worshiping of the ancient world, he sallies forth in a plea to be sensitive to the *vulgo*'s expectations. The resulting "state of the art" is, in actual fact, much more than the occasional piece most critics consider it to be. The very title is significant: "El Arte nuevo de hacer comedias en este tiempo."[11] It is well to ponder a little on the three elements of this title: "Arte nuevo"—the new art; "hacer comedias"—to make or "do" comedy; "en este tiempo"—these days.

Lope sets this new art against the old (by which he meant the models of Terence and Plautus and Aristotelian poetics as expounded by the Italian humanist Robortello). For Lope, however, classical precepts were wholly unsuitable if one wanted to make things work, or in other words, if one needed to live: "Whoever writes according to the art will die without fame nor money to his part." ("Que quien con arte agora las escrive muere sin fama y galardón"). Instead he proposes a new art which, on close inspection, is not as new as he would like to suggest, since it is squarely rooted in the *ars rhetorica* which he learnt at school.

As a pupil of the Jesuits, Lope took part in the frequent plays that were given in the Colleges; indeed he claims to have written his first play at the age of 12. The performance of plays was part of the normal school curriculum: in fact, the Jesuits had taken over this practice from the German *Scola Latina*, as they realized their enormous potential not only as an educational asset, but also as an effective tool of propaganda. As such, these plays, be they performed in Jesuit colleges or in Protestant grammar schools, were meant to impress the community and to attract potential benefactors and parents of new pupils, often in competition with other schools.[12] To this end, schoolmasters and pupils practised all the rules pertaining to the three principles of rhetoric which were to instruct, to delight and, above all, to move ("docere, delectare, movere"). It is very probable then, that Lope, in turning away from the academic *ars poetica*, consciously or unconsciously returned to the rules of the *ars rhetorica* which he had learned from his master of rhetoric.

For Lope, as for the rhetorician, the proper reception of the discourse was of prime importance and this, more than anything, is the message of his "Arte Nuevo." The opening lines of the treatise make this abundantly clear: "You ask me how to write plays that are well received by the common people " ("Mándanme . . . que un arte de comedias os escriva/ que al estilo del vulgo se reciba").

And indeed, the *ars rhetorica* is an eminently audience-oriented art: beyond the poet and his discourse, it aims at the all-important listener, recipient of the message. And this was the single most controversial point Lope de Vega dared to make: give the public what it wants, play on its sensibilities, manipulate if you must, but at all times keep the public in mind.

This was of course the approach the religious theatre had adopted all along and which Lope adapted to the secular drama. Thus, in spite of the resistance of his academic contemporaries, Lope's formula proved to be the more successful as it aimed, not at the skills of the poet, but the sensibilities of the recipient: "al estilo del vulgo"—"the people way."

The second part of the title also shows how Lope saw the theatre in a very different light from the *ars poetica*. He does not call his treatise the art of *writing* but of *doing* theatre: "hacer comedias." Clearly, drama for Lope was different from literature in that it is "doing things with words," a simultaneous interaction between the author, the players and the public. Lope's greatest achievement perhaps was his awareness of the fact that a play differs from a novel or poem in that it is all action, without, however, a narrator to explain or to further that action.[13] For that reason the playwright needs to use all the visual and acoustic aids afforded by a live performance to get his message across. It so happened then, that the new playhouses gave him ample scope to ponder on the limitations and possibilities of the theatre's time-space continuum. On the one hand he realized that playwrights had to adapt the length, structure and cohesion of their discourse to the two hours permitted by a well-run theatre, on the other, the improved acoustics and visibility now allowed the author to play with words and unspoken signs. And so it became possible to convey double meaning or produce dramatic irony, to make the most of asides, to create incongruency between what is seen and what is heard, and to experiment with backstage sound effects. In short, all the tricks reserved specifically to the playwright and all of which aim at instructing, delighting and moving the audience.

With all this in mind then, Lope recommends, in the first place, a good story, preferably about love and honour with virtue rewarded. For Lope, the greatest sin is to bore one's audience and so, to avoid them "looking surreptitiously to the exit" he advises that suspense should be kept up until the last act. Moreover, to engage the audience's participation to the full he suggests misleading them with the truth, to make them guess the meaning of the *double entendre* and to entertain them with puns. Language should fit the character, including that of the peasant, while obscure or highsounding verse should be avoided and satire should be subtle. As far as form is concerned, he discards the unities of time and place as implausible, but maintains unity of action to produce a well-rounded whole. The play should consist of three acts, the first exposing the plot, the second complicating it and the third containing the *dénouement*. Finally, because the action should always seem plausible, Lope bans gods, magic, allegory and choruses from the stage, while the role of the messenger becomes redundant thanks to the freedom to develop the plot without Aristotelian constrictions of time or place.

Because of these revolutionary changes, Lope turns into the undisputed master of the dramatic arts in Spain and comes to be seen as the Father of the National Theatre.

There is another reason why Lope deserves this honorary epithet and that is a detail hinted at in the last part of the title to his treatise. He promises to write an art for "este tiempo," that is to say "this day and age." Lope was aware that an enormous change had come over Spain. The 16th century had come to a close, a century in which the pen had served as weapon in order to attack, to prove and to clarify, and in which the theatre often had been a means of making a point. As a result the pre-lopesque poets wrote a didactic, highly committed and often sententious drama. By contrast, Lope insisted on the entertainment value of his art, and indeed, he shies away from the *pathos* of the tragedy to concentrate on the *ethos* of comedy. His poetry is more lyric than epic and song and dance enliven the action. But that does not make him a superficial playwright, as some literary critics have opined, nor does he become the spokesman for a repressive *régime* as some sociologists of literature like to think.[14]

It is true that many of the more than 1,800 plays attributed to Lope and of which some 400 are still extant bear the mark of hasty composition in response to an ever increasing demand. But many of Lope's plays have stood the test of changing times and tastes: *Peribáñez, Fuenteovejuna, El caballero de Olmedo, El perro del hortelano, El villano en su rincón*, and many more, are still being performed and are staple reading in any course on Golden Age Drama.

However, Lope's achievement goes beyond being a "Monstrosity of Nature" or even "Father of the National Theatre." He inspired others and created a school which produced plays such as *El burlador de Sevilla* by Tirso de Molina, *Las mocedades del Cid* by Guillén de Castro and *La verdad sospechosa* by Ruiz de Alarcón, plays that were gladly taken over by Molière and Corneille under the titles of *Don Juan, Le Cid* and *Le Menteur*. Meanwhile, Spanish plays were translated and performed in the capitals of Europe and left their mark there. In short, Lope's impact went well beyond the national borders of Spain, a fact easier to state than to explain.[15]

Lope's breakthrough, perhaps, was due to his "declaration of independence" from theory, because that was what the contemporary *"ars poetica"* amounted to: literary theories as battleground for academic debate. Lope's rebellion against the academicians and theoreticians of his time, however, was more than an act of defiance. It was a first step towards the development and practice of a genuine dramatic art. Thanks to Lope's awareness that good theatre only functions within the framework of a receptive audience, Spanish drama was able to develop independently from any "law of art" as the young Cervantes would put it.

As we have seen, the *auto sacramental* was the first to aim at full audience participation, an approach they had in common with the early school plays. Although the goals of the religious theatre were different from those of the secular drama, the technique of *comedia* and *auto*, thanks to Lope's innovations, would in the end be surprisingly alike. It is possible, then, that Lope's success as a playwright was due (but never acknowledged) to the approach to the theatre he had first encountered in his Jesuit College. And so he may well have learned from his master of rhetoric how to write a play "the people way" ("al estilo del vulgo"), a technique he was to describe half jokingly, half seriously, in his *Arte nuevo de hacer comedias en este tiempo*.

NOTES

1 J.P. Crawford, *Spanish Drama before Lope de Vega*, 2nd revised edition (Philadelphia, 1967); N.D. Shergold, *A History of the Spanish Stage* (Oxford, 1967); J. Jacquot, ed., *Dramaturgie et société. Rapports entre l'oeuvre théâtrale, son interprétation et son public au XVIe et XVIIe siècles*, 2 vols. (Paris, 1968); Margaret Wilson, *Spanish Drama of the Golden Age* (Oxford and London, 1969); Edward M. Wilson and Duncan Moir, *The Golden Age: Drama 1492-1700* (London, 1971); M. McKendrick, *Women and Society in the Spanish Drama of the Golden Age* (London, 1974); R.E. Surtz, *The Birth of a Theater. Dramatic Convention in the Spanish Theater from Juan del Encina to Lope de Vega* (Madrid, 1979); F. Ruiz Ramón, *Historia del teatro español*, I (Madrid, 1979); *Historia y crítica de la literatura española*, Francisco Rico, ed.: *Renacimiento* (Barcelona, 1980) and *Barroco* (Barcelona, 1983); The *Bulletin of the Comediantes*, the *Publications of the Modern Language Association* and *The Year's Work in Modern Language Studies* include

valuable bibliographies on Golden Age Theatre.

2 A.A. Parker, *The Allegorical Drama of Calderon* (Oxford, 1943); J.-L. Flec-
niakoska, *La formation de l'auto religieux en Espagne avant Calderon* (Montpellier,
1961); B. Wardropper, *Introducción al teatro religioso del Siglo de oro* (Salamanca,
1967); D. Th. Dietz, *The Auto Sacramental and the Parable* (Chapel Hill, 1973);
L. Fothergill-Payne, *La alegoría en los autos y farsas anteriores a Calderón* (London,
1977).

3 N.D. Shergold and J. E. Varey, *Los autos sacramentales en Madrid en la época de
Calderón 1637-1681* (Madrid, 1961). Pedro León and John Warden, *Three
Mythological Plays by Calderon* (Toronto University Press, in press).

4 Othon Arroniz, *Teatros y escenarios del siglo de oro* (Madrid, 1977); John J. Allen,
The Reconstruction of a Spanish Golden Age Playhouse: el Corral del Príncipe, 1583-1744
(Florida, 1983); David Castillejo et al., *El corral de comedias* (Madrid, 1984).

5 Henri Mérimée, *l'Art dramatique à Valencia* (Toulouse, 1913); Rinoldi Froldi,
Il teatro valenzano e l'origine della commedia barocca (Pisa, 1962), (Spanish transla-
tion: *Lope de Vega y la formación de la comedia* [Salamanca 1968]); John G. Weiger,
The Valencian Dramatists of Spain's Golden Age (New York, 1976).

6 Anthony Watson, *Juan de la Cueva and the Portuguese Succession* (London, 1971);
Richard F. Glenn, *Juan de la Cueva* (New York, 1973).

7 H.J. Chaytor, *Dramatic Theory in Spain* (Cambridge University Press, 1925);
D. Moir, "The Classical Tradition in Spanish Dramatic Theory and Practice
in the Seventeenth Century," in *Classical Drama and its Influence*, M.J. Ander-
son ed. (London, 1965), 191-228; F. Sánchez Escribano and A. Porqueras
Mayo, *Preceptiva dramática española del Renacimiento y el Barroco* (Madrid, 1967);
M. Newels, *Die Dramatischen Gattungen in dem Poetiken des Siglo de Oro* (Wiesbaden,
1959). (Spanish translation: *Los géneros dramáticos en las poéticas del siglo de oro*
[London, 1974]).

8 B. Wardropper, "Comedias," in *Suma cervantina*, J.B. Avalle-Arce and E.C.
Riley eds. (London, 1971), 147-69; Joaquín Casalduero, *Sentido y forma del teatro
de Cervantes* (Madrid, 1966); M. Durán, *Cervantes* (New York, 1974).

9 S. Morley and C. Bruerton, *The Chronology of Lope de Vega's Comedias* (New
York and London, 1940); R.D.F. Pring-Mill, Introduction to his edition of
Five Plays (New York, 1961); F.C. Hayes, *Lope de Vega* (New York, 1967).

10 A.A. Parker, "Reflections on a New Definition of Baroque Drama," *Bulletin
of Hispanic Studies* 30 (1953), 142-51; A.G. Reichenberger, "The Uniqueness
of the Comedia," *Hispanic Review*, 38 (1970), 163-73; J. Parr, "An Essay on
Critical Method Applied to the Comedia," *Hispania*, 57 (1974), 434-44; T.A.
O'Connor, "Is the Spanish 'comedia' a Metatheater?" *Hispanic Review*, 43
(1975), 275-88; E. Forastieri Braschi, *Aproximación estructural al teatro de Lope
de Vega* (Madrid, 1976).

11 Juana de José Prades, ed., *El arte nuevo de hacer comedias en este tiempo* (Madrid,
1971); Juan Manuel Rozas, *Significado y doctrina del "Arte nuevo" de Lope de Vega*
(Madrid, 1976).

12 E. Purdie, "Jesuit Drama" in *The Oxford Companion to the Theatre*, 3rd ed. (London, 1976), 508-15; Nigel Griffin, *Jesuit School Drama, a Checklist of Critical
Literature*, Research Bibliographies and Checklists, 12 (London, 1976); M.
Fumaroli, *L'âge de l'éloquence: Rhétorique et "res literaria" de la Renaissance au seuil
de l'époque classique* (Geneva, 1980).

13 M. Pfister, *Das Drama, Theorie und Analyse* (München, 1977); Elke Platz-Waury,
Drama und Theater, eine Einführung (Tübingen, 1978); L. Fothergill-Payne, "Del
carro al corral," *Revista canadiense de Estudios Hispánicos*, 72 (1983), 249-61.

14 José María Díez-Borque, *Sociología de la Comedia española del siglo XVII* (Madrid,
1976); Charlotte Stern, "Lope de Vega, Propagandist?" *Bulletin of the Comediantes*, 34, 1 (1982), 1-36.

15 E. Martinenche, *La comedia espagnole en France de Hardy à Racine* (Paris, 1900);
J.A. van Praag, *La comedia espagnole aux Pays-Bas, au XVIIe et XVIIe siècle*

(Amsterdam, 1922); Hilda U. Stubbings, *Renaissance Spain in its Literary Relations with England and France* (Nashville, 1968); Henry W. Sullivan, *Calderon in the German Lands and the Low Countries. His Reception and Influence, 1654-1980* (Cambridge, 1983).

Shakespeare and the Comedy of Revenge

James Black
The University of Calgary

Renaissance revenge tragedy is a widely recognized and clearly definable literary form whose most famous—indeed supreme—example is Shakespeare's *Hamlet*.[1] Fredson Bowers, tracing the development of revenge tragedy up to and past *Hamlet*, into its Jacobean decadence, convincingly argues that in *Hamlet* the form had developed as far as it could go.[2] Certainly after *Titus Andronicus*, his early attempt in the genre, and *Hamlet*, Shakespeare wrote no more revenge tragedies. But in the blazing sunset of his career, with *The Tempest*, he devised or accomplished a new genre—a Renaissance revenge comedy.

The Tempest is one of only three Shakespearean plays not extensively adapted from existing sources,[3] though certain minor analogues and conjectural sources have been found or suggested. Shakespeare clearly saw and in part used the Bermudan pamphlets with their accounts of the miraculous escape of the *Sea-Adventure* in 1609. These documents are Sylvester Jourdain's *Discovery of the Bermudas* (1610), the Council of Virginia's *True Declaration of the State of the Colonie in Virginia* (1610) and William Strachey's letter, the *True Reportory of the Wrack*, dated 15 July, 1610 though not published until 1625. Shakespeare's use of atmosphere and incidents from these accounts being relatively minor and having little to do with plot beyond the shipwreck and miraculous preservation of those on board, other analogous European works have been canvassed as sources. Among these are [Jacob] Ayrer's (d. 1605) *Die Schone Sidea* and the two Spanish works: Antonio de Eslava's *Noches de invierno* (1609) and Diego Ortunez de Calahorra's *Espejo de Príncipes y Caballeros* (1562, translated into English 1578, 1601). At least, it appears there are elements in these works analogous with plot incidents in *The Tempest*, and some scholars have argued with especial enthusiasm that Eslava's story is a source, but the Arden editor of Shakespeare's play considers the structure of source possibilities (which include Bulgarian, Byzantine, Latin and Italian as well as Spanish and German analogues) to be "a mare's nest."[4] *The Tempest* also has certain parallels with Commedia dell'arte scenarii, and these parallels are discussed by K.M. Lea in her *Italian Popular Comedy*. I shall be returning to Commedia possibilities, but it should be emphasised that aside from the clear borrowings from the Bermudan pamphlets all "sources" of the play are suggested or reputed only. One possibility which I think has not been canvassed adequately—and the oversight may have something to do with the enthusiasm with which source-hunters have searched outside Shakespeare—is Shakespeare's own work. Though it has no full sources, *The Tempest* has precursors in the revenge tragedies of the time, and is especially influenced by *Hamlet*.

As Ashley H. Throndike defined it, revenge tragedy is "a tragedy whose leading motive is revenge and whose main action deals with the progress of this revenge, leading to the death of the murderer and often the death of the avenger himself."[5] Thorndike notes that the revenge motive appears in the anonymous *Alphonsus of Germany* (c. 1590) and in Shakespeare's *Titus Andronicus* (also c. 1590), but after examining precursors of Shakespeare's *Hamlet* (including the earlier or Q.1 version) he suggests that Kyd's *Spanish Tragedy* and the Q.1 *Hamlet* are the main sources of later developments in the genre.[6] "From 1599 to 1604 . . . [revenge] plays were popular on the stage and . . .Marston, Chettle, Tourneur and Jonson, as well as Shakespeare, were employed in supplying the stage demand."[7] But although Sheakespeare's *Hamlet* owed its existence primarily to a marked stage fashion for revenge tragedies, Shakespeare's hero leaves "the old stage type and [rises] into that ideal sphere where imagination and reflection dwell alone."[8] As Bowers explains, the dramatists' imaginations were helped along by their reading of Italian *novelle* in translations and imitations by William Painter, George Pettie and George Turberville. In these works the Italianate revenger is a leading and impressive figure. He also flourished in Italian histories such as Guicciardini's account of *The Warres of Italie*, translated by Geoffrey Fenton in 1579. Guicciardini's is typical of the kind of "history" of continental practices which fascinated the English. He notes "the readinesse of [Italy] to . . . broiles and innovations, with the present divisions and factions of the Italians";[9] and sets out to describe how Italian princes turn "to the damage of others, the power which is given them for the common good."[10] "From the *novelle* and the non-fictional accounts of Italian life the Elizabethans took almost every dramatic device that was to be found in Seneca, and more besides," says Bowers.[11] By the 1590's stereotype Italians, Spaniards and other continentals dominated the English tragic stage with their vendettas and bloodlust. *Hamlet* is the supreme achievement of the revenge genre because Shakespeare made the issue turn on the character of the revenger; only in *Hamlet*, as Eleanor Prosser has it, do we "find the tragic issue of [revenge] to be rooted in an ethical dilemma that is universal."[12]

As the epitome of revenge tragedies, *Hamlet* has all the apparatus of the type: (1) Revenge is the fundamental motive for the action. (2) The revenge is supervised by a ghost —usually the ghost of someone who has endured a blood wrong. (3) There is justifiable hesitation on the part of the revenger, who is weaker than his adversary and who, on the failure of legal justice, supposedly lacks a suitable opportunity for straightforward action. (4) Madness is an important dramatic device. (5) Intrigue used against and by the revenger is an important element. (6) The action is bloody and deaths are scattered through the play. (7) The contrast and enforcement of the main situation are achieved by parallels. (8) The villain is an almost complete Machiavellian. (9) The revenge is accomplished terribly, fittingly, with irony and deceit.[13] As will be seen, all of these elements, with one exception, appear in one way or another in *The Tempest*. The exception is that of bloody action: there are no actual deaths in *The Tempest*, though deaths are surmised and threatened.

Among the features of revenge tragedy just listed, the most interesting characteristic is the weakness and hesitation of the revenger. It is mainly in this aspect that the plot of Shakespeare's *Hamlet* differs from its predecessors and successors, in that the hero has serious ethical considerations about what he is to do. In the standard revenge tragedy the revenger bides his time to collect proof and watch for his opportunity. This is the method of Titus Andronicus, who is at his weakest in III, i when, desolate and maimed, left with his violated daughter Lavinia and well-meaning but helpless brother, he begins to move against the Roman Emperor and Empress and the Empress' evil sons and henchman. By a sequence of accidents and planning Titus achieves a ghastly revenge on Saturninus and Tamora, making the latter eat a meal whose ingredients are her sons' heads, bones and flesh, and killing her before the Emperor kills him.

Now, there is a side to the business in *Titus Andronicus* which, in the frantic destructive energies—and the indestructibility—of some of the characters is almost comic. When the arch-villain Aaron the Moor is planning the rape and mutilation of Titus' daughter he gives a perfect exhibition of what Hamlet will call (in bad acting) "damnable faces" (*Hamlet III*, ii, 246):

> What signifies my deadly-standing eye,
> My silence and my cloudy melancholy,
> My fleece of wooly hair that now uncurls
> Even as an adder when she doth unroll
> To do some fatal execution?
> No, madam, these are no venereal signs:
> Vengeance is in my heart, death in my hand,
> Blood and revenge are hammering in my head. (II, iii, 32-9)

There is critical controversy over just how seriously certain parts of *Titus Andronicus* are to be taken. The New Cambridge editor requests the reader to note the florid images which Shakespeare employs in various places to convey the plight of Titus' daughter, and to "ask himself whether he can conceive Shakespeare writing this stuff in earnest."[14] He writes about another conceit (again on Lavinia's plight) which, he feels, "shows us the author pulling our leg"; and he concludes that *Titus Andronicus* is in parts "burlesque and melodramatic travesty . . . a huge joke which, we may guess, Shakespeare enjoyed twice over, once in the penning of it, and again in performance."[15] The New Arden editor of *Titus* argues against this conviction of a burlesque intention on Shakespeare's part, though he admits that "it would be rash to say that a uniform attitude of deadly seriousness is presupposed."[16]

Is *Titus Andronicus* in places a kind of revenge farce, then? Without attempting here to answer this question, I would nonetheless point out that, although the Italian histories, which lent their flavour or atmosphere to the Elizabethan revenge tragedies, have been read with great seriousness by Bowers and others, these histories are not necessarily always uniformly serious. Some of their characters, dreadfully violated on one page, miraculously are up and about their own depredations on another, displaying the resilience and energy—and the comic possibilities—of morality-play Vices. Consider for instance Guicciardini's account of the Cardinal D'Este and his brother Julio, rival lovers of the same young woman:

The Cardinall Hippoloto d'Este, loving fervently a young maide his kinswoman, who for her part was no lesse amorous of Don Iulio the bastard brother of the Cardinall, and confessing her selfe to the Cardinall, that that which above all other things made her affection so vehement to his brother, was, the sweete aspect and beautie of his eyes: the Cardinall being full of wrath, having spied a time when he should go out of the towne on hunting, set upon him in the field, and plucking him from his horse, caused some of his pages to plucke his eyes out of his head, for that they were the companions of his love, and he had the heart to behold the doing of so wicked an act; which afterwards was the cause of very great scandals among many of the brethren. Such was the end of the yeare a thousand five hundred and foure.[17]

Then, a few pages further on from this example of Italianate villainy, we find that

Ferdinand brother to Duke Alphonso and Iulio, whose eyes the Cardinall had violently caused to be plucked out (but by the readie helpe of Physitions were restored without losse of his sight), conspired together with the said Iulio the death of the Duke.[18]

As I have suggested, in the serious contemplation of the blood and thunder with which continental texts apparently filled the imaginations of Renaissance English audiences, critics overlook the comic possibilities of some of these endlessly-energetic and apparently indestructible depredators. The mind which neatly parallels the tragedy of Romeo and Juliet (a tragedy turning on vengeful acts) with the robust knockabout of "The most lamentable comedy . . . of Pyramus and Thisbe" is a mind that could have noticed the comic possibilities in Italian stories and histories, which often are written in King Cambyses' vein.

One comic possibility exploited by Shakespeare is the matter of a solemnly-enrolled but thoroughly reluctant and frustrated revenger—Benedick in *Much Ado About Nothing*. At the climactic moment in *Much Ado* (IV, i), when Hero has been rejected at the altar by Claudio, Beatrice turns into a Clytemnestra and, when Benedick protests that he will do anything to show his love for her, demands that he "Kill Claudio." At this moment and for the remainder of the scene, the action and comic development of *Much Ado* hang in the balance and, as R.A. Foakes puts it, "we the audience, are exposed to the idea of a growth and spread of evil."[19] Loving Beatrice as he does and convinced at last of her deadly seriousness, Benedick can only accept the revenge mission—"Enough, I am engaged; I will challenge him" (IV, i, 331-2) and goes off to find his victim. Two scenes later, white-faced (V, i, 129) and uncharacteristically laconic, he issues what he intends to be a deadly challenge. But just as it has taken Beatrice some time to convince Benedick of her seriousness about wanting Claudio killed, Benedick can't get across to Claudio the idea that he seriously wants to duel with him. He goes off the stage without receiving any answer to his challenge. And just as the gravity of the situation comes home to Claudio and Don Pedro who have been laughing Benedick's words off, Dogberry and his watch enter with Borachio and the revelation of Don John's villainy toward Hero. The duel becomes unnecessary, the happy ending is secured, and the dramatist has had a brief fling at introducing revenge into a comedy. In doing so he has, as Alexander Leggatt puts it, moved "temporarily outside the shelter of the normal world of comedy into a world of deeper and more painful feelings . . . .   In the scene of Benedick's challenge, the license of comedy is temporarily suspended."[20] The comic resolution of Benedick's temporary dilemma—he must visit revenge on his friend to prove his love—is all the more striking in being accomplished by the clowns, who are unwitting *dei ex machina*. Nonetheless, for that space while Beatrice's vengeful imperative, "Kill Claudio," is Benedick's law the play has turned toward revenge tragedy and its possibilities.

In the complex of motivations which drive Shylock, in *The Merchant of Venice*, first to make and then to enforce his bond, vengeful anger at the loss of Jessica is an important element: "If you wrong us, shall we not revenge?" (III, i, 66-7. See also 11. 68-73). And although comic resolutions, here and in *Much Ado*, head off the tragic potentiality, vengeful energies clearly are at work among the characters in Shakespearean comedy. Such energies threaten the comic reconciliation in *Twelfth Night* when Feste's claim to have accomplished his revenge is answered by Malvolio's parting malediction:

FESTE . . . Do you remember, 'Madam, why laugh you at such a barren
    rascal? And you smile not, he's gagg'd.' And thus the whirligig of time
    brings in his revenges.
MAL. I'll be reveng'd on the whole pack of you. (V, 1, 374-77)

Revenge threatened, then, can be part of the complication in a Shakespearean comedy; revenge prevented gives comic satisfaction, though in *Twelfth Night* a sense of unease seems deliberately to be left as revenge, however comically achieved, is seen to tend to set off further reaction. Where comic reconciliation is achieved in spite of an impulse to revenge it usually is because the revenger is foiled, like Shylock, or has a redundant cause, like Claudio. Malvolio appears to have the will (and the name) to retaliate, but given his social place he has no power. The prerequisites for carrying out a revenge mission are neatly summed up by Hamlet as "Cause, and will, and strength, and means" (*Hamlet*, IV, iv, 45). Ironically, though he claims to have "Cause, and will, and strength, and means" to carry out the task of avenging his father, Hamlet is at the time he speaks very far from having strength and means to fulfill this mission. In revenge tragedy the horrors come from the interchange and uses of power, and revenge may be accomplished as bloody instructions return to plague the inventor. The suspense in the genre comes from the relative weakness of the revenger. This is why, in *Hamlet*, one of the most startling moments—startling because it comes so early in the play, III, iii—is that scene where the prince surprises Claudius at prayer and for a long and indecisive time stands with drawn sword over his kneeling unwary adversary—exactly as Pyrrhus in the Player's recitation of II, ii stood over King Priam before hacking him to pieces. There is a long tradition of critical argument over Hamlet's renun-

ciation of opportunity here, and over the reason he gives for that renunciation. From the 'Mouse-Trap' play he has evidence of Claudius' guilt,
and the recreation of his father's murder performed twice over in that play
has excited him. Now he has cause, and strength, and means—and what
Shakespeare calls in Sonnet 94 the power to hurt:

> They that have pow'r to hurt, and will do none,
> That do not do the thing they most do show,
> Who moving others, are themselves as stone,
> Unmoved, cold, and to temptation slow,
> They rightly do inherit heaven's graces,
> And husband nature's riches from expense;
> They are the lords and owners of their faces,
> Others but stewards of their excellence.
> The summer's flow'r is to the summer sweet,
> Though to itself it only live and die,
> But if that flow'r with base infection meet,
> The basest weed outbraves his dignity:
>> For sweetest things turn sourest by their deeds;
>> Lilies that fester smell far worse than weeds.

In pulling back from doing hurt Hamlet does not "inherit
heaven's graces." He goes directly from this renounced opportunity to
the killing of Polonius, thus becoming "the villain in [Laertes'] cause
which images his"[19] and tying himself irrevocably to his "double-sided
nature and double-sided task."[21] Finding Claudius apparently at
prayer, Hamlet shows he has not the will to revenge in cold blood; his
tragedy is that he will do no hurt, but does it.

Prospero, on the other hand, with cause, and strength, and
means turns potential revenge tragedy into revenge comedy, acting out
the sonnet's theme. The fundamental motive for the action of *The
Tempest* is Prospero's revenge. As Milan was taken from Prospero, so
Caliban fancies that Prospero has taken the island from him—"This
island's mine, by Sycorax my mother, Which thou tak'st from me"
(I, ii, 333-34)— and therefore Prospero's intrigue against his usurping
enemies is imaged in an intrigue against him by Caliban. Although
Frank Kermode, the New Arden editor of *The Tempest*, maintains that
the chief opposition in the play is between the worlds of Prospero's
Art and Caliban's Nature,[22] the action turns as well on the struggle
withing Prospero's own all-too-human nature. For Prospero has a
justified resentment and a deeply-entrenched recollection of the wrongs
which have been committed upon him and his daughter Miranda. The
resentment is kept fresh by the recollection.

Aids to memory are standard props of the sensationalist revenge
tragedies. In Kyd's *The Spanish Tragedy* the revenger Hieronimo carries
a handkerchief stained (and apparently always freshly so) with his
son's blood: "It shall not from me, till I take revenge" (II, v, 51-2).
He also appears with a book, reading and expounding a lesson of
revenge (III, xii, 1f). In *Hamlet*, memory needs no aids: it is a theme
of the play. The revenger is urged by the Ghost of his father to
"Remember me," and responds:

Remember thee!
Ay, thou poor ghost, whiles memory holds a seat
In this distracted globe. Remember thee!
Yea, from the table of my memory
I'll wipe away all trivial fond records,
All saws of books, all forms, all pressures past
That youth and observation copied there,
And thy commandment all along shall live
Within the book and volume of my brain,
Unmix'd with baser matter.   (I, v)

"Heaven and earth, Must I remember?" (I, ii, 142-43) Hamlet rhetorically asks in his first soliloquy. He cannot choose but remember as he sees the wrong done to his father imaged in life—Claudius as his mother's husband and as king—and in art—in the the speech the Player once spoke to him from a never-acted play; in 'The Murder of Gonzago;' in the cameo pictures of the new king which the Danes wear. Memory is another Ghost which haunts Hamlet and prompts his revenge.

Memory also haunts Prospero. The long expository second scene of *The Tempest* is an extended illustration of how "the dark backward and abysm of time" (*The Tempest* I, ii, 50) is preserved in his mind. Probably no other Shakespearean character besides Hamlet has such a gift or curse of total and passionate recall as Prospero has: the length and near-monologue quality of his first scene attest to this. Frank Kermode attempts to ascribe Prospero's irascibility in this scene to his descent from a bad-tempered giant-magician of folk tale.[23] Such an explanation takes no account of the simple and all important fact that the one day in which the play's action takes place concentrates all Prospero's feelings about the former day of his and Miranda's victimization and about all the days and years since then. "Twelve year since, Miranda, twelve year since" (II, ii, 53), he emphatically begins his story: and as the story unfolds he repeatedly admonishes his daughter and the audience, "I pray thee, mark me" (1. 67), "Dost thou attend me?" (1. 78), "Thou attend'st not?" (1. 87), "I pray thee, mark me" (1. 89), "Dost thou hear?" (1. 106). In its urgent imperiousness, Prospero's tone is reminiscent of the Ghost's charge to Hamlet: "Mark me . . . . My hour is almost come . . ." (*Hamlet*, I, v, 2), "Lend thy serious hearing to what I shall unfold" (11. 5-6), "List, list, O, List!" (1. 22) In each of these scenes in *Hamlet* and *The Tempest* the voice of the past speaks urgently to the present, proclaiming a wrong and announcing that the time has come to deal with the wrongdoers. As the Ghost of Hamlet's father is obsessed with the wrongs done him, so too is Prospero; as the Ghost recalls his victimization in intimate detail, so too does Prospero, who blames his brother not only for his venality but also for the fact that he "made such a sinner of his memory To credit his own lie" (11. 101-02). Prospero's memory is not confused or edited. Sharp, detailed and fierce, it gives this long expository scene its energy. Remembrance is the ghost which haunts *The Tempest*: it is a ghost from a revenge play.

Reinforcing Prospero's angry remembering is the fact that Caliban also is an aggrieved rememberer. He has a selective recall of how Prospero first befriended him and then usurped him. Ariel, on the other hand, is free

of memories of former terrors and of what he owes Prospero. It is of course
an expository device that Prospero should remind Ariel of his debt, but
Prospero's forcefulness in doing so illustrates once again his own all-too-
circumstantial recall:

Pros. Dost thou forget
        From what a torment I did free thee?   (11. 250-51)
Pros. Hast thou forgot
        The foul witch Sycorax, who with age and envy
        Was grown into a hoop? Hast thou forgot her?
Ari. No, sir.
Pros. Thou hast . . . . I must
        Once in a month recount what thou hast been,
        Which thou forget'st.   (11. 257-64)

Even allowing for Prospero's excitement at the arrival of this long-studied-for
day, Prospero's language is strikingly belligerent. The belligerence seems
justified, for as Hamlet's father was the victim of "foul play" (*Hamlet* I,
ii, 255), Prospero and Miranda were "By foul play . . . heaved hence"
(*Tempest* I, ii, 62). Beginning with reassurances to Miranda, who is ter-
rified for the ship in the tempest, his story builds through the account of
what was done twelve years before into stronger and stronger recrimina-
tion toward their wrongers: "that a brother should Be so perfidious!" (11.
67-68); "Thy false uncle" (1. 77); "in my false brother Awak'd an evil
nature" (11. 92-3); "mine enemies" (1. 179). Soon the story is "beating
in [Miranda's] mind" (1. 176) just as it beats in her father's (IV, i, 163).
This strong working in the mind is potentially dangerous, as Prospero tells
Alonso when at the end of the day Alonso tries to comprehend all the things
that have been happening: "Do not infest your mind with beating on The
strangeness of this business" (V, i, 246-47).
    This "beating in the mind" is paralleled in the play with the force
of the sea, and it is clear from the exchange with Ariel that the force and
terror of the shipwrecking storm were in every detail specified by Prospero:
"Perform'd to point . . . To every article" (11. 194-95). When he is
angered by Caliban's truculence and invective, Prospero responds with equal
violence of language, calling down (like King Lear when he is raging) a
barrage of natural afflictions:

Cal. As wicked dew as e'er my mother brush'd
        With raven's feather from unwholesome fen
        Drop on you both! a south-west blow on ye
        And blister you all o'er!
Pros. For this, be sure, to-night thou shalt have cramps,
        Side-stitches that shall pen thy breath up; urchins
        Shall, for that vast of night that they may work,
        All exercise on thee; thou shalt be pinch'd
        As thick as honeycomb, each pinch more stinging
        Than bees that made 'em.   (I, ii, 323-32)

And,

Pros. If thou neglect'st, or dost unwillingly
    What I command, I'll rack thee with old cramps,
    Fill all thy bones with aches, make thee roar,
    That beasts shall tremble at thy din. (11. 370-73)

With Ariel he already has threatened that

    If thou more murmur'st, I'll rend an oak,
    And peg thee in his knotty entrails, till
    Thou hast howled away twelve winters (11. 294-96)

And for Ferdinand, in the same scene, it is, "Come,"

    I'll manacle thy neck and feet together:
    Sea-water shalt thou drink; thy food shall be
    The fresh-brook mussels, wither'd roots and husks
    Wherein the acorn cradled. (11. 463-67)

Frank Kermode says that Prospero exercises "the supernatural powers of the holy adept" and achieves "an intellect pure and conjoined with the powers of the gods."[24] This is a retrospective view, and eventually a reasonable one, but it is not easy to credit on the evidence of Prospero's first long scene, where he dominates by force, memory and invective. The violence in the exchanges just quoted is re-echoed through the play in the plans of murder and ravishment which Caliban hatches with Trinculo and Stephano. Their plot, as R.G. Hunter points out, is a comic analogue both to Alonso's original crime and to Antonio's and Sebastian's frustrated attempt to repeat it.[25] Generally in discussions of this aspect of the play Prospero is seen as far above the conspirators, but the Prospero who rages at Caliban in Caliban's terms is not this remote mage. His grievance is Caliban's grievance—a sense of having been misled, usurped and exiled. Caliban is a revenger—however ridiculous and fumbling his plotting may be, he has a sense of "cause and will" inspiring him to do hurt, and he has terribly violent intentions. And Prospero is associated with Caliban's darkness, as he admits; "This thing of darkness I acknowledge mine" (V, i, 275-76). The audience is kept in suspense in the first act as this man with "power to hurt" keeps his own counsel:

    Know thus far forth.
    By accident most strange, bountiful Fortune,
    (Now my dear lady) hath mine enemies
    Brought to this shore; and by my prescience
    I find my zenith doth depend upon
    A most auspicious star, whose influence
    If now I court not, but omit, my fortunes
    Will ever after droop. Here cease more questions. (I, ii, 177-84)

    Now, the senexes of classical comedy and the Pantalones of *Commedia dell'arte* often froth with ridiculous belligerence over suitors whom they perceive to be unworthy of their daughters. In *Commedia dell'arte* pastorals the Magician who broods apart is averse to wooing and marriage on his island or sea-coast.[25] Clearly, Prospero is not far removed from these traditions in his first encounter with Ferdinand, who sees him as "compos'd of harshness" (III, i, 9). In Shakespearean comedy, revengers are rather given to splutters of frustration—Benedick trying to convince Claudio that his challenge is serious—or storms of recrimination—Shylock raging in the street over his lost turquoise and a wilderness of monkeys (*Merchant of Venice* III, i, 113-23). But although Prospero ultimately will engineer a comic outcome at the cost of swallowing his resentment, his recall of grievance and his reactions to Ariel, Caliban and Ferdinand show him on the play's terms to be a haunted and potentially dangerous man of (as we often forget) Italianate nature, with a cause for revenge. With this cause, he has what the conventional revengers of drama lack—power to hurt.

This power may be exercised at will in the play's setting, a remote island which could be an ethical wilderness. The wicked Antonio recognizes such a possibility almost as soon as he finds his feet on dry land. When King Alonso of Naples, the idealistic old courtier Gonzalo and their other companions are charmed asleep, leaving only Antonio and Alonso's brother Sebastian awake, Antonio promptly sees an opportunity for Sebastian:

> My strong imagination sees a crown
> Dropping upon thy head. (II, i, 203-04)

Believing that Ferdinand, the heir of Naples, is drowned, recognizing that his sister Claribel is married in Tunis, "Ten leagues beyond man's life" (II, i, 241), and that they on the island are "sea-swallow'd," as distanced from Tunis and Naples as those places are from one another by "A space whose every cubit Seems to cry out" that no record or suspicion of their deeds will ever surface (II, i, 252-55), Antonio persuades Sebastian to let him murder Alonso while Sebastian simultaneously kills Gonzalo. Convinced, Sebastian says, "As thou got'st Milan [by disposing of Prospero] I'll come by Naples" (II, i, 286-87).

The ethical bare stage or wilderness which the villains so keenly identify is the equivalent of the unweeded garden which is Hamlet's Denmark: "Things rank and gross in nature Possess it merely" (*Hamlet* I, ii, 136-37). Titus Andronicus recognizes the state of moral emptiness even more clearly: "Dost thou not perceive," he asks his brother,

> That Rome is but a wilderness of tigers?
> Tigers must prey, and Rome affords no prey
> But me and mine.   (*Titus Andronicus* iii, i, 53-6)

The "tigers" of Prospero's island, Antonio and Sebastian, think themselves able, as Antonio puts it

> To perform an act
> Whereof what's past is prologue; what to come,
> In yours and my discharge.   (*Tempest* II, i, 247-49)

"What's past is prologue" and Sebastian's "As thou gotst Milan, I'll come by Naples'' (II, i, 286-87) clearly indicate that the villains are not so much acting a new crime as re-enacting a form of the original blood wrong—a brother's attempted murder—while the avenger watches through his art (II, i, 292). This is a form of the revenge tragedy's play-within-a-play. The villains' sterile repetition of the past is brilliantly contrasted by the *other* play-within-the-play, Prospero's Act IV masque, which is all about fertility and the future. Antonio, who thus in his re-enactment has confessed and confirmed his guilt, as Claudius does in *Hamlet III*, is the complete Machiavel. Ruthless and unrepentant, he goes back in Shakespeare beyond Claudius to Aaron. Only when it suits him will Aaron remember having heard of ''a thing within [religious individuals] called conscience'' (*Titus Andronicus* V, i, 75). When Antonio proposes to serve Sebastian's brother much as he served Prospero, Sebastian wavers at first:

Seb. But for your conscience.
Ant. Ay sir; where lies that? If'twere a kibe,
    'Twould put me to my slipper: but I feel not
    This deity in my bosom: twenty consciences,
    That stand 'twixt me and Milan, candied be they,
    And melt, ere they molest!   (*Tempest* II, i, 270-75)

''Then tell me,'' Prospero already has asked Miranda, ''if this might be a brother?'' Her reasonable reply is that Antonio and Prospero need not be alike, for ''Good wombs have borne bad sons'' (I, ii, 117-18, 120). But Prospero's excited wrath and Antonio's remembered and presently-confirmed evil dominate the first two acts of the play. By the beginning of Act Three we have a drama of Italian brothers, with parallel enforcements of an evil strain and an examination of the use and misuse of power and opportunity—three of the brothers already being guilty of actual or contemplated usurping villainy. The dramatic energy of the play to this point appears or threatens to be revenge and, were Prospero to show the same tigerish disposition as his adversaries, he could be ready to emulate them in destructiveness when he is sure that

    My high charms work
    And these mine enemies are all knit up
    In their distractions: they are now in my power.   (III, iii, 88-90)

Ironically, the traditional hesitation of the Renaissance stage revenger would bring about the destruction of Prospero's foes. As we have seen, left to themselves with no apparent law they quickly propose to murder one another. Prospero does not need to kill them, he merely needs not to strive officiously to keep them alive. In II, i he prevents the murder of Alonso and Gonzalo: dramatically this could be to draw out Alonso's, Antonio's and Sebastian's punishment. It is only in the third act, when we see him observe the courtship of Miranda and Ferdinand and hear his language soften, that there appears the likelihood of grace rather than revengeful destruction:

Pros.   Fair encounter
   Of two most rare affections! Heavens rain grace
   On that which breeds between 'em! (III, i, 74-6)

But Ferdinand has been carefully isolated from the older generation, and at the end of this act Alonso, Antonio and Sebastian still are Prospero's "enemies" and as already mentioned, fully in his power. Even after the betrothal-masque for the young couple there is a resurgence of Prospero's fierce indignation at Caliban for his conspiracy and for his nature, on which "Nurture can never stick: on whom my pains, Humanely taken, all, all lost, quite lost" (IV, i, 188-90). This description (in which, incidentally, a cry from the storm in the first scene is echoed: see I, i, 51) also applies to Antonio. With renewed indignation comes a reminiscence of the earlier violent language:

   Go charge my goblins that they grind their joints
   With dry convulsions; shorten up their sinews
   With aged cramps: and more pinch-spotted make them
   Than pard or cat o'mountain. (IV, i, 258-61)

This violence is directed at Caliban, Stephano and Trinculo, but it does not bode well for the aristocratic villains, as Prospero immediately turns to contemplate with menacing satisfaction the situation whereby

    At this hour
   Lies at my mercy all my enemies:
   Shortly shall all my labours end. (IV, i, 262-64)

 On this foreboding, or at any rate ambiguous, note the fourth act ends. Prospero seems to be, as the play's own phrase for moral indecision has it, in standing water. (Tempted by Antonio, Sebastian non-committally replies, "Well, I am standing water": Antonio's response is "I'll teach thee how to flow," and he does, II, i, 216-17). Will Prospero "flow" toward preserving Ferdinand and Gonzalo but take his satisfaction on the others? At this point he can be compared to Hamlet, standing over the helpless Claudius with "power to hurt." But Prospero, like Hamlet and like the type of man apotheosized in Sonnet 94, will not take advantage. The moment of sea-change from potential tragedy to comic resolution is at hand, and when Prospero agrees with Ariel that he should and will forgive his enemies the violence which in the play's language has been associated with the sea, ebbs: "Though the seas threaten, they are merciful" (V, i, 178). The turn into comedy is accompanied—perhaps consciously marked—by references to a turning tide:

   . . . Ye that on the sands with printless foot
   Do chase the ebbing Neptune, and do fly him
   When he comes back. (V, i, 35-37)

Most strikingly, it is a tide of reason and of cleansing power:

> Their understanding
> Begins to swell; and the approaching tide
> Will shortly fill the reasonable shore
> That now lies foul and muddy.   (V, i, 79-82)

The process of sea-change is fully accomplished in Alonso (this metamorphosis was announced, as a sea-change, in Ariel's dirge in I, ii). As Prospero recognizes, it does not take effect in Antonio (V, i, 78-79, 130-34). Having forgiven the villains, Prospero shows that he has thrown off not only revenge but also the memory of injury, telling Alonso not only to beware of infesting his mind with beating on the strangness of this business, but also saying,

> Let us not burthen our remembrance with
> A heaviness that's gone.   (V, i, 199-200)

This weight of memory is the last burden which Prospero puts off. With this renunciation the ghost of the past is exorcised (save of course for the important but irreparable matter of Antonio and Sebastian still being "themselves," V, i, 32), and Gonzalo's benediction is proclaimed in the very next lines. The benediction sums up only the reconciliations issuing from the adventure, underlining Prospero's determination to "think of each thing well" (V, i, 251).

Reading *The Tempest* for its associations with and possible origins in *Commedia dell'arte*, K.M. Lea shows many striking parallels with the Commedia, but has difficulty accounting for what she calls the awkwardness of construction which allows the flow of stage movement in the Italian tradition to be interrupted at a crucial moment by a revenge plot (she has in mind Caliban's revenge intrigue):

At the moment when we might expect [comic scenes of mishandled magic] in *The Tempest* the Masque of Juno and Ceres is summoned, and then just as they reach their height the revels are rudely interrupted by Prospero, who dismisses the dancers and prepares to defend himself against a conspiracy. . . . If it were not that every time we read the play we are spellbound by the loveliness of his apology we might resent the intrusion of a revenge which now seems beneath his dignity.[26]

Lea suspects a faulty interpolation of the masque here. Like many other commentators on *The Tempest* she overlooks the possibility that the revenge intrigue and counter-intrigue are part of the main—if not the main—business of the play. As a comedy of revenge *The Tempest* embodies nearly all the conventions of its tragic counterparts, especially *Hamlet*: revenge as a fundamental motive; a "ghost"; intrigue by and against the revenger, and dramatic parallelling; a Machiavellian villain and, as in *Hamlet*, a hero on whose character the issue of revenge turns—in this case to forgiveness. *The Tempest* might even be said to have the revenge tragedy device of play within a play, or rather to *be* a play within a play, for as a drama of potential revenge its one-day's (or between-tides) events are framed on one side by a story from the dark backward and abysm of time and on the other by that dark forward: the possibility that Prospero will act by the revenger's code. He does not do so, and consequently can project his hopes for his daughter into the future, embodying them in the masque. The brave new world may be new and brave only to Miranda (V, i, 183-84), but Prospero has turned away as well as he can from the bad old one.

As early as *Titus Andronicus* Shakespeare had begun to bring tragedy and comedy close together. In doing so he was carrying on a form of literary experimentation which had been conducted in Italy during the sixteenth century. Louise George Clubb has described these experiments in the combining of generic elements:

The practice of conflating individual units of action, character, and language from different sources had, even in the early *commedie*, sanctioned fusions of Roman comedy and pieces of the *Decameron* and Petrarchan imagery. In time, the principle of *contaminatio* levied parts from more numerous and disparate sources and eventually led to combining generic elements and aims chosen challengingly for their seeming incompatability within the limits of regular comedy and of regular tragedy.[27]

There emerged from these experiments a *commedia grave*, which "included matters thought by Renaissance theorists to be fit for tragedy: characters of noble rank, threats of serious danger, of death or spiritual peril, occasions for heroism and pathos."[28]

Clubb suggests that there is some reason for believing Shakespeare was aware of Continental theatrical trends, and she discusses his "testing of generic possibilities" in *Romeo and Juliet* and *Othello*.[29] In my view, *The Tempest* combines "generic elements and aims chosen challengingly for their seeming incompatibility within the limits of regular comedy...." Shakespeare has taken the elements of revenge tragedy and reconstructed them as tragedy's binary opposite.

It is rather appropriate that *The Tempest* seems to have no major sources and few analogues of substance, for in its ethical dimension it is unique. Only the playwright who had carried the revenge tragedy as far as it apparently could go would carry it farther still, by taking its conventions and, with *The Tempest*, sea-changing tragedy into revenge comedy.

NOTES

1 Fredson Thayer Bowers, *Elizabethan Revenge Tragedy 1587-1642* (Gloucester, Mass., 1959), 278.

2 Bowers, 278.

3 See Stanley Wells, "Shakespeare Without Sources," in M. Bradbury and D. Palmer, eds., *Shakespearian Comedy*. Stratford-upon-Avon Studies 14 (London, 1972), 58-74.

4 Frank Kermode, Introduction to the New Arden *The Tempest* (London, 1968), 58-74.

5 Ashley H. Thorndike, "The Relations of Hamlet to Contemporary Revenge Plays," *PMLA* XVII, 2 New Series X, 2, 125.

6 Thorndike, 126.
7 Thorndike, 127.
8 Thorndike, 217.
9 Geoffrey Fenton, trans., *The Historie of Guicciardin: Containing the Warres of Italie.* Reduced into English by Geoffrey Fenton. Third Edition (London, 1618), 16.
10 Fenton, 1.
11 Bowers, 266.
12 Eleanor Prosser, *Hamlet and Revenge* (Stanford and London, 1967), 252.
13 In its essentials this list is borrowed from Bowers, 71, 268.
14 John Dover Wilson, Introduction to the New Cambridge *Titus Andronicus* (Cambridge, 1948), liii.
15 Wilson, lvi.
16 J.C. Maxwell, Introduction to the New Arden *Titus Andronicus* (London, 1968), xxxiv.
17 Fenton, 257.
18 Fenton, 266.
19 R.A. Foakes, Introduction to the New Penguin Shakespeare *Much Ado About Nothing* (Harmondsworth, 1968), 19.
20 Alexander Leggatt, *Shakespeare's Comedy of Love* (London, 1974), 179.
21 Both quotations in this sentence are from Harold Jenkins' Introduction and Longer Notes to the New Arden *Hamlet* (Methuen, 1982), 156, 515.
22 Kermode, xxiv.
23 Kermode, lxiii.
24 Kermode, xlvii.
25 Robert Grams Hunter, *Shakespeare and the Comedy of Forgiveness* (New York, 1965), 231.
26 K.M. Lea, *Italian Popular Comedy: A Study in the Commedia Dell'Arte 1560-1620.* 2v. (New York, 1962), I, 201.
27 Louise George Clubb, "Shakespeare's Comedy and Late Cinquecento Mixed Genres." In *Shakespearean Comedy*, ed. Maurice Charney (New York, 1980), 130.
28 Clubb, 130-31.
29 Clubb, 135.

Hooft, Bredero and Dutch Comedy: Translation—With a Difference

Yehudi Lindeman
McGill University

I

The Golden Age of Dutch Renaissance comedy produced several great masterpieces in the genre; Bredero's *Moortje* (1615) and *Spanish Brabanter* (1617) and P.C. Hooft's *Warenar* (1617) are still cherished and performed today on account of their originality, charm and native wit. Curiously, these and other comedies of the period are either translations (*Moortje* from Terence's *Eunuchus*; *Warenar* from Plautus' *Aulularia*; Hooft's *Schijnheiligh* from Aretino's *l'Ipocrito*), or else lean heavily on foreign models. Even Bredero's *Brabanter*, everybody's favourite Dutch Renaissance comedy, relies for its structure and much of its dialogue on the sixteenth-century Spanish novella *Lazarillo de Tormes*.[1]

I am suggesting that this paradox can be solved. A certain mode of Renaissance translation resulted—under the proper conditions—in a new work of remarkable native power. It is normal to think that one can't have it both ways. I will show how certain authors managed to have it both ways. Hooft and Bredero were able, through a creative *tour de force*, to follow their models faithfully and yet create theatrical works that were as powerful, alive and original as any "original" text from which they derived their inspiration.

To substantiate my insights I will introduce a theoretical paradigm which, though fully discussed elsewhere, will be recapitulated in minimal detail.[2] My theoretical point concerns the once popular notion of *enargeia* or visual heightening. Derived from classical and medieval rhetoric, it is a recipe that calls for vivid, visual representation in prose or verse. While it was self-consciously employed by authors as different as Dante, Sidney and Montaigne, its clearest theoretical exposition can be found in the works of George Chapman, the celebrated translator of Homer.

Beginning with Chapman's observations, I will show that an adequate understanding of *enargeia* renders the otherwise implausible successes of Bredero and Hooft more intelligible. For the notion of *enargeia* is itself associated with two disparate elements. First of all it demands the translator's unconditional loyalty to his "source text" as he absorbs and decodes it. At the same time it also refers to the kind of visual imagination that is able to lift the new version (or "receptor text") to an unprecedented imaginative height.[3] This new text may or may not be dynamically equivalent (or even superior) to the text of the original document, but that is less important than the nature of its artistic independence in relation to the source text.

Thus, in Bredero's *Brabanter*, Robbeknol's factual resemblance to Lázaro is easily confirmed. But the relation between the two is a complex one. While the character is obviously modelled after that of the luckless servant in *Lazarillo de Tormes*, it also transcends it in many ways. What finally matters is that Robbeknol is an entirely convincing new literary creation whose continued popularity in Dutch literature (and on the Dutch stage) is as assured as that of Falstaff in English.

Finally a word about my critical/theoretical assumptions. Concerning my paradigm all that needs to be said is that I am employing the habitual conceptual terminology of several generations' theorizing on the subject of translation. I am not using a new tool; I am merely sharpening an old one. But if their paradigm suits our analytical needs, many new insights may be gained, especially into those Renaissance texts that draw extensively on prior literary models, from Wyatt's sonnets to Shakespeare's *Coriolanus*.

II

O jeemie, o jeemie
't Is Costers Academie!

The jingle still survives today. This is how lower-class Amsterdammers saw the efforts of a handful of burghers to establish a new "academy." They mimicked their accents and debunked their intentions in the best and nuttiest Amsterdam tradition. Maybe a tinge of respect is mixed in with the ridicule as well, for the new academy flourished at once as it combined the function of a fledgeling University with that of a National Theatre. And though it couldn't match the fame of Leyden as an institution of higher learning, it is worth noticing that it used, from its humble start as "Atheneum illustre," modern Dutch as its language of instruction. Leyden, on the other hand, would go on teaching in the "old" Latin language for centuries to come.

Loosely translated the ditty says:
O Lordie, O Lordie,
Look at Coster's New Academy!

As it happened, the new Academy was the result of vehement quarrelling inside the old Chamber of Rhetoric. "The Eglantine" (the colourful name by which the old Academy was known) had produced all major theatre productions until 1617. By this time the dissent within its ranks culminated in a schism and a large number of members left, led by the triumvirate Hooft, Bredero and Coster. Of the three men Samuel Coster (the one in the dittie)—though least remembered today—was the undisputed leader.

Under Coster's inspired leadership the new Academy was off to an excellent start, producing in its first year Hooft's and Bredero's most famous comedies, *Warenar* and *The Spanish Brabanter*. Coster's own play, the farce *Teeuwis the Farmer*, had been produced by the "Eglantine" in 1612. In it a farmer has come to deliver wood at the manor house of his Lord, but finds himself sleeping with the Lady instead (he is young and good-looking, she desires him, and the Lord is away on business). The deal turns sour for the farmer when he is forced to leave behind his horse and his cart. When he returns to address the Lord about his losses and to explain how he was unfairly robbed, he retrieves all that he had lost. In the end the farmer has the best bargain and the last laugh. The subject matter is more farce than comedy, but the play has five acts and a very real intrigue. As a result, it is seen by some critics as the beginning of modern Dutch comedy.

To the same genre belong two of Bredero's short comedies, the *Farce of the Cow* (acted in the Nes by the old Chamber of Rhetoric) and the *Farce of the Miller*. A thief gets a gullible farmer to sell a fat cow for him. To the farmer's chagrin, he finds that he has bid up his own cow for the thief's gain. At least three people are cheated by the clever thief, who walks off with the money, two pewter plates and a costly overcoat without rousing any suspicion. Though the story is medieval, there is a modern angle in the over-all tone and in the perspective that the farmer is able to bring to the occasion. Ungrudgingly he admits that, though it may take him a year to replace his losses, that thief was such a clever fellow that "I have to laugh about so much trickery." To this the inn-keeper (who lost her plates) agrees, adding that "as one makes one's bed, so one must lie in it." (*Farce of the Cow*, 641 and 655.)

The real transformation in Dutch comedy, however, takes place during the years 1615-18 with the creation of a number of full-length comedies. These include Bredero's *Moortje* and *Brabanter* and Hooft's *Warenar* and *Schijnheiligh*. This transformation occurred as the Dutch republic grew into a world power through the expansion of its commerce and its holdings overseas: the East India Company was founded in 1616, followed by the West India Company in 1619. The meteoric rise of the republic was made possible through a truce with Habsburg Spain (1609-21) with which the rebelling Dutch provinces had been at war since 1568. However, by 1619 the divisions inside Holland had led to such violent political quarrels that it was perceived by many as the end of an epoch. These national convulsions culminated in the imprisonment of the world famous jurist Hugo Grotius, and in the gruesome public execution of the first minister of the republic, the great Van Oldebarneveld.

The same years also saw the unprecedented expansion in influence, affluence and size of the city of Amsterdam. Between 1612 and 1622 it doubled its population (from 50 000 to 100 000). At the same time it was rapidly becoming the leading port of Europe, its Baltic trade making it a rich staple port for grain, and its trade in spices and manufactured goods assuring its position as the word's leading transit port. Much of this had become possible after the decline of Spanish-Catholic Antwerp, ever since the Protestant-Dutch rebels successfully blockaded it in 1585, thus essentially closing it by force. The truce with Spain signalled the real boost for Amsterdam. As David Brumble says in his introduction to *The Spanish Brabanter*, in these years Dutch shipping came to dominate Europe because "Dutch ships were the most economical;...Dutch warehouses were the most numerous; Dutch interest rates were the lowest."[4] Meanwhile large numbers of Protestants and Spanish Jews had fled Antwerp to seek refuge in the North, bringing with them a lot of capital and international business expertise, most of which benefited the ever-expanding city of Amsterdam.

The years 1610-18 are known as the second phase in the long life of

P.C. Hooft (1581-1647) and also as the happiest years of his life. In 1610 he had married Christina van Erp and from all we know the marriage was an extremely happy one. This is the period of Hooft's rising fame in public office (he had had a good start as the son of one of Amsterdam's most prominent families): it was also the period in which Hooft composed his great historical tragedies, including *Geraert van Velsen* (1613) and *Baeto* (1617). *Warenar* (1617) was written during a pause in the composition of *Baeto* and with the stated intention of using the profit from its anticipated financial success for the production of the more "serious" tragedy.[5] Hooft's career as a playwright came to an end with the composition, in 1618, of the *Schijnheiligh*, a translation of the *Ipocrito* by the Italian poet and playwright Pietro Aretino.

In 1618 Hooft, as if pulled away from the pleasures of his youth, decided to consolidate his creative energy and started work on the *Netherlandic Histories*. While the *Histories* would make him the republic's greatest historian, his translations also continued to earn him fame. Besides Plautus and Aretino he translated parts of Homer's *Odyssey*, Virgil's *Aeneid* (books one and four), and all the works of Tacitus. His patriotic zeal for documenting Holland's national history was matched by his sense of mission with regard to the purity, inner strength and outward flexibility of the Dutch language. Yet his permanent position in Dutch literature is the result of his great poetic gifts as expressed in a body of lyric poetry of unequalled beauty—and in the *Warenar*.

III

According to Hugo Grotius, Hooft's translation of Plautus' *Aulularia* (or The *Pot of Gold*, as it is also known) "surpasses the original in many parts."[6] *Warenar* expands Plautus' text from 788 to 1486 lines. Part of this expansion is due to the more compact nature of the Latin language (as compared to Dutch). Part is the result of Hooft's completion of the Latin text, which breaks off before the end.[7] The less obvious cause for the increased length, however, is the particular manner in which Hooft substitutes the atmosphere of Amsterdam for that of Plautus' Athens.[8] This is not to say that Hooft takes great liberties with the plot; rather that the local colour and the characters themselves are adjusted according to the needs of the occasion. In this respect, the whole comedy is "verduytschet" (as it says on the title page of the first edition), meaning "turned into Dutch" or "adjusted to Dutch conditions," as the case may be.

One such adjustment concerns the use of language, which is full of phrases in the Amsterdam dialect.[9] Then there is the use of popular Amsterdam humour. It causes Casper to express admiration and awe at the verbal dexterity of his companions from the north. Those "Hollanders are so full of wit," the man from Brabant exclaims (457).

In the following example the adjustment affects both the length of the receptor text and the tone. Staphyla, the female household slave of the miser

Euclio, is having an argument with her master. Here she is leading him on by her controlled use of sarcasm:

EUCLIO: ...even if Lady Fortune herself should come to the door, don't let her in.
STAPHYLA: By God, she will be very careful herself not to enter our house.
   In fact, she has never come to our house, even though she lives in the area.
   (100-102)

Staphyla is merely being sarcastic, partly (one assumes) because her social position would not allow her to go much beyond that. On the other hand, Hooft's maid-servant Reym, with her quick Amsterdam tongue, is not only openly disrespectful, but also leads her master on with vulgar, scurrilous glee:

WARENAR: Look out, even if Lady Fortune comes for a visit, I warn you, your duty is not to open the door...
REYM: Lady Fortune? Don't worry, she likes to stay far away. Lady Fortune knock on our door? You're full of air. The smell of your stairs is enough to make her run.

And as if this weren't clear enough, the patrician Hooft adds some graphic details of his own, none of which are in Plautus:

And if our house were, by chance, on her route,
she would make sure to walk on the other side:
one look at the entryway would make her puke.   (152-54; 155-57)[10]

Warenar remained very popular for over a century after its first performance, and reappeared in the Dutch repertoire early in the twentieth century. One main reason for its popularity is, no doubt, the character of Warenar himself. This celebrated manifestation of the latin *senex* stands in the way not only of others' happiness, but of his own as well. Nervous and worried about his gold (will anybody rob him of it?), he is the twenty-four hours a day slave to the "reality principle." This fact is accentuated by Hooft even more than by Plautus:

STAPHYLA: ...he lies awake at night, without cosing his eyes.   (72)
REYM: He lies awake all night, and gets up fifty times.   (114)

What we find in the last two sets of examples are simple additions. At the same time these additions have the special function of making the Dutch more colourful, more visually rich and imaginative than the Latin. Meaningful, and usually visual, detail is added in the Dutch version. This makes the characters, especially Warenar, come more alive: the Dutch draws our attention not just to Warenar's house, but to the unbearable smell of its stairs and the poverty-stricken look of its entrance door (both in contrast to his great but secret wealth), while inside the house itself we seem to see or hear Warenar tossing and turning in his bed, then getting up once again to make sure his gold is still where he left it.[11]

Hooft's text also adds something that is quite possibly characteristic of

Dutch comedy during this period, namely its irony and its light, rather mocking tone. His general tone is not just more playful than Plautus' more bitter, jeering comedy; it also contains a degree of self-mockery that may be hinted at in the Latin, but is never given full expression there. Here Staphyla, in despair, confides to the audience that all will be lost as soon as Warenar finds out about his daughter, who is about to have a baby, father unknown:

STAPHYLA: The best thing for me to do is to hang myself with a noose around my neck, so that I become like a long, limp capital "I."   (76-78)

Hooft utilizes the hint implicit in that limp body swinging from the ceiling to create an image in which despair vies with self-deprecation. This rather changes the tone:

REYM: I might just as well hang myself from the nearest hook, inside a poulterer's shop, like a holiday turkey: what a sight, and what a hell of a bird that would be!   (122-24)

Suggesting half despair, half self-mockery, the image of that bird in the poultry shop gives the passage an accent of psychological realism that goes beyond Plautus.

It should be clear by now why and in what way Hooft's comedy could become an original Dutch comedy in its own right: although some of the Latin passages are skipped altogether in Hooft's version, more often existing passages are enriched and enlivened in an obvious effort to make the translation more colourful, robust and vital than the source text. Thus Grotius' preference for *Warenar* over the *Aulularia* is justified. Also, as my examples show, the additions in the receptor text are quite plausibly triggered off by some element or other in Plautus' text. In other words, it may be postulated that most additions were prompted by some elusive element in the translator's source text. This is an important insight, especially if we remember that it was Hooft's professed goal (see title-page) to adjust the Latin text to local Dutch conditions. Even if it was Hooft's purpose to make the Dutch text more lively as a picture of what might happen should an Amsterdam miser be placed in the position of his ancient counterpart, the new situation would still be firmly anchored in the source text, not just verbally, but in its implicit emotional connotations as well.

That this is indeed the case, one last example will show. Here the servants are gossiping and exchanging tall stories about Warenar's excessive cheapness, which surpasses normal human behaviour. In Plautus' text, one such story is about Euclio's reaction to an incident in which a bird flies off with his dinner, lifting it right off the dinner-table. Crying, the indignant miser runs out of the house to the court house. "Wailing and in tears," he seeks the judge, in a serious attempt to "get the bird sub-poenaed by the court." (316-19) There is no mention of any specific locale. In Hooft's version, Warenar is walking home from the market with a few miserly fish in a net, when suddenly

swoop, there is the stork,
who swallows a little sprat right through the net.
Now he is up in arms, as if that little fish
were a ton of gold; through Bird Lane he flies,
across the Chapel Bridge, right up to the burgomaster,
reciting every detail, crying the blues,
demanding the immediate arrest of the stork...   (486-90)

This is certainly Plautus-with-a-difference: not only is the adjustment to local Dutch conditions complete; with the mention of the specific route, local colour itself has become dominant. This indicates how the Dutch text (here, as elsewhere, regrettably cited in English translation) can at times yield an entirely new work that is fully emancipated from its source text.

With the enhanced pictorial quality and the freedom of Hooft's version sufficiently established, we are now in a position to ask questions about the process of Hooft's translation itself. For instance, is there any theoretical principle at work that could help explain this particular mode of heightened visualization? How does it work? What are its antecedents? What is the cognitive process in this type of translation?

IV

Fear is a bad servant and a worse master, but sometimes it can spur the accomplishment of the near-impossible. Frustration or even despair about the possibility of achieving successful translation from one language into another was the spur that drove some authors of the sixteenth and early seventeenth century to explore ways of obtaining the impossible: masterful verse translation. If the age old pun on traduttore = traditore (the translator is a traitor) was generally accepted, then the obvious challenge was to produce a receptor text (to use the modern terminology) that would remain *faithful* to the source text. But how could that kind of fidelity be achieved without causing irreversible harm to the final product? A brief glance at some of the strategies devised by various Renaissance authors to solve this tantalizing question should suffice. I refer those who seek more detail and greater depth to my fuller treatment of the suject elsewhere.[12] For our present purpose it is enough if we can find out something about the way in which Hooft may have read his source text.

The question of "how" can readily be answered, for there was (in the Renaissance, at least) a good deal of consensus on the matter. Concerning the subject of fidelity, it was agreed that a good translation can only be produced by an author who fully experiences the living force of the source text, with the emphasis on "experiences" and "living force." Or, as Flora Amos observes about the generation of sixteenth-century writers influenced by Cambridge scholar John Cheke, success is contingent upon a writer's power to feel the "vital, permanent quality" of the original text.[13] One of the most famous writers under Cheke's tutelage was Thomas Hoby, who translated into English Castiglione's *Book of the Courtier* (1561), a work characterized by its robust and colloquial strength. F.O. Matthiessen notes how the "vividness that Hoby achieves reveals how fully he was caught by the force of the book."[14] Clearly what is needed for a vigorous and lively product to emerge is the sort of fidelity that derives from deep and sympathetic immersion in the source text. This being the case, is there any authority that provides a more detailed picture of the mental or cognitive process that makes possible the composition of a strong and vital receptor text?

George Chapman, the great translator of Homer, identifies the power to compose successfully as *Enargia*. It is what he calls the "cleerenes of representation," which lends to a writer's text not only its surface polish (its "luster"), but also its "motion, spirit and life."[15] Translation that is both faithful and forceful is predicated on the need to "reach the spirit" of Homer's Greek, says Chapman, writing in 1609; but those unable to search Homer's "deepe, and treasurous hart" cannot expect to arrive at satisfactory translation.[16]

Enargia or (more properly) *enargeia* is a term used in ancient rhetoric, meaning to describe things vividly. In the late classical treatise *On the Sublime*, the term is related to "imagination" (*phantasia*) and the ability of an author to have a picture clearly present before his mind's eye *and* to "bring it vividly before the eyes of [his] audience."[17] I propose the adoption of the term *enargeia* to indicate successful, i.e., vivid, imaginative but faithful translation, especially with reference to the Renaissance period. This then is the paradigm governing successful translation: the author must immerse himself in the source text ("in the hart of [one's] subject," to quote Chapman once again)[18] in order to bring to the process of re-presentation a visual articulation that heightens and intensifies that which one experienced imaginatively by reading the original text. Successful translation results from an intense spill-over from the mind's screen into the new language. This occurs through a visualizing/conceptualizing process that mediates between the activities of thoughtful reading and recreating.

I suggest that Hooft and Bredero drew on not just *enargeia*, but an entire visual epistemology, which had become especially useful to their generation of late sixteenth- and early seventeenth-century authors and translators. It was this inheritance that made possible their faithful, yet visually enhanced quality of composition and translation that resulted in dramatic works with the self-confident air of original masterpieces.

V

Gerbrand Adriaensz. Bredero (1585-1618) was born in a house on the Nes in Amsterdam. Next door was the building where the old Chamber of Rhetoric held its meetings. The comedy *Moortje* would be performed in a building on the same street. When Bredero was seventeen, his father (a rather prosperous artisan and businesman) decided to move the family to a larger house on one of the canals. Here Bredero was to live until his early death at age 33.

The name Bredero is today a household word in Dutch. His popularity rests on his comedies and his playful and moving lyric poetry, though it is for the latter that his is most loved. Of his comedies, *The Spanish Brabanter* is everybody's favourite. As it brings to life the exciting, ever-expanding atmosphere of the city of Amsterdam, it is in fact Holland's most popular Renaissance comedy. Even though for socio-political reasons the play is set one generation earlier, it is more than likely the proud, dynamic and expansive Amsterdam during the twelve-year truce with Spain (1609-21) that is actually celebrated in it.

If *The Spanish Brabanter* is most often praised by the critics for depicting the feelings of a wide variety of Amsterdammers, it is most often remembered by its audiences for its portrayal of the servant Robbeknol. This luckless descendant of the *servus dolosus* of Latin comedy gradually assumes a life of his own as he falls more and more under the spell of his master. This is the "Brabanter" of the title, the colourful "nobleman" and penniless impostor, Jerolimo. In the end Robbeknol seems to surrender to his master's fantasy world to the extent that the world of illusion merges with the life of struggle and material reality the servant has known so well throughout his hard life. Meanwhile we, the audience, find ourselves equally hard pressed to distinguish between Jerolimo's fantasy and Robbeknol's reality.

The Spanish Brabanter is indebted for its narrative structure to *Lazarillo de Tormes*, the earliest picaresque novel. Robbeknol himself is an almost-carbon-copy of Lázaro, especially in the details of his early life, where the art of begging, listening and surviving in a cruel or indifferent world has been mastered to perfection. Here is an example that illustrates the close resemblance between the Spanish and the Dutch. Lázaro, we may recall, through his author addresses the noble patron to whom the book is dedicated; Robbeknol speaks to the feigned nobleman Jerolimo. The narrator is referring to the role played by his stepfather, who (in both versions) was a Moor:

> When he first started coming I was scared of him and didn't like him because of his colour and the way he looked, but as I saw that whenever he came we ate better I began to take quite a liking to him, because he always brought bread, pieces of meat, and firewood to warm ourselves with in winter...

One day it is found out that his stepfather had been stealing

> about half the oats that he was given to feed the animals. He 'lost' bran, firewood, curry combs, aprons and the horsesheets and blankets; and when he didn't have anything else he removed the horseshoes.[19]

Here is the Dutch:

Before, I'd howled and screamed whenever he came near–
For very fear I'd shiver when I saw him come.
I'd cry, "A thunderstorm is coming up–
It's so dark there yonder!" I thought he was the Devil
Or some hobgoblin, but the more I saw of pastries, bread,
And other treats, and wine as well as food,
The more he seemed an angel, not a man.   (109-16)

Then one day his employers, having observed him for some time,

...laid for him—spied and watched,
Until they'd seen him grabbing, stealing
Oats and hay, and bridles, brushes, bits and spurs,
And blankets, bear hides, and more than I can name–
Even shoes right off the horses' hooves.
All these he sold to smiths and waggoners at half their worth.   (132-37)

The matter-of-fact tone is very nearly the same in both versions, while the
details are also quite similar. What is added in the receptor version is first
of all an elaboration on the theme of fear: "I'd howled and screamed,"
"I'd shiver" are striking dramatizations of the more neutral "I was scared
of him" and "I didn't like him" of the source text. Likewise the stepfather's
blackness and the boy's reaction to it are dramatized: "A thunderstorm
is coming up / It's so dark...." (112-13) But besides these vivid elaborations there is also, in the receptor text, a conceptual clarity that locates,
through mental association, the thought of "Devil" for the stepfather's "colour and the way he looked." Then an angel is invented to match it: "I
thought he was the Devil / ...but the more I saw of pastries, bread... / The
more he seemed an angel, not a man." (113-14; 116) This gives us our
first glimpse of the dramatic tension in the play between "illusion" and
"reality."

Here is another example. The master is leaving after giving Lázaro
orders to look after the house. At the end of that long passage, Lázaro reflects
on the illusory quality of his master's behaviour, and how things in this
world are often not at all what they seem to be:

He walked out of the door, dignified and erect.... He rested his right hand
on his hip with a swagger. 'Lázaro,' he said as he left, 'look after the house
while I go and hear Mass. Make the bed and go fill the water-jug.... And
mind you lock the door when you go; I don't want to find anything missing
when I come back. Put the key in the crack so that I can get in if I get back
while you're out.' And he walked up the road with such a swagger that
anybody who didn't know him would have thought for sure he was a near
relative of the Count of Arcos, or at least his personal valet. 'Blessed art thou,
O Lord,' I stood there saying, 'you send the illness and then the medicine.
Who could meet my master and not think...that he has had a good supper
and slept in a comfortable bed...and who would think that that nobleman
spent all day yesterday without taking a bite of food except that crumb of
bread that his servant Lázaro had carried for a day and a half under his shirt

and where it couldn't have képt very clean.... And how many men like him must be scattered around the world, who suffer for the sake of their ridiculous honour what they certainly wouldn't suffer for Your sake?'[20] Here is the Dutch, in Brumble's English version:

JEROLIMO: Well, Robbert, now make the bed, I'll trust the house to you.
        Haul water, be watchful that nothing might be stolen.
        Should you go out, do shut the door and lay the key
        There upon the ledge, that I might enter when I come,
        And be careful that the rats don't get our stores!

ROBBELKNOL: If a mouse should happen in, he'd starve.
        How grandly he struts; such elegance.
        Wouldn't you think he was his highness' self?
        Or at least one of his council? So haughty's his appearance.
        God, you send the disease, but then you send the cure.
        Whoever saw his lordship walking spry and brisk
        Would never think he'd not a penny in his purse.
        He who seems so courteous and cheerful? Who'd ever know
        That he's eaten neither yesterday nor today—
        Excepting a wedge of bread I bore here beneath my shirt,
        Which served me as my pantry—and that was gray with mould.
        O God, your works are wonderful.
        Who'd not be fooled by such a show of weal?
                                    But Lord in heaven
        Only knows how many such there are in the world
        Who'd suffer more for idle honor and display
        Than for God's holy laws.   (530-47 and 556-59)

One can see at a glance terms that were added by Bredero, and they all point in the direction of a receptor text more pictorial and vividly descriptive than the Spanish original. A mouse that would starve, "not a penny in his purse," a wedge of bread that is "gray with mould," all of these are elaborations of a by now familiar type. For the rest, the two versions are obviously rather close to each other. Even when we make allowances (once again) for nuances lost in translation from 16th-century Spanish and 17th-century Dutch into modern English, the additions seem minor. The very tone of voice in Bredero's dramatization of a fictional narrative is rather close to the original.

What then is added in Bredero's dramatic portrait of Robbeknol that is substantial? Even Robbeknol's outcry, "But Lord in heaven / Only knows how many such there are... / Who'd suffer more for idle honor... / Than for God's holy laws," (556-59) mirrors the Spanish Lázaro's prayer for those who "suffer for the sake of their ridiculous honour." What *is* new and striking in the receptor text is the immediately following comment made by Robbeknol. We find Robbeknol describing a new, quite different kind of reality rising up inside himself, as a result of watching the amazing behaviour of his master Jerolimo:

Well, my thoughts have gone a'wandering again;
For certain I was nigh translated to a higher sphere.
Now I'd best go in and shut the door—
I suppose I've got to do my work.   (562-66)

This self-reflective statement comes immediately after the philosophic out-cry about those who put up such a brave show of wealth and well-being in order to deceive the world. It does not seem to be based on anything in the Spanish text:

I stood there like that at the door, watching him and thinking about these things.... Then I went back into the house and went right through it, upstairs and down.... I made that ghastly bed, took the jug and went down to the river....[21]

The only reference that could have prompted the new, imaginative flight of the Dutch servant's mind, is in Lázaro's phrase "watching him and think-ing about these things...." This shows that the antithesis between thought and reality is already implicit in the source text. It remained however for Bredero's artistic eye, or insight into the Spanish servant's mind, to bring to the Dutch creation the strong dramatic tension between fantasy and reality.

Herein then lies confirmation of the presence of *enargeia* or heightened pictorial quality in the receptor text. But rather than being an addition or elaboration of a stylistic nature, this kind of expansion concerns the inner dramatic workings of the new creation as a whole. The theme of illusion versus reality is instilled into Bredero's version of the picaresque tale as an organizing principle as the writer boldly underlines something which in the source text was no more than a dim notion.

As a result of the presence of this new organizing principle, the character of Robbeknol not only gains in artistic depth in comparison to his model Lázaro, but also acquires a kind of transcendental validity. It brings him surprisingly close to that other involuntary juggler with illusion and reali-ty, Sancho Panza. This no less Spanish servant had equal occasion to reflect on the behaviour of his master, also a nobleman of no common sort. Since *Don Quixote* was published only a few years earlier (completed 1615), the possibility of some kind of connection between it and Bredero's play is more than mere speculation.

As he is transported to a different reality, Robbeknol's worries (the worries of one who has suffered much in the material world) are temporarily dissipated. In Jerolimo's presence, or at least under his growing influence, they seem to disappear, to be replaced, even if only for a moment, by a strange other-world of fantasy and noble illusions. It should come as no surprise that this fantasy world, with its emphasis on escape and its con-tempt for the mundane, is so close to the "holiday world" that has been traditionally shared by characters and audiences of comedy, since its early Greek and Roman beginnings.[22]

NOTES

1 G.A. Bredero, *The Spanish Brabanter*, translated by H. David Brumble III (Binghamton, N.Y., 1982). All the quotations will be from this edition.

2 See my article "Translation in the Renaissance: A Context and A Map," in *Canadian Review of Comparative Literature* (Spring, 1981), 204-16.

3 I am drawing upon the useful terminology ("source text" and "receptor text") employed by Eugene A. Nida and Charles R. Taber in *The Theory and Practice of Translation* (Leiden, 1974).

4 *The Spanish Brabanter*, p. 14.

5 See the letter to Hugo Grotius of January 17, 1617.

6 See Grotius' letter to P.C. Hooft of January 24, 1617, in *De briefwisseling van P.C. Hooft* (Culemborg, 1976), I, 294.

7 The ending of Plautus' *Aulularia* is lost. The part where the Roman text breaks off corresponds to approximately line 1240 in *Warenar*.

8 For a variety of reasons, the place of action of Plautus' Roman plays is normally "a street in Athens" or some other Greek town.

9 This point has received much critical attention. For a brief analysis of the presence of the Amsterdam dialect in *Warenar* see the introduction to the edition of J. Bergsma (Zutphen, n.d.), viii ff.

10 The translations from Plautus' Latin and Hooft's Dutch are mine.

11 My argument is not made any easier by the fact that all comparisons appear in English only. The reader is thus confronted with a double language barrier between the original Latin text and Hooft's Dutch version. Later on in the paper the same barrier must be overcome when Alpert's English version of *Lazarillo de Tormes* is compared to Brumble's translation of Bredero.

12 See note 2 above.

13 Flora Amos, *Early Theories of Translation* (New York, 1920), p. 125.

14 See F.O. Matthiessen, *Translation: An Elizabethan Art* (Cambridge, Mass., 1931), pp. 42 and 45-46.

15 *The Poems of George Chapman*, ed. Phyllis Bartlett (New York, 1962), p. 49.

16 Chapman, pp. 392 and 393.

17 See the ancient treatise *On the Sublime* (Loeb text: Cambridge, Mass., 1927), pp. 170-171 (XV, 1-2).

18 Chapman, p. 49.

19 *Lazarillo de Tormes* in *Two Spanish Picaresque Novels*, translated by Michael Alpert (New York, 1969), pp. 25-26. All page references are to this edition.

20 *Lazarillo de Tormes*, p. 54.

21 *Lazarillo de Tormes*, p. 54.

22 Cf. Erich Segal's emphasis on the notion of holiday versus duty in his *Roman Laughter* (Cambridge, Mass., 1968), especially in chapter II.